S0-GQF-419

Counterings
Utopian Dialectics
in Contemporary Contexts

Literature Advisory Boards	Studies in Speculative Fiction, No. 17

Studies in Speculative Fiction

Robert Scholes, Series Editor
Brown University

Studies in Modern Literature

A. Walton Litz, Series Editor
Princeton University

Consulting Editors
Joseph Blotner
University of Michigan
George Bornstein
University of Michigan
Jackson R. Bryer
*University of Maryland
at College Park*
Ronald Bush
California Institute of Technology
Keith Cushman
*University of North Carolina
at Greensboro*
Richard J. Finneran
Newcomb College, Tulane University
Daniel Mark Fogel
Louisiana State University
Carolyn G. Heilbrun
Columbia University
Paul Mariani
*University of Massachusetts
at Amherst*
Thomas C. Moser
Stanford University
Linda Wagner
Michigan State University

Nineteenth-Century Studies

Juliet McMaster, Series Editor
University of Alberta

Consulting Editors
Carol Christ
*University of California
at Berkeley*
James R. Kincaid
University of Southern California
Julian Markels
Ohio State University
G. B. Tennyson
*University of California
at Los Angeles*

Other Titles in This Series

No. 1
*Feminist Futures: Contemporary
Women's Speculative Fiction*
Natalie M. Rosinsky

No. 3
The Scientific World View in Dystopia
Alexandra Aldridge

No. 5
Utopia: The Psychology of a Cultural Fantasy
David Bleich

No. 7
*Red Stars: Political Aspects
of Soviet Science Fiction*
Patrick L. McGuire

No. 13
*Italo Calvino: Metamorphoses
of Fantasy*
Albert Howard Carter, III

No. 16
*Le Guin and Identity in
Contemporary Fiction*
Bernard Selinger

No. 18
*Sanity Plea: Schizophrenia in
the Novels of Kurt Vonnegut*
Lawrence Broer

17650928

Counterings
Utopian Dialectics
in Contemporary Contexts

by
Kingsley Widmer

PN
3448
W7
W53
1988

U·M·I Research
Press

Ann Arbor / London

OHIO UNIVERSITY LIBRARY

WITHDRAWN

Copyright © 1988
Kingsley Widmer
All rights reserved

Produced and distributed by
UMI Research Press
an imprint of
University Microfilms Inc.
Ann Arbor, Michigan 48106

Library of Congress Cataloging in Publication Data

Widmer, Kingsley, 1925-
  Counterings : utopian dialectics in contemporary contexts / by
Kingsley Widmer.
    p. cm.—(Studies in speculative fiction : no. 17)   Bibliography: p.
  Includes index.
    ISBN 0-8357-1861-1 (alk. paper)
    1. Fiction—20th century—History and criticism. 2. Utopias in
literature. I. Title II. Series.
  PN3448.U7W53   1988
  813'.5'09372—dc19   88-6085
                                                                            CIP

British Library CIP data is available.

WITHDRAWN

Contents

vi   Contents

Acknowledgments

Since I have been reading and discussing utopianizing writings for more than three decades, this book is obviously continuous with my previous writings. I have consciously drawn on several dozen earlier published essays, review articles, chapters, and a monograph but have usually repeated only a few sentences, sometimes a few paragraphs, never an entire piece. Nothing is reprinted in anything near its original form. Even what has been reused has usually been modified, and in more than a few instances, I must humblingly admit, considerably changed. Thus it seemed most appropriate to cite the earlier publications in conventional notes, in spite of sometimes appearing to be my own major source.

Conventional annotation, however, fails to aknowledge the explicit or implicit help of editors, a number of whom kindly asked for the writings. Most of them displayed, I should grant however belatedly, considerable tolerance not only for my contentiousness and rhetorical idiosyncrasies but for the manuscript muddles of a dyslexic who, with a utopianist distaste for servants and services (indeed, the whole dehumanizing division of labor), did all the typing and other preparation of his manuscripts. I suspect that one editor, whom I shall leave in polite anonymity, expressed the feelings of a number of them when he returned a much penciled article with the irritated comment that my "learned and provocative" work had been grievously undermined by an "incompetent secretary" who not only couldn't spell but wandered off into stylistic barbarisms.

The incompetent secretary apologizes to the following editors (in random order): Charles H. Anderson, Michael G. Cooke, Barry N. Schwartz, Warren French (especially), David Madden, the late John Crowe Ransom, A. M. Mirande, Jeffrey Meyers (especially), David Manning White, Stanley Schatt, Herbert Weisinger, the late Don Cameron Allen, George Wickes, C. A. Patrides, the late G. Salgado, Harold M. Hodges, the late Maurice Beebe, John Bryant, Sondra J. Stang, Charles Rossman, John V. Cody, the late E. E. Bostetter, James Cox, Edward L. Kamarck, Mark Spilka, Milton Swenson, Albert F. Gegenheimer, the late Harry T. Moore, K. Das, Dennis Jackson, the late Carey McWilliams, Ross Wetzsteon (especially), Howard J. Ehrlich, Colin Ward (especially), William Phillips, the late Mark Schorer, Thomas F. Staley, Charlotte Stewart, Penny Williams (especially), the late Karl Keller, Arthur Efron (especially), Kenneth Eble, Lawrence Poston, Sylvia Bowman, and Eleanor Widmer (especially).

No doubt some who helped are unknown to me by name, and others too conveniently forgotten by the incompetent secretary. Apologies within an apology. And to others who provocatively disagreed with me and have been relegated to a footnote.

On the other hand, I have no acknowledgment to make to any institution, its officials, monies, or ambience. Except for the standard use of several university libraries, none aided, or abetted, me in any intellectual efforts. Probably just as well.

1

Diatopianism:
Some Dialectics of Utopianizing

Introduction: Counterdefining

Inconveniently, no doubt, I have no adequate simple yet general theory of utopian narrative, or even of utopianism more broadly. In the course of discussing a few handfuls of utopian writings selected from some hundreds I know a little about, I have found occasion to dig around some general-simple theorizings. But my countering cultivation of them does not intend a full-bloomed theory of utopian narrative, not least because I doubt the value of such plantings, mere academic bushes, in providing an adequate sense of the larger landscapes of utopianizing. It is the forests and fields of utopianizing, which I see as resulting from fundamental human imperatives and concerns (at least in Western culture—of others I am too ignorant to comment), that engage this essay. Among the flowers, and weeds, of the utopian impetus are some variety of utopian narratives. These provide a shifting focus for arguments and counterarguments about a broader cultivation of utopianizing sensibility.

Inevitably, in the utopian fields the practice of literary criticism is also the practice of social criticism. Or, since I am dealing with the written artifacts, social-cultural criticism. In practicing the critical vocation, it seems necessary to be critical, raising differences and difficulties wherever one goes. That certainly does not mean that my discussions pretend neutrality—scientist camouflage—but my obvious libertarian biases are also treated critically (if somewhat more mildly) along with other views. After all, what could be more appropriate to images of counter social orders than a continuous countering?

So let me start by countering what appear to be some representative general-simple theories of the utopian, with the purpose of suggesting that the gen-simps are not only inadequate but misleading. Take a well-known and often cited case, Michael Holquist's clever "How to Play Utopia: Some Brief Notes on the Distinctiveness of Utopian Fiction."[1] These loose ruminations, with insubstantial bits of More's *Utopia* for most of the illustrations, claim to provide a general theory: "My thesis is that the relationship of chess to battle is roughly parallel to the relationship which obtains between utopias and actual society." Piggy-backing the thesis on a couple of incidental metaphors of games (though not chess) in More and Plato, Holquist insists on the overriding response that utopia is "a simplification, a radical stylization of something which in experience is of enormous complexity"—an actual society. Of course, but read a random handful of utopias and one might as quickly conclude that they also vary greatly in complexity. And, of course, radical simplification is true of all intellectual social-political patterns (theories of divine ordinance, natural law, social contract, historical materialism, etc.). And most fictions, comic or tragic or realistic, are also simplifications. So either we have a too easy truism, or we are being led by the nose to something slier.

The trick is that, since utopian fictions are simple, we need not consider any issue of relation to society but just the more simplified analogy of games. Since chess will not carry one very far off the board, the gaming theorist slips into an even looser yoking of utopian "games" with the "playful." Now there surely are verbally playful elements in many utopias, from the punning neologism for the mode to, frequently, the names of nonpeople and nonplaces. (It is contagious, and we commentators often catch it.) Playful, too, are many of the narrative devices, such as strange voyages and quaint discoveries. Furthermore, some of the more overtly satiric nowheres not mentioned by Holquist, such as those by Aristophanes, Swift, Huxley, Burgess, Vonnegut, and Barth, are savagely playful in their double-takes and other mockeries. Literature, we can certainly agree, often has strong elements of play—play-acting, the play of language, playful tactics; the fanciful unfolding of patterns, the gaming of and against conventions, the juggling (and dropping) of forms, tropes, myths—and utopian literature does some of the same things as other literature. But most games, on board or field, do not seem to be playful in any of these senses— punning, jocular, satiric, ironic, and so on—and require rather strict ways of engagement and consistent moves. Games, being only games, can afford to be literalist.

Utopianism, quite undistinctively, employs common linguistic and other literary devices. It also, using play in a quite different sense, is play with ideas. But play-with-ideas little resembles play with a pawn, puck, or other game piece, except in the prejudices of the anti-intellectual. Indeed, the play-with-ideas that approximates alien game rules is usually, and not incidentally, of the more fatuous sort, as with gambling or sports analogies for the reductive dismissal of human injustice or suffering ("You have to play by the rules"; "Too bad, but that's how the game is played").

The utopia-as-game argument lacks even minimal consistency, maintaining on the same page as play-with-ideas that the laws of utopias correspond to non-idea games, "arbitrary, but infinitely open to recombination." Surely game rules are arbitrary and closed, which is why they are appealing. Throwing away kings, altering counters, doing away with opponents are all rather discouraged in board games, though often crucial to utopianizing. In sum, utopian recombinations can only be understood beyond confined game rules and in relation to, as it were, suprarules (which are never quite rules) of politics, religion, technology, social ideology, and the like. The gen-simp theory crassly voids these in playing cute board games with large utopian issues.

Granted, there is little merit in belaboring a weak and irrelevant set of tropes, except for the basic falsification. Just as one cannot fight real wars by playing chess (though in fact some real-world commanding strategists attempt to approximately do so),[2] so "you cannot erect actual communities based on the logic of utopia." That is the supposed intellectual checkmate. I do not object to the switch from "literature" to the quite broader "logic," for that just unmasks the real issue: utopianizing is socially wrong. But why justify it with a grossly counterfactual claim? Obviously there have been thousands of "intentional communities," not to mention parts of large societies, from city plans to whole constitutions to revolutions, which have employed, with whatever degree of consistency and adaption, some ideal-place logic. Holquist's "cannot," then, really means a righteous "should not," for, he pronounces, when people try to apply utopian thinking to actual society, "the consequence has inevitably been pogroms." Patently wrong. Since pogroms went with the vicious order of traditional Russian tyranny (quite unutopian) but may be plausibly extended to the pseudo-utopian Soviet Union, the essay is a rather loaded political gesture. The admonition against relating simplified utopian "games" to complex real worlds is a not very honest effort to denature and denigrate any pertinence of the utopian sensibility to society. While the case might be made that certain utopian ideas in certain circumstances are dangerous, or in some other way undesirable, it is doubtful on the face of it as well as historically that all utopian ideas in all circumstances can be rejected on the same grounds. Too varied and complex a field of pertinent social ideas. Gen-simps here seem to intend simple intellectual genocide.

"How to Play Utopia" has been cited many times in the last two decades by informed literary critics, and almost always approvingly. While that no doubt is a credit to nice manners (and to dubious taste in academic games), such an attitude falsifies much of the purpose and meaning of utopianizing. Since I, too, find *some* utopianizing dangerous or otherwise distasteful (as my specific discussions will make clear), I must find the sly, indiscriminate, denaturing dismissal worse than wrong.

A more recent ambitious and influential theorist of utopian narratives (who praises "How to Play Utopia"), Darko Suvin, might merit a different assessment for "Defining the Literary Genre of Utopia."[3] He at least approaches the subject with the broader role of knowledgeable apologist for science fiction (hereafter, usually labeled sci-fi to give appropriate emphasis to its formulaic predominance). More candidly than Holquist, Suvin frames his definitions with an acknowledgment that the issue is complicated by the widespread identification of the utopian with "attempts at a radically different social system." To be sure, and Suvin displays considerable social awareness in other chapters of his book. But for academic purposes he wishes to finesse social issues, and so he blandly poses the claim that "utopias are verbal artifacts before they are anything else." One might as well object right there to a sort of deconstructionist fallacy. You do not have to be a Platonist of some kind to observe preliterary and extraliterary utopian impetuses. Also, utopianizing does not necessarily start out in the form of "verbal artifacts" (leaving aside the question of whether other literature does). Architect city planning provides centuries of obvious examples (which, with others, I will return to),[4] for, even when a planner writes about his utopian vision of the city, there is evidence, frequently implicit, sometimes direct, that a nonliterary visualization is at work. (To image a frustrating object—a chair, a wrench, a condom—in a radically different way may provide everyday confirmations of this.)[5] And so with other activities, of which we might plausibly speak of a utopian way of responding, pre- and extra-literary. In short, that "any utopia is a *verbal construction*" seems a fallacy of misplaced concreteness. While a natural bias for us compulsive verbalizers, and a specialist bias of the literary professional, it may be, if utopianizing rests on broad human impetuses (as I am holding), a reductive notion.

But even assuming for the moment the verbal-artifact premise (thus privileging us literary scholar-critics), Suvin makes, with rather roccoco scholarship, a series of curious distinctions. For example, utopia is a verbally constructed world "located in *this world*. Utopia is an Other World immanent in the world of human endeavour, dominion, and hypothetic possibility—and not transcendental in a religious sense." It is a "this worldly other world." I would like to agree, but does the secularism in fact always apply? Probably to More (in spite of the ambiguous Christian humanist context and authorship); to Plato, with some essentialist qualification (isn't his Republic finally relegated to divine mind?); to Voltaire, Diderot, and Enlightenment utopias generally (of course); to much nineteenth-century utopianizing, including Fourier, Marx, Morris, and Bellamy (unless "socialism" be construed as a religion). But much utopianizing comes out of a religious context and goes in religious directions, such as with the millennial prophets. Broad exclusionary categories may be desirable (I will later try some) but should be admitted as problematic.

Suvin sets off a formal definition, which includes (besides a peculiar Brechtean theory of "estrangement," which I am ignoring here) several other qualifications: "Utopia is the verbal construction of a particular quasi-human community where sociopolitical institutions, norms, and individual relationships are organized according to a more perfect principle." "Quasi-human" lets in sci-fi robots (as in Capek's *R. U. R.*),[6] though much sci-fi and other dystopias—and all ambiguous worlds?—seem excluded by "more perfect principle."

But the apparently careful definition moves to some unconsidered jumps. Unquestioningly following Northrup Frye's literary typologies, Suvin assumes utopias to be prose narrative "anatomies" (Menippian satire), though in practice that is often rather an antiform, and far from all utopias are prose fiction. With even more sweeping formalistic demand, he also insists on a pervasive ordering: "a formal *hierarchic system* becomes . . . the supreme value in utopia." That, I will variously argue (with libertarian bias), is what is wrong with many of them, though fortunately not all suffer from it.

While Suvin's emphasis on "a radically different location"—for both different-than and affective distance—seems standard (though restrictive of utopian elements that appear in other contexts, as in a number of "realistic" novels), his exclusion of "pastoral" and similar radically different places is another matter. Pastoral utopianism he takes, with considerable circularity, to be insufficiently structured, hierarchical. The counterview, which he little confronts (and which I will belabor below), is that the pastoral is not only historically pervasive but may provide the primary traditions of utopianizing, present as well as past. Without the Golden Age values—those neolithic propensities not all that evolutionarily far behind us and still so fundamental to human community—utopianizing is radically denuded and misunderstood.

It is equally denuding, in both literary and other ways, drastically to sever positive from negative utopias. Suvin has ulterior motives for this, assigning the more critical values to a special set of conventions, those usually summarized as sci-fi. Since they appear to have a special historical pertinence to this time and place, they are hypostatized into the dominant rubric. Thus utopia becomes merely the positive, the ideal, *"sociopolitical subgenre of science fiction."*

Such "englobing" of utopia by expanded sci-fi conventions seems more fashion and special interest than substantial argument. Conceptually as well as historically, one can probably make a better case for sci-fi conventions providing subdivisions (and some interesting examples) of a broader utopianism, from which they derive. Suvin nowhere pauses to consider the arbitrariness of sci-fi conventions, including the dehumanizing manias such as technological fetishism, techno-jargonized language, abstracted psychology, and the pathology of cosmic space fixation in its flight from the earthy human.

Part of the purpose of such a typology as Suvin's is to escape "loose" utopianizing. Sardonic and comic utopianizing, from Diogenes through Rabelais (he fudges a bit on that one) to much in the present, is conveniently excluded. While Suvin's exclusions and categorizings aim at conceptual neatness (and academic aggrandizement for sci-fi), the costs seem high. The results include a lack of responsiveness to considerable non-sci-fi writings, especially in the present, and to much of the variety of the utopianizing impetus. Granted, broader and looser approaches (such as mine) may make the subject less manageable, more idiosyncratic, for both advancement and denigration. But if utopianizing centrally includes countering what prevails, the broader, however loose, may have inherent interest and justification.

One more example of gen-simp confining by genre of utopianizing: Gary Saul Morson's "Utopia as a Literary Genre."[7] One of the more fully developed and sophisticated discourses of that sort, Morson's study argues for properly placing utopias in a broader system of genres, though most must find any such system weakly hypothetical. But his main and simple strategy is to fall back on requiring the prose piece to be a "literary work in the tradition of previous" recognized instances (meaning mostly More-Plato) of the depiction of "an ideal society." While the utopia must also "advocate" that ideal society, "tracts" (the majority of cases?) are excluded as nonliterature. Parody, in spite of so many utopias displaying it, is methodologically eliminated, as are antiutopias or any other paradoxical variation.[8] Purism is the purpose. Ambiguous cases are levered in or out of the genre by subdefinition. Thus *Utopia* (in its disparity between cautious More and his spokesman Hythloday) "was designed by its author to be read in a tradition of deeply ambiguous works." This may not only be dubious about More, who seems finally earnest about his attacks on "enclosures" and other inequalities, but, since More provides much of the genre's definition, the utopia grouping itself becomes ambiguous, as do the other qualities of advocacy for an ideal society to which this account is hostile.

In spite of this essential ambiguity, the theorist wants drastically exclusionary categories. Satiric utopias, such as Butler's *Erewhon,* are reversed to nonutopian nowhere, as are "imaginary journeys and unreal societies" (that last rather begging the question). Methodologically, and against the empirical evidence, Morson holds that a work cannot be both utopia and antiutopia (I shall argue that the more interesting are often both).[9] "Novels," by a restrictive assumption of psychological and social verisimilitude, go against didactic purposes, and hence there cannot really be a "utopian novel." The "Masterplot" for utopia is Plato's Allegory of the Cave (though that lacks many of his other utopian requirements) because of its epistemological dualism. Apparently the many antidualistic, and anti-Platonic, utopias should disappear in this submerging of a responsive theory of society into an abstract theory of knowledge. While Morson's argument impresses us with its range of ostensible distinctions and examples, it is mostly mere genre dogmatizing of a socially repressive cast.

Given such casuistry, a problem with utopian forms turns into a subdefinition, with the split in More's *Utopia* (between the reformist and radical as well as the two parts) becoming itself a type. More generally, the difficulties with the genre come to define the genre. "Designed to overcome epistemological complacency, utopias render habits of classification and interpretation problematic."

But what might seem admirable skepticism turns into italicized definition: *"utopias lie on the boundary between fiction and non-fiction because they are about that boundary."* They are what they are by not being what they are, which includes images of society not being about society but about not-imaging. Platonic shadows, indeed. If this seems to be a catch-22 argument, that is because utopias themselves specialize in, and thus can additionally be defined by, the "double-bind." Certainly the genre theory can be so defined.

Since I have at hand rather different binds, including works and purposes contrary to the reduction of utopianizing in literature to little board games, or to subspecies of historically mandated sci-fi specialisms, or to the ingenious casuistry of genre-theorizing, such gen-simp theories of utopia are, shall we say, mere pedantic myopics, and all too squint-eyed. But what of the other available critical strategies? We could possibly manage some of the varied literature about countersocieties by reducing it to "dreams" and "fantasies," which, indeed, provide the ostensible costuming of many utopian works. Possible justification or denigration: Here are the ideal dreams, or here are the sick fantasies.

On the latitudinarian side, which might be represented by one of the most knowledgeable of commentators, utopias are the record of the historically conditioned sweeping dreams "no great civilization has lived without."[10] Frank Manuel concluded his later massive survey: "Western civilization may not be able to survive long without utopian fantasies any more than the individual can exist without dreaming."[11] On the reductive side (for a crass lesser example), the utopian is engaging in an "infantile wish for a kind of nutritional merging," which, in its somewhat more mature forms, works to "compromise the conflict of love and authority by transferring the first infantile compromise onto the relationship between the individual and the rest of mankind" in the projected fantasies identified as utopian in literature.[12] While the latitudinarian leads to the relativist historical typologies of utopias, the quasi-Freudian leads to smug clinical typologies of "immature utopian personalities" (the authors). The latitudinarian and the psycho-fundamentalist do at least agree on the centrality of utopian dreaming.

As with all literary modes (and probably most other forms of human signification, from games to religion and science), fantasy projections can be found, whether as visionary social ideals or as limiting personal symptoms. But is there one that is peculiarly utopian? The knowledgeable historical relativist not only does not find any such projection but denies it, absorbing utopias into their contexts. The relentless clinician looks only for it, for the reductive psychogenesis. Surely there are strong pathological elements in many utopian stories and schemes (I will later pursue several of them, such as resentment). But the illnesses may be less in utopias than in, say, the repressed sexuality of sentimental romances, or the cosmic familial displacements of religious allegories, or the ritualized sadism of Western and sci-fi "shoot-em-ups," or the defensive-avoidance syndromes of academic studies. If one were to isolate a characteristic syndrome of many utopias, a leading one might be compulsive fixations on cleanliness and order (perhaps the source of Suvin's defining "system"), be they Swift's cleanly rational horses or the neat rocket homes of futuristic sci-fi. A purification mania?

It may also be held that there is, almost by definition, a megalomania in even thinking about an alternative society, though that fearful response seems to me more than a little mad. Surely there is a regressive defense compulsion in only psyching utopians and utopias. Just possibly, "inadequately resolved motives" could appear more clearly in utopias because they are often contentious ("hostile") and because we can bring so many reality-tests of the commonsense sort to bear on the presentations of a different society. That very countering, in both the utopianizing and our responses to it, seems to me one of the more durable characteristics of the utopian.

So far, I have tried to suggest some de-defining of the utopian by arguing against some representative commentators. However, I do not intend to deny that there are various utopian conventions, used and abused in various kinds of tales, novels, fables, fantasies, documentaries, tracts, and mixtures of them. In twentieth-century syncretistic Western culture, of course, most utopias will be heavily indebted to a variety of literary manners. Just as there is no adequate gen-simp genre for the poem or novel, there is none for the utopia. While I doubt that there was ever any inclusively long-term genre, surely (as many of my examples below should indicate) there is not one now. To lock into genre theories, or game or clinical or formalistic reductions, may be more than descriptively dubious: it is misleading as to the crucial attitudes and purposes and significances of much utopianizing. Certainly some uses of the mode, like romance or detective fiction or pornography, are primarily formulaic, as is evident with a majority of sci-fi. Genre considerations might be useful in such cases, though if "pure" (without ideological concern), that analysis would be rather superficial. And even when discussing the binds of formula, as with the "format" imprisonments which debilitate so much of TV programming, we should at least ask what social mystification, and other interests, the patterning serves.

No doubt a sense of utopianistic writings may be helped by some knowledge of their varieties, present even more than past, of their conventions, and the sense of the play for and against them, but that is hardly the *ding-an-sich*. If it be countered that this essay does not properly confine itself to the literary thing in itself, then I deny that there is such a definable thing. The gen-simps tend to reify random instances of nowhere into a denuded nothing. Defensively, of course, I do not claim more than provisional use of the materials and terms. No chapter here is about "utopia," but about Diatopianism, Revtopianism, Femtopianism, Primatopianism, and Entopianism. While I have used some of the literary works and issues others define as the genre or history or fantasy of utopia, I have also gone elsewhere. Even if that be nowhere, it might be intellectually useful, or counteruseful.

Some Variant Introduction, and Lawrence vs. Lawrence

With no simple and general definition of utopianizing (as partly explained in the preceding section), my nomenclature will have to be indicated as the argument jogs along. Ignoring Thomas More's learned word play (good-no-place), it seems that what was the more-or-less ideal no-place, utopia, has by the late twentieth century twisted to some contrary directions, including eutopia (good-place) and dystopia (bad-place). But the division of the images of a speculative society into positive and negative often seems to miss the more complex points of ongoing utopianizing. Granted, some goody-no-places appear blandly affirmative, which usually means that they are neither very lively fictions nor significant thinking. And some satiric no-no-places appear grimly dismissive, which is not much better. Interesting utopianizing will hardly be so easily painted into dankest black and mere off-white, the uncolorings of sensibility. Could it be, then, that conventional distinctions into (in effect) eutopia and dystopia are not all that real?

Part of the issue here may be larger than utopianizing. While subgenre distinctions, like those of genre, may be useful when deftly danced around, taken in themselves they tend to be as flat-footed for the mixed realities as the lock-step genre marching. For general examples: few pertinent modern critics would any longer simply set off comedy from tragedy. Or the heroic from the grotesque. Few aware reflections on humor, for at least a couple of generations, would just present laughter as only affirmative, genial, happy, and exclude the black, sick, bitter, sardonic, and even tragic.[13] Or understand tears as only signifying woe, and not also rage, joy, confusion, and much else. The ancient reifications are mostly obtuse to the muddle, if not the complexity, of human feelings. Varieties of "depth psychology" have taught us at least that. How impertinent, then, the subgenre mania which, simplistically categorizing on an arbitrary selection, holds traditional alternate societies to be only eutopic and twentieth-century utopias to be different enough to require a separate division into dystopia. More than a little variety is being missed here.

The eutopia-dystopia issues seem almost too easy to redo, a setup for some ponderous critic to come along (I am not the first) and announce that utopias and utopians are mixed company, uncertain, ambiguous, dialectical, and much else that will hardly qualify as simple and straight.[14] One can then recompute the modes as marginal or "mixed" or on the "boundary" (Morson), which is mostly just genre sleight-of-hand, or dress up the evident with some fashionable scientism, such as reader-response software, which supposedly gets around uncertainty as to what it is by data (mostly arbitrary) on how it is taken, which then becomes what it is. So let us grant that the ontology of utopia is uncertain, at least in general, and considerably ambiguous as to whether it is to be responded to as positive or negative.

To redo present categories, of course, is also to redo the past. Looking again at More's *Utopia* (1516), we may now see that it has, if not a lot of problems, a lot of irony, such as that between the humanist secularism (represented by the decency of greater equality and less work—the six-hour day for all), and the vicious Christianized class society, of which More was certainly an integral part.[15] Or consider a bit further an apparently simpler case, Voltaire's *Candide* (1759) and its "El Dorado," that eutopian mountain fastness in South America of deistic decency, humanized science, economic equality, and free-for-the-taking diamond and ruby stones, so easily turned into sour bread in the outside world.[16] Why did simple Candide leave such a good place? He was absurdly romantic (Cunegonde not yet recognized as the hag and nag of the end of the tale); and he was a modern Western high-achiever (more gratified to be invidiously rich in a bad world than equal in a decent one); and he was, as surrogate for his always-present author, bored with the eutopian. In Voltaire's context, and countering, the positive utopia is, in several senses, a brief episode in a larger process of enlightenment.

That is true rather literally for Candide who, in the following sharply contrasting episode with the mutilated slave in Guyana (a rhetorical high point of the fiction), first expresses real doubt about the Panglossian best-of-all-possible worlds (as well as Western colonialism and entrepreneurial economics).[17] In the pattern of *Candide,* the eutopic world of El Dorado is not primarily an immutable best-of-worlds but an informing polarity on the way to the disenchanted cultivation of a communal garden which serves to counter the dystopian world at large. That is Voltaire's shrewd, and still pertinent—indeed, it might be taken as paradigmatic—utopianism. Voltaire's Enlightenment utopianizing dialectically yokes eutopic idealism and dystopic disillusionment for a modest but morally sharp utopian ending.

Some such dialectical process has repeatedly recurred in later utopianizers. We need but recall that the satiric *Brave New World* (1932) was followed by a series of partial utopianizing fictions and essays (*After Many a Summer Dies the Swan,* etc.), ending with the highly eutopic *Island* (1961). That last turned what had been negative motifs in the early dystopia—pharmacological states of mind, synthetic religion, sexual openness, benign conditioning—into concluding positives.[18] Dystopian countering also, of course, continued; the happy isle of Pala succumbs to the grim powers of oil corporations and U. S. Marines, representative antiutopian forces in our world. The counterutopianizing, the dialectics within Huxley, was no literary caprice since he had repeatedly presented his harsh satire and his positive utopianizing (decentralist economics, libertarian ethics, the contemplative "perennial philosophy"). Both directions link Huxley with what is probably (as I shall explain later) the major utopianizing complex in Western culture.

Dour George Orwell was temperamentally a different case. Yet he also combined the dystopian with the positive utopian, however often ignored. While *Nineteen Eighty-Four* (1949) is one of the bleakest satires of near-future totalitarian "socialist" empire, Orwell always avowed democratic socialism, and, indeed, idealistically put his life on the P. O. U. M. line for it in the Spanish Civil War *(Homage to Catalonia)*. Obviously his positive and negative utopianism draw on the same values and moral righteousness. The countering, the personal and public dialectics of eutopia/dystopia, seems crucial.

But rather than belabor with many examples the inseparability of negative and positive utopianism in the same sensibility, let me concentrate a bit more fully on one illustration, D. H. Lawrence. Though usually not much discussed in utopian terms (genre blockage in the critics?), he displayed an obsessive bent to utopianizing, as one would expect of a writer sharply dissatisfied with the ordering of our world. At a rather literal level, his utopian tendency took the form of his recurrent plans to found an ideal community in the United States. Rananim, as he called it, was to be an escape from the British Great War world which so enraged him. He wanted (as he wrote in a letter) not only removal but "a sort of communism as far as the necessaries of life go, and some real decency."[19] Rather insistently for a war year (1915), and then again later, he attempted to enlist about twenty literary and artistic friends for his commune, planned for Florida. A decade later, he did temporarily establish a communal situation with some painters on his ranch north of Taos, New Mexico. However, such efforts only amounted to gestures by a man increasingly ill and despairing. But much of Lawrence is incomprehensible without a sense of him as a persistent exacerbated utopianizer, positive and negative.

This utopian bent unfolds in a pattern of literary dialectics only in the later period of his writing. A long story, "The Man Who Loved Islands" (1926), twists some stock conventions of utopia into a sardonic fable.[20] A well-to-do, cultivated English dandy, Cathcart, takes possession of an island in order to create a "world of his own," the perfect place. "Why should it not be the Happy Isle at last?" So he becomes the "Master" of an autonomous island farming and fishing colony, with thirteen others (mostly employees). In spite of expertise and earnestness, things go wrong: a cow falls over a cliff; he lives in too high, expensive, a gentlemanly style; the employees swindle the Master; in sum, he and his rationalized egotism have quite failed to take into account the impetuses from the "timeless world" of human and other natural irrationalities, which therefore become a pervasive "malevolence." Most importantly, Lawrence mocks dehumanized idealism—a favorite focus (often in Nietzschean-style attacks on Platonizing upper-class intellectuals). Such "goodness" includes the denial of fuller human responsiveness: "anyone who wants the world to be perfect must be careful not to have real likes and dislikes. A general good will is all you can afford." And that "form of egoism" leads to the loss of the authentically human. After four years of decline and disenchantment, the Master sells his utopia to a hotel chain for a "honeymoon-and-golf island," one of the modern travesties of the paradisical isle.

But the nihilistic Lawrence, who so acutely diagnosed the nihilism of others, is far from finished with his utopian. Cathcart gives up creating "a world" only to take himself to another, much smaller, island "refuge" and the lesser eutopianism of mere private life. Crucially, in terms of Lawrence's central dialectic of desire-and-negation, his utopian is doomed because he no longer responds with passion but operates on a calculus "without desire," which is to be without real purposive life.[21] But one does not easily escape the human condition; Cathcart is trapped by an adoring and manipulative woman servant into a pseudo-desire created by his "pity" and her "will." He ends up married, with a daughter and resident mother-in-law. The ideal of the good life turns into an imprisoning matriarchal "suburb."

He flees to yet another island, a small, bleak, isolated rock, a solitary hermitage, the ultimate utopian withdrawal. His accelerating nihilism denudes him more and more; he eliminates animals, language, self, until he even "ceased to register his own feelings." Trapped in his purity and compounding winter snows, he merges with the cold in complete annihilation. Such is utopianizing idealism that has lost the fundamentally human.

This relentless fable of utopianizing absolutism works like a logical paradigm: a descending order of three islands, three stages of ideal worlds (small colony, family refuge, solitary hermitage), and three denudings of passional life. The roles also unwind: he who would be the dandy "Master" becomes mere suburban familial "Mister," and then vestigial mere man mastered by the implacable elements. Too fine in his "nausea" with life, he has rejected too much. Given forcefulness by Lawrence's parody of his own nihilistic longings, as well as of conventional utopian modes, "The Man Who Loved Islands" of the mind more finally than life is also an acute mockery of life-denying forces, plausibly linked with some utopianizing.

Who should know better than Lawrence? The weakness of the tale is its lack of sympathy for its utopianizer (though certainly the parallels with Lawrence suggest a covert identification), a disproportionate authorial revulsion which might be understood as a self-attack. A few months previous to this dystopian fable, Lawrence had finished a long and lavish utopian narrative, *The Plumed Serpent* (1925).[22] This futuristic Mexican fiction of a revolutionary new society created by two religious-political ideologues (which, partly out of my own repulsion, I will not lengthily detail here) is a fervently ugly utopian account. Even charitably viewing that fiction as a "thought-experiment" requires an ingenious apologia for the dominant two thugs with their mean and resentful revolutionary movement. So does Lawrence's serving up synthetic spirits of mythology, Aztec-mystagoguery on resentful rocks. The *Serpent* exalts repressive revenge on female sexuality, various brutalities including murder, and quite unthought-out social ordering pervaded by authoritarianism. In spite of some intense descriptive bits, and occasional touches of Lawrence's intelligence, much of the writing must be characterized as hysterically ritualistic rhetoric serving a forced religiosity and a mean sense of society. It is a vengeful eutopianism. It should remind readers of some of the less often acknowledged motives for creating ideal societies. I suggest that we see an inner dialectic of dystopian penance when Lawrence so soon turns to "The Man Who Loved Islands" of the mind more than responsive life. Dystopianizing Lawrence was countering nastily eutopianizing Lawrence.

And he reversed the dialectic again in his next, and last, novel, *Lady Chatterley's Lover* (1928, but first drafted the same year as the dystopian novella).[23] There has been considerable disagreement on how to conceptualize, including genre-ize, that fiction. With rather too much caricature, didacticism, and poetry to be taken as "realism," and rather too much gritty documentation and harsh tendentiousness to be taken as "romance," it can be discussed (as I and others have done) as partly that loose utopian form identified as "pastoral." In one of the approximate pastoral patterns, sensitive lovers retreat from a falsely sophisticated society to a *locus amoenus* such as a sacred wood (here the Wragby Park remnant of Sherwood Forest), engage in erotic discovery and ritual (not only the sex but the twining flowers in pubic hair and dancing naked in the spring rain, etc.),and are rejuvenated more generally into passional awareness. The metaphors play upon a Golden Age mythos (counterposed to the harsh iron-industrial age mines, mechanized wheelchair of the master, and gray cities). The orgasmic woods provide a sanctuary (the keeper's cottage and the pheasant hut) with pagan religious overtones, which Lawrence calls "phallic consciousness." The lovers not only identify with rustic life but pursue an arcadian model of the return to a prelapsarian emotional wholeness, including an insistent rejection of the corrupt civilization (but that non-primitivistically provides the consciousness of characters, author, and readers). Such sophisticated pastoral may be credited with a reversion to a pagan withdrawal-and-return transformation, a religious-erotic renewal or conversion of personal life, and also a change of social allegiance to at least, as it were, a temporary counterculture. The Lady, now pregnant, and the exgamekeeper are planning a permanent mating and a new life as farmers in a different land. At least a considerable part of Lawrence's strident but poignant cross-class love story can be understood in terms of such pastoral resonances as an erotic eutopianism.

Lawrence, I have argued, chose the pastoral emphasis (as he moved to the third version of the novel) so as *not* to write a proletarian, "realistic," social fiction. In consequence of that form-ideology choice, he socially alienated and marginalized his protagonist (an evolving process from working-class Parkin in his first version through uncertain Seivers in the second to Mellors in the third). He arrived at the defiant emphasis, with some awkwardness, on his own role of the outsider intellectual. Mellors is that not only because he so angrily refuses all class identifications but also because of his modernist apocalyptic rhetoric—"the whole damned thing is doomed"—and utopian avowals and perspective.

In a couple of noted passages in the novel, Lawrence's Mellors condenses his vision of the good society into the trope of the community where the men all wear "close bright scarlet" trousers.[24] While the rest of the adumbration of the counter society is thin, it includes the dominance of handicraft production (specifically against early twentieth-century industrialism), autonomous small communities (as against mass society), rural-natural conditions (as against megalopolis), egalitarian-exchange economics (as against commercial-class exploitation), communal arts such as "the old group dances" (as against, quite specifically, the modern mass media, such as Clifford's radio), and sensually positive pagan worship such as of "the great god Pan" (as against Christianity and other moralized "higher cults"). However quaint the use of the Renaissance costuming image of red tights as his utopian metaphor, the vision is a large and serious one.

Several issues should be noted here. The social anger running through the novel is not (contra a good many critics) mere irascibility but the edginess of that larger social view. Lawrence demands that the regenerative eroticism be viewed as going beyond personal experience and a mere arcadian interlude to a large eutopian alternative. Such utopianizing can readily be identified as more than individual. It displays elements of Golden Age mythology, Renaissance pastoral traditions, William Morris and a heritage of anti-industrialism, etc. and thus participates in a major literary, and larger historical, utopianism (and one which I will repeatedly return to). The pastoral-utopian ideas of the artful community and impassioned life propose a full-scale countering of Western civilization's technology, socioeconomic orderings, religion, culture, and character. No less.

Lawrence, then, is a significant twentieth-century utopian. But it drastically reduces the sense of it to sunder the late eutopianizing from the rather meanly different counterutopianizing of *The Plumed Serpent* or the dystopianism of that fine fable, "The Man Who Loved Islands." Certainly the dialectical movement from a revenge utopia to an antiutopia to a pastoral eutopian (however pyrrhonistic) resolution seems important. Granted, fuller recognition of *Lady Chatterley's Lover* as a pastoral-utopian culmination does not dissolve some of the problems of the fiction and the ideology. The tonal disparities, such as the repeated switches from tenderness to stridency, point to a quite scarred regenerative eroticism which inflames into hatred and male bigotry (most crassly in the subordination of women and the gratuitous vituperation against lesbianism—part of the feminist issue I will keep returning to). The rather forced, and uncertain, stock family-on-the-farm-to-be semiaffirmative ending suggests desperation. So does the quaintly cast and elliptical eutopianizing. But utopianizing is crucial to it (though one would never learn that from a majority of the critics).

We might learn from Lawrence a sense that eutopian/dystopian emphases are but provisional parts of a larger utopianizing dialectic. In such self-argument to give social enlargement to private experience, the utopianizing sensibility repeatedly counters what is, including itself. Whether rancorous utopian mythology, sardonic dystopianism, or pastoral-utopian extension of lovers, an alternate society as well as self is at issue. A sense of some such dialectic seems rather more pertinent than many conventional literary concerns (genre, form, textuality, moral categories, and so on). Lawrence's utopianizing dialectics certainly are not the only ones meriting consideration (thus I preceded them with a look at Voltaire's rather different ironic process), but they do point to larger matters, larger awareness.

Counterutopianizing in Some Contemporary Fictions

To complicate, if not irretrievably muddle, literary definitions, let us briefly consider a few recent utopianizing narratives. These are examples of works which, however formally classified, insistently take utopianism as subject. They certainly employ techniques, such as those used for verisimilitude, and emphases, such as the complication of character, which accord with some commonly accepted senses of the "novel." Admittedly, then, they are only utopianizing in subject, in ideas, in derivation (partly), and in concern, which may be insufficient to meet usual formal and genre definitions of "utopian narrative." But that may be fortunate.

Consider Paul Theroux's *Mosquito Coast* (1982), which is taken up here because it is so well known.[25] Competently limned in part, though portentously melodramatic (as is the 1986 Peter Weir movie version with Harrison Ford), it includes a vivid descriptive manner (Theroux is a quite effective, though meanly uncompassionate, travel writer). It tells of an obsessive contemporary American utopian, Allie Fox, and of a couple of years of his utopian adventuring. Cleverly employing some *bildungsroman* devices, it is told from the point of view of his thirteen-year-old son, Charlie, a home-schooled apprentice antiutopian who only slowly comes to realize that his father is mad (a classic manic psychopath, he had, we are passingly informed early in the story, been in a psychiatric hospital). His madness takes the form of whole-hog utopianizing his life, family, and all around him. *Mosquito* buzzes, often at a caricatural level, with a whole series of utopian themes. Fox is an alienated Harvard dropout, an idiosyncratic mechanical inventor—"no man on earth more ingenious"—who had tried pastoral self-sufficiency in Maine and apparently failed. In the novel's introductory interval, when he is a handyman-eccentric in rural Massachusetts, he desperately wants to escape the stupidly commercialized, increasingly incompetent, decadent America, and so takes his family of six to primitive Honduras. There he quickly builds an ideal rural community—his family plus a number of simple locals—in the jungle.

That would-be eutopia, the larger part of the novel, appears an ingenious "masterpiece of order," especially as an elaboration of "appropriate technology" (*MC* 195), that major countering focus of contemporary utopianizing (see below).[26] But he is given an arrogant megalomania in not only teaching and practicing "survival skills" but in his claims to "rebuilding civilization from the smoking ruins" (*MC* 142), which he predicts. Illogically, he is also given a madness which equates ice with civility. He caps his community with an ornately ingenious ice-making plant—portentously seen by his son as a hot-cold paradigm of "Father's head"—which is weirdly inappropriate technology. The crazed Yankee tinkerer-salvationist makes faltering attempts, in scenes rather badly overdone, to impose his ice-power civilizing on the primitive Indians. Though feeling a "little like God" (*MC* 202), he is upset when natives worship only the outer form of the ice-machine. He has discovered that "advanced technology is indistinguishable from magic" (*MC* 193). Since he has been shown as righteously antireligious, he is defeated in his utopianizing even before his ice-plant, town, and more, are blown up when he cleverly traps marauding guerrillas within it.

Instead of curing his mania, this incident accelerates his survivalism. He then imposes a simpler eutopia, confined to his family's scavenging a marginal existence on a tropical lagoon. Harshly ingenious again, he manages, and reenforces the new order by righteously announcing "the destruction of the United States" by nuclear war and fire; hence, there is no alternative. But his grim new place is soon storm-flooded out. Then he maniacally drives his family into the jungle for yet another go at the miserable good-place, this time at the simplest primitive level of the Indians. Forcing his way up the river—"How can I be wrong if I am going against the current?" (*MC* 322)—he now rejects (in authorially imposed incoherence) all the technology he once fervently avowed. "Science fiction gave people more false hopes than two thousand years of bibles" (*MC* 324). Melodramatically combining warfare against his two devils of technology and religion, he fires the private airplane of a missionary (televangelist Spellgood) with whom he had earlier done righteous verbal battle. Betrayed by his distraught son, who wants to escape utopianizing, father Fox is critically wounded by a rifle shot. In satiric parallelism, the smug fundamentalist Christian has downed the righteous fundamentalist utopian. Shortly thereafter, in spite of the heroic efforts of his compassionate, natural, submissive (and quite undeveloped and unbelievable) wife, the mad utopianist dies, pecked to death by the scavenging vultures he has always righteously hated.

In a poignant episode during the most successful Fox-topia, the covertly rebellious eldest son creates his own little counterutopia a couple of miles into the jungle, a children's good-place for his siblings and other families' kids. There they pretend stores and money, religion and prayers, "returning to all the things father hated" (*MC* 168). With similar countering insight, it is shown that, when the father is away, the mother naturally turns to the "traditional methods" instead of technological gimmicks for providing the necessities. Less persuasive are the various explanations for the techno-foxy utopianist, since he is given little of the traditional novel-of-character's backgrounding. He sees himself (as so many contemporary utopians do) as a countering force to corrupt and decaying America, though sometimes failing because he is "too ambitious. I can't help being an idealist" (*MC* 276). His narrating son comes to despise his father as the most selfish of men who "needed comfort" and always "thought of himself first" (*MC* 276). So "when it looked as though America was doomed, he invented a way out." But since the father mostly suffers manic discontent, and was a failed utopian long before, only the self-centeredness seems plausible. (And even there we may observe the novelist's heavy dependence on trite traditional realism and its inappropriate emphasis on self-interest.) His forever patient wife sees him as simply a "perfectionist." A resentful younger son sees him as just an endless talking "farter" who always wanted his own way. His utopianizing is certainly shown as manipulatively autocratic, which leads to considerable meanness and hastens his downfall. A compassionate native follower wisely sees the larger-than-life adventurer driven by the desire for "sperience" and "spearmint" (*MC* 279, 294), the hunger for intense experience and experiment which may be taken as fundamental utopianizing motives. The author covertly seems to judge him not only as selfish and mad but, through repeated ironic metaphors of "the last man" (*MC* 6, 15, 161, 374, etc.), perhaps as the sardonic Nietzschean conception of the devolution of the heroic Western archetype in a nihilism of values.

Near-paralyzed from his bullet wound, utopianizing Fox makes a final argument based on arrogant rejection: "It's a bad design, the human body" (*MC* 465). While this may be true enough (it is a longtime atheistic reverse argument-from-design), it is treated as a final exemplum of his hubris that the given world is not good enough. After all, he had always just wanted to make a better world since God "made a hash of this one" (*MC* 105). His last gnomic utterance of blasphemy: "Christ is a scarecrow!" And this the mad utopianizer has sacrificially become, though the vulture that plucks out (improbably) his endless utopianizing still-live tongue shows him no respect.

The adolescent son's "testing" complete (the puritanic father was always cruelly imposing tests), he has in his conclusion reversed his father's commandment, *"Don't look back" (MC* 266, and repeatedly). The son counters: "Yet for me the past was the only real thing, it was my hope—the very word *future* frightened me" (*MC* 343). He feels "glorious" in his escape from mad utopianism with all its discolorations and in his return to the brightly lit, crass, usual world. Moral: maturity is antiutopianism.

Theroux conveniently demonstrates that utopianizing is used by conservatives, however obsessively incoherent in combining pro- and anti-technology, contemporary survivalism and communalism, selfishness and apocalypticism, and the rest. This is utopian-fascinated antiutopian fiction which employs common novelistic (French realist) techniques of undercutting self-interest psychology in a quasi-*bildungsroman* pattern, though rather thin on character and heavy with improbablities (jungle ice-plant, vultures eating the living, and the melodrama). A grotesque version of *The Swiss Family Robinson?* It does rather more than that, in spite of starting reductively with a psychopath. Perhaps the more pertinent analogue would be L.-F. Céline's mad utopian inventor exploiting his adolescent protégé in *Death on the Installment Plan* (1936); his parallel grotesque ending frees the young Ferdinand horrendously to discover the deathly ordinariness of the world. Theroux's less consistent misanthropy is, of course, watered with the heavy familiar sentimentality of the popular writer. While his sometimes suggestive mockery has combined antithetical traditions of the utopian, such as high-tech and pastoral, so have a number of other contemporary utopianizers (see chapter 4 below), often with disastrous practical as well as intellectual results. Such pop-antiutopianizing as Theroux's, of course, also testifies to the fascination in our time with the utopian themes of ecological apocalypse, alternate social order, ingenious community, simple living, rebellious protest, heroic flight, survivalist self-sufficiency, deschooling and related cultural deconstructing, and the other themes he disdainfully employs yet confirms.

But is such caricaturing really utopian fiction? It obviously mocks traditional as well as contemporary (including sci-fi) utopianizing within more conventional fictional and social values. But except to abstracting formalists, who ignore tangible subjects and ideas, the question must seem obtuse. The fiction is what the fiction does. Granted, my premise for utopian literature includes the "anti-" as part of the thing itself. Dialectically, there is little justification for being simple-minded, or for excluding the widespread varied contemporary responses to utopianizing.

Take the reverse, positive, usage, as (briefly) with John Fowles in *The Maggot* (1985).[27] In shape and much of the material, this is an English historical romance, set in the early mid-eighteenth century, though Foweles in his "Prologue" objects to the historical novel designation. Instead, he describes the work with an obsolete meaning of "maggot," literarily "an obsession with a theme." The theme is the power and virtue of radical dissent in the Protestant tradition. As his "Epilogue" concludes, "Dissent is a universal human phenomenon, yet that of Northern Europe and America is, I suspect, our most precious legacy to the world" (*Maggot* 406). I, too, am persuaded of that, and concur that radical utopianizing is central to it.

With elaborate indirection as well as historical costuming, Fowles unfolds his fanciful story of Rebecca Lee, prophetic parent of Mother Ann Lee, the quite exceptional historic visionary—woman of great "spirit, courage, and imagination" (*Maggot* 467)—who founded and led the movement of Shaker utopian communities (eventually there were dozens of them) in America. Forerunner Rebecca is presented as a poor Quaker turned whore who converted, almost in spite of herself, to socially radical Christian millennarian prophecy.[28] In her conversion experience in an Oxfordshire cave, she literally sees another "maggot," what we bemusedly recognize as a twentieth-century UFO (anachronistically described in terms of plastics, alloys, and electronics) displaced to the eighteenth century (*Maggot* 361 ff.). This futuristic maggot-like thing carries her to a visionary city, June Eternal. Only briefly sketched, it is readily recognizable as a traditional form of eutopia. Country and city have been pastorally fused. Work has become the pleasure of life—"They worked because they would, not that they must" (*Maggot* 379). All live communally, dine communally, and have all goods in common. What is peculiar, and almost distinctive to the Shaker ordering, is that the sexes are separated, and celibate.[29] Should we understand this central manifestation of the Christian revulsion to the fallen flesh as also rooted in an ex-prostitute's sexual reaction? It remains unclear. (Historically, it did free women from the brutal confines of endless procreation and early death, and did not stop the Shakers, in a largely non-Shaker world, from going on with considerable success for generations—as well as implicitly responding to our two-century malaise of overpopulation.)

As for the rest, June Eternal—the name and condition a distinctively British fantasy—is the eutopian city of "Christian justice," which means of radical equality, not in grimness but (as we perceive in Shaker art) in beauty and joy. Such utopianism, of course, is cognate with two centuries of Protestant dissent, and one of its greatest creations. Near the end of the novel, the author steps in to announce defensively that he is an antireligious atheist, yet one who admires such dissenting Christianity, however usually scorned as "quaint and utopian" (*Maggot* 462). He had earlier insisted (as we atheists are wont to do) on the social logic of Christian doctrine: "If all are equal in Christ's sight . . . why are they not in human sight? No degree of theological obfuscation or selective quotation justifying the Caesars of this world can answer that" (*Maggot* 395).

Nor can religious-moral casuistry justify male rule over women. In a feminist correction of trinitarianism, Rebecca Lee is succored by "Holy Mother Wisdom" who reveals June Eternal to her (*Maggot* 383). Rebecca later prophesizes that "when the Lord Jesus comes again, He shall be She" (*Maggot* 459). Such feminism has long been a central aspect of radical utopianism, though, historically, Shaker women's equality existed within a still-limited hierarchical order (and much of the work was still assigned by traditional gender roles).[30] Overall, the point Fowles makes is that, without its radical dissent and utopianism, Christianity is socially contemptible. It can only be redeemed by those demands for the earthly "founding of a more humane society" (*Maggot* 405).

In the fiction, the recovery of earlier feminism is yoked somewhat incongruously with the fascinated delineation of eighteenth-century whoring (and such discoveries as that women didn't wear underpants), as is the larger egalitarianism with the vicious class society of the time which provides central characters and decor.[31] The novel is also straight-jacketed by the dominant form of lengthy lawyerly depositions, and the lawyer-detective's quest (an unsolved mystery) for the Lord who led Rebecca to her conversion. The tiresomely set and redundant depositions obscure a bit the theme and too much limit the author's best play of intelligence. June Eternal can hardly receive adequate development in the depositions for the hostile establishment attorney. The most incisive remarks (including some quoted above) are authorial commentary from outside the pattern of the fiction, which shows numerous such strainings. *The Maggot,* then, is awkward fiction, and, it seems to me, not Fowles' best. Whether viewed as twisted historical romance or dissenting utopian maggot, its parts do not quite come together. Yet however inadequately presented by the skittishly sophisticated novelist, it is intriguing for his sense of the larger import of the visionary radical utopian, who, Fowles advises us, does no less than "adumbrate the relation of fiction to reality" (*Maggot* 463). That might serve as out motto for what utopianizing often does more generally (and justify our detailed concern with often inadequate literature).

In taking two quite different examples from 1980s mainstream novelists, Theroux and Fowles, am I suggesting a new contemporary role for literary utopianizing? No doubt some of the elements show a strongly topical cast— apocalyptic flight from, rather than to, America *(Mosquito Coast); male insis-tence on female equality *(The Maggot);* and, more generally, sophisticated mixtures of fascination and skepticism with the utopian. But the popularity of literary utopianizing is not really that new, except in the thinly rinsed minds of some literary historians. While the recognized literary concern, perhaps more than its larger social-cultural impetus, may show tidal variations, and cast up different flotsam and jetsam, the currents have long continued at the established cliffs.

Step back a full generation, to before the 1960s (from whose dissenting movements it is fashionable to explain supposedly revived utopianizing). This is the period in which nondissenting intellectuals were loudly announcing the end of utopianizing (taken as the "end of ideology" in the opposite sense from the famous definition of Karl Mannheim).[32] The off-tells (official intellectuals) explained that the positive hopes of utopian ideologies were no longer germane (most thankfully, though sometimes with a a touch of nostalgia) to a culture made dourly pessimistic by endless hot-and-cold war, overpopulation, uncontrollable technology, reactive social-political views, and, indeed, an obvious desperate pragmatism in the age of anxiety. Utopianism had had its day.

But though the cultural weather seems variable, the days keep coming, including the utopianizing impetus and its literary artifacts. During the end-of-utopias rain the literary utopias were many, and even popular. For example, one might take (assuming a strong literary as well as political stomach) Ayn Rand's best-selling *Atlas Shrugged* (1957), an immensely long, bombastic tract in trite fictional form pushing an extreme version of entrepreneurial capitalism.[33] It depends in part on an essential non-place as well as social nonsense. This "Utopia of Greed" (a phrase plausibly summarizing much of the view) is also called "Galt's Gulch" and is located in a Colorado mountain valley protected by magical rays. Here a conspiratorial cult of embittered "egotists" has established a utopian refuge under the charismatic authority of a soap-opera hero, John Galt. (The Aynrandean simple-minded rationalistic individualism, of course, lacks most richness of individuality.) As Rand explained elsewhere, her fictional credo was dominated by the purpose of providing an image of "the kind of social system that makes it possible for ideal men to function," and that is "laissez-faire capitalism."[34]

But in countering modern collectivism, and various forms of compassion, Adam Smith's Invisible Hand has been turned to the tricky and mean. The heavy, trite rhetoric justifying the capitalist eutopia (as with Galt's four- or five-hour radio address) is dominated by contempt and hatred. Resentment, we are reminded again (as also in part with Theroux's unappreciated inventor and Fowles' abused whore), can be a major motive for utopianizing. In addition, as with so many twentieth-century utopias, Rand's is not intended to be eternal. The Utopia of Greed is only temporary as the capitalists scramble toward renewed positions in the society that they absurdly deny depending upon. To true believers in a mystical notion of the "market," that piety, not individual development, centers the ideology. While this pop-utopianizing is of little literary interest, it did spawn a cultish movement.[35] Self-fishy Aynrandism, combined with more traditional liberal political economics, still continues under the misnomer "Libertarianism" (including a political party as well as an ambiguous, broad left-right intellectual wing—it does emphasize some liberties—of the Republican Party), as if economic exploitation were the essence of freedom. But it may be salutary in reminding us that utopianizing can be turned to a variety of motives and purposes.

Reactive, "conservative," motives dominate the 1950s utopian allegories of William Golding (touched on below). They also launch an odd assault on pacifism and feminism in Bernard Wolfe's *Limbo* (1952), which blithely includes a couple of nuclear wars, a 1990s sci-fi dystopia in a postnuke vestigial America run by male voluntary multiple amputees (a religious ritual of masochistic pacifist ideologues), plus an earlier eutopianism of a primitivistic Happy Isle in the Indian Ocean run by a penitent lobotomist (with a warmly submissive native wife).[36] Psychoanalysis and cybernetics are deployed to prove that men should be aggressive and women should not—a prefeminist feminist backlash— but pronouncements (and a True and False chart) insist in a mostly sloganeering prose that it should be "healthy" aggression. The hip-bombast might only need some slight updating in decor to provide a mixed eutopia/dystopia for popular fears in the 1980s. The more things change. . . .

Somewhat better known utopianizing from the 1950s is Kurt Vonnegut's *Player Piano* (1954), which utilizes some traditional nowhere conventions (such as from *Brave New World*) to project a satiric "technological utopia" in the American near future. While quite journalistic in its style and stereotypical characters (though hardly the collection of caricatures and wisecracks apparent in his later cartoon utopias), it does raise some thoughtful issues about the impenetrable rules set by a corporate-style technocratic elite in a possible, highly automated society. The parallel theme of dehumanization from the loss of conventional job-identities seems to me less persuasive, given what the majority of jobs already were. But it carried out with some perception the utopianizing critical function.[37]

A utopianizing work of the same period that has been more praised as literature is Walter M. Miller, Jr.'s three novellas, eventually combined into *A Canticle for Leibowitz* (1959).[38] The linked stories, six centuries apart in sequence, follow a not-quite-complete twentieth-century nuclear holocaust. The slowly recovering remains produce a Medieval-style Dark Age, then a scientific-political renaissance (including the rediscovery of electricity, as in an earlier Rand utopia, but with comic wit), and a neomodern age of high-technology ending in a more complete nuclear doom. That is only slightly ameliorated by a devoutly religious party rocketing off to utopianize a star and, one must suppose, yet again to reenact the absurd sequence of human history and devolution.

The astutely detailed, and often wry, accounts of each epoch are told from the successive viewpoints of traditional Christian (Roman) fanatics in a Southwest American abbey, which is incongruously dedicated to one Leibowitz, a twentieth-century Jewish engineer, eventually canonized for trying to save books from the vengeful antiintellectuals (McCarthy-period style) after the "Flame Deluge."[39] While most of the society has apparently returned to the pastoral, the saving "remnant of human culture" under religious auspices creates new heroic martyrs, recreates the old amoralist science-technology, and insures the repetition of doom.[40] But the irony is subordinated to doctrine. For, as the last martyr-abbot concludes, civilization "always culminates in the colossus of the State . . . drawing about itself the mantle of godhead." And what induces that is human sin, "not suffering but the unreasoning fear of suffering, *Matis doloris*. Take it together with its positive equivalent, the craving for worldly security, for Eden, and you might have your root of evil. . . . To minimize suffering and to maximize security were natural and proper ends of society," but they have been perverted by human wickedness to total ends and in the process produced "maximum suffering and minimum security."[41] For the bad creation that so insistently allows this process to repeat itself, we should (apparently) "forgive God." But the utopianizing impetus allows without requiring forgiveness, or the recognition that God is properly damned and doomed.

Surely this diverse handful of utopianizing fictions over the past generation suggests the radically protean quality of the impetus. What do they have in common? An alternate vision of society, eutopian or dystopian—or mixed and muddled. Science fiction conventions? They all have a bit of high-tech—historically displaced, or magical, or pathological, or prophetic, or at least problematic (though only the Miller is usually discussed as sci-fi, because of its publishing genesis). Sci-fi, and older utopian conventions, are used, in combination with conventional realism, historical romance, religious fable, social tract, etc., without being defining. But social ideology seems rather more the issue in all of them. And ancient questions of how to live, which is what the utopianizing impetus is really about.

Countering the Counterings

Since I have suggested an expansive view of literary utopianizing, it might be prudent also to pose some possible limits. While the utopian can be more widely found than frequently acknowledged, it certainly should not be found everywhere, not quite everywhere. That, I hasten to add, does not proscribe speculative and fanciful noplaces from appearing in all sorts of times and places (as the previous examples suggest). Images and arguments of alternate societies can, and do, show up as parts of "realistic" novels, historical romances, moral allegories, fictionalized political and religious tracts, etc., without being totally determining of the literary experience. And without being definable by any single ideology. In a highly syncretistic culture like ours, it often makes sense to view the utopianizing as part rather than parcel of the literary experience and ideological purpose.

Is utopianizing, then, merely a synonym for fantasizing? That does not seem helpful. Such fantasies as, say, heavens of perfect and eternal bliss, or sexual projections of constant orgasmic satisfaction, certainly shed little light on what a society is, or can be. Even here, of course, the restrictions can hardly claim finality, since heavens-on-earth and pornotopias (to be discussed later) seem recurrent. We might therefore grope for some more general principle of demarcation, some separation between utopianizing and fantasizing parallel to Coleridge's "imagination" and "fancy." But is not that rather a distinction of quality than of kind? Some projects seem "serious" or "significant," and others less so. No doubt sometimes one woman's mere fanciful fantasy is some man's most imaginative utopian leap.

But with all due regard for the problems of relativism and reification, some approximate differences, tendencies at least, between, for example, fantasyland and idealland might be suggested. From my perspective, Tolkien's quaint land of the Hobbits may suggest a kind of social ordering, but it is one so lacking in critical spirit and so pale in social substance as not to be anyone's eutopia or dystopia. Or, for a more recent example, consider Russell Hoban's *Riddley Walker* (1982).[42] Its futurist scene and neoprimitive society might suggest the utopian. But this mannerist confession of a postnuclear adolescent, tiresomely done (I think) in synthetic dialect, also mostly concerns ritualization. While ritual has a place, negative or positive, in a social vision, its dominance is another matter. What makes D. H. Lawrence's utopian *The Plumed Serpent* so hard to take, many commentators agree, is the heavy quantity and hysterical style of made-up ritualism (ceremonies, songs, dances, poems, etc.). In contrast, what gives Miller's *Canticle for Leibowitz* some of its literary effectiveness is the use of quite traditional Roman Catholic ritualism, on which he can play for wryness and incongruity, for irony as well as communal faith, many centuries in the future. The effectiveness of ritual must partly depend on prerational recognition, inculcated assent. To try to invent much of it, instead of merely varying what is recognized, may be beyond most literary art. The synthetic, in ritual as in language (not to mention all other usages), has obvious limits this side of the insistently arbitrary. When there is much ritualization, it takes over, not only as a stylistic problem but as social mystification, which, of course, is an essential function of rituals. If overdone, I am suggesting, ritualism will defeat other ends of utopianizing, and intelligence. Literature heavy in ritualizing will be thin as eutopia. Not incidentally, the more effective literary use of ritualization, in all its arbitrariness, appears satirically in dystopias, such as *We, Brave New World,* and *Nineteen Eighty-Four.*

Certainly there are complex matters here, which I do not mean to dismiss. But rituals, less the product of individual art and assertions than of communal mergings and continuities, are not responsive utopianizing. Ritual performances—say, at a sporting event or military formation, a club or academic installation, a funeral or memorial occasion, an award ceremony or religious service—mystify, transcend, obfuscate the mere realities, such as competition, force, achievement, death, suffering, and so on. Undoubtedly mystification has its utilities, but they do not include much social criticism or alternative.

One might wish to extend this argument to religious utopianizing in general (previously cited arguments emphasize the secular nature of the utopian), yet several of the contemporary utopias I use to illustrate other points, such as *The Maggot* and *A Canticle for Leibowitz,* centrally employ historic religions. And effectively. Yet most historical discussions of the utopian tend to separate out the millennial.[43] Surely in terms of religious as well as utopian tropes, Revelation has little connection with the Garden of Eden. Judgment Day ends all societies, including the imaginative utopian. Religiously inspired utopianism must be of a different sort than transcendentalizing fantasies, though sometimes in practice they do get contradictorily mixed. Which brings us back to some worldly distinctions between utopianizing and fantasizing.

Perhaps a modern religious example will set off some of the differences. One major direction of utopianizing, at least since Francis Bacon's *New Atlantis* (1614), has been scientism, that is, faith in science as a salvational religion.[44] It became a watershed issue in all sorts of nineteenth-century utopian counterings. Saint-Simon, Comte, and Bellamy were pietists of scientism, Fourier and Morris heretics. Engels' Marxism furthered the positivistic side by speciously distinguishing between "utopian socialism" and "scientific socialism," the latter patently the more dogmatically pretentious direction. It usually tends to the authoritarian, not only in the faith in the scientistic as palliative, progressive, and redemptive, but in casting its practitioners as high priests, a ruling technocratic elite. That role not only appears in Bacon's House of Solomon (an ambitious scientific institute) but might plausibly be traced back through the alchemist, the more technically clever magus or shaman, or indeed any priest with medical or similar pretensions. It becomes utopian when it determines the social shaping, but it becomes fantasy when it transcends the human.

The distinction might be applied within one representative utopianizer. H. G. Wells, certainly one of the most influential utopian propounders as well as fictionists, will serve.[45] In *A Modern Utopia* (1905), he specifically acknowledges Bacon's emphasis on science-as-power.[46] And Wells means power in the literal social sense, with elitist rule by a scientific-minded "voluntary nobility," which is acknowledged to be a "caste." They are shown—or rather, in the heavily essayistic narrative, asserted—to be the rulers of the "World State" of the future (another ominous notion of great influence). It is a highly technologized and bureaucratized welfarist ordering, with public work projects, statist rehabilitation of the deviant, endless education—97 percent go to college (even outdoing the California of three generations later). In spite of some skeptical dialogue, *Modern Utopia* does optimistically burble with scientific piety.

But that politically dubious technocracy of his first modern utopia is far from the last word for the prolific Wells. Among his variety of utopian proposals, in and out of fiction, the apparently most libertarian may be one done nearly two decades after the first, *Men Like Gods* (1923).[47] Unlike the earlier one, it is more egalitarian and supposedly has no central State. However, that may be rather hypocritical since rule has in effect been displaced into uniform scientistic indoctrination, in which "education is our government" and "runs everything." That would seem to be an authoritarian State by just another, a pedagogically honorific, control. But even that may be less the crux than that in his utopia more than a hundred generations in the future, after elaborate "eugenic" development (i.e., what is now called genetic engineering), there is "a cleansed and perfected humanity." In contrast to the earlier people-pretty-much-as-they-are, plus science schooling, there is now a world of "demigods," beings bred into not only higher intellect but direct psychic communication, and other boring fantastic powers.[48]

This, I argue, should be viewed less as eutopian projection than as scientistic fantasy. Wells, though he does not acknowledge the difference, has crossed over into religious transcendence. While no simple formula may adequately define *homo sapiens* for social and cultural purposes (I am not going to repeat, albeit at a higher level, the gen-simp fallacies of the genre critics), there must be limits for human possibilities which at least allow the significant grounds for our disagreements on politics, economics, psychology, art, language, love, and much else. Fundamentally change the premises by changing the beings—not just the conditions, not just the emphasis—and the arguments (and utopias are arguments) tend to the meaningless.[49] As with heavily other-worldly religions, this scientistic-other-world depends on acts of faith and magic, not on acts of recognizably human intelligence, will, and sensibility.

Even granting the possibility of the man-into-demigod future, would it be of any interest to us? By definition, "perfected" beings—or "angels," if one prefers a more ancient image—do not correspond to our language or other experiential tests. What we have, then, is speculation so arbitrarily pure as to be essentially false to the human. When anything goes, it does not go from here. Surely such fantasy can be read, though mostly for symptomatic value. As a recurrent form of the pathological escape from the human (as also with some of the Wells-influenced science fiction), it might be of some interest, although only if reconstructed in terms of human disease. While we might be properly reluctant to set a hard line where meaningful imaginative construct turns into meaning-shifted-to-symptom fantasy, some recognition of the difference seems unavoidable. Wells is an interesting case because he mixes utopianizing and fantasizing, though certainly he is not the only one. Since in Wells these elements mix rather than merge, we can still discriminate rather than simply reject. But when fantasy dominates (with a nod to Hegel's dialectic), quantity becomes a lack of quality, and we have departed from intelligent imagination.

As I understand Wells, the impetus that turned his utopianism to fantasy (as I am using the terms) was magical belief, what used to be called "faith in progress" but may be better thought of as "perfectionism." As he writes in *Men Like Gods,* "thanks to a certain obscure and indomitable righteousness in the blood of the human type," we must move towards perfection.[50] Obscure, indeed: the only bloody substance here is faith. But given his skeptical intelligence shown elsewhere, it must have been a forced and precarious faith. At least we can easily read that back from his last discussion of the subject, *Mind at the End of Its Tether,* where, in post-World War II despair, he announced: "Homo sapiens . . . is in his present form played out," and our "universe is not merely bankrupt . . . it is going out of existence. . . . The attempt to trace a pattern of any sort is absolutely futile."[51] The other side of faith, the despair over the lack of any guaranteed pattern, left him no perspective at all, and confirmed the scientistic religiosity of his earlier view.

Apparently, too, at that serious level of concern, he could no longer fall back on fantasies. Literary fantasies, which do not much interest me here in their own right, might fit Michael Holquist's misdefinition of utopias (discussed earlier) since they tend to be games, at their best consistent deductive structures from fantastic premises. Since noted utopianizing writers, from Wells through Le Guin (discussed in the next chapter) and beyond, also practice fantasy writing, there is an understandable confusion between the two different impetuses. Some considerable separation seems necessary between utopia and fantasy literature.

And between utopianizing and fantasizing the future. Since, again, the context and concern here are larger than the literary artifacts, we might follow Wells and his scientistic religiosity, and desperation, into the larger world of fantasizing. One of the best known American fantasizers of the past generation, R. Buckminster Fuller, messianically proclaimed that the choice was either his engineering paradise or nothing, as in *Utopia or Oblivion* (1969).[52] In his *Operating Manual for Spaceship Earth* (1963), he had insisted that the issue was the re-creation of the "total world society." Such tropes may also be indebted to Wells (so popular in Fuller's youth) since such political (as well as engineering) totalism was previously uncommon, at least in secular utopian traditions (though of course it may be found in the millennial). Fuller's global political transformation was simply to be the natural by-product of a "world-round industrial retooling revolution."[53] Mechanics masters all.

What in fact Fuller did was to deploy grossly simple design analogies to everything. The very limited merits of his geodesic and dymaxion devices (the resulting buildings I have seen are often not very good for their human purposes, not even in very limited physical senses), and his other engineering templates, were expanded with religious fervor into total metaphors. Claims that they would resolve psychological and social issues were megalomania. When he pronounced that properly programmed computers would take care of all political issues, and that there were no real difficulties with overpopulation, resource limitation, or technocratic authoritarianism, he was not utopianizing but fantasizing. As in fantasy games, there was little limit to the deductive moves.[54] Even a sympathetic anthropologist has to admit that Fuller did not even try to understand how humans behave but simply imposed a technology and "expect[ed] men to adapt" to whatever it required.[55] His implicit desire must be to escape from human freedom and variousness, not even by critique and alternative but by technomysticism.

Other technomystics take flight from the human by fancies of genetic transformation (as Wells did in *Men Like Gods*), psychic reconditioning (B. F. Skinner's *Walden Two* [1948] is the most notorious, though a relatively mild, example), and even approximations of immortality, as in Wells' "demigods" or as it also appears in Olaf Stapledon's "Fifth Men," who have a life-span of fifty thousand years in his speculatively suggestive but humanly (and novelistically) incoherent *Last and First Men* (1930). Eternal life had not been traditional (so far as I can find) in earlier utopian literature. One scholar links it to the rise of new biological theories in the nineteenth century.[56] But it should probably be linked to alchemical and Faustian promises of "new knowledge." The religiosity of scientistic immortality rises concurrently with the decline of Christian faith in literal immortality. It has now taken on programmatic claims. For example, Alan Harrington in *The Immortalist* (1977) concludes his optimistic medical projections with "Notes on a Utopia beyond Time" in which he blandly announces that in the future living forever will answer most problems.[57] Earlier, in crude jottings entitled *Up-Wingers* (1973), the manic flights of F. M. Esfandiary included "Everything is now possible," not least cosmic consciousness, "super-utopias," and literal immortality.[58] Such symptoms of scientistic mania can hardly be argued with, though they may suggest a renewed pertinence of some traditional literature. The literate (which probably does not include the immortalists I am citing) might recall the anecdote from Petronious' *Satyricon* (first century, but T. S. Eliot used it as epigraph to *The Waste Land*).[59] It is about the Sibyl at Cumae to whom Apollo had granted eternal life but not eternal youth (some things being beyond plausible gods, and plausible doctors). The forever aging lady cries for death. Immortalist fantasts might take heed, for if any characteristic at all is not regenerated, deathlessness may become exponentially horrendous. Even a few centuries of arthritus, or a "drinking problem," or just bad memories, might be hard to take.

Some of the technotopians (as we might call those in the scientistic fantasy modes yet claiming utopianism) may be viewed as engaging in a little discussed literary type, the comic routine disguised as speculative fiction-philosophy. For example, a routine of Timothy Leary, guru of the Swiss-cheese-brain-generation, included the scientistic super-utopian pronouncement that new technologism "will eliminate the prescientific problems of poverty, territorial conflict, disease, aging, death, pollution, over-population."[60] Curious how mortality becomes a secondary problem in a series rather than a defining human condition. The "New Scientists" will resolve all problems, and apparently create no new ones, except perhaps the ugly literalism of the devotees who forget that even in fairy tales wishes are limited.

More deadpan comical at times is Leary's devotee, the avowed right-libertarian science fictionist and burlesque prophet Robert Anton Wilson. In *The Illuminati Papers* (1981), he scores some odd ideological points, such as demonstrating that science fiction is a worldwide paranoid conspiracy. He, too, embraces endless technological fantasies, new drug-induced forms of "consciousness," and instant "immortality"—"some people alive today will never die."[61] However, he may self-destruct in what he defines as his own great "Utopian" project: "a worldwide War Against Stupidity."[62] This continuation of Wells' "campaign against the dull" has the virtues of considerable learning and of skepticism about conventional thinking but becomes self-burlesque in the perfectionism.

One may kindly hope that these self-parodying sons of Wells find a nicer final tether than their master, who was capable of reckoning critical despair, and dying. While it may be comforting to think in only one direction, nondialectically eliminating most human problems, the vision of living forever with cosmic consciousness in a perfect world is simply dull. Such quaint extremes of technotopianism remind us that utopianizing is only intellectually interesting when it maintains a tension with present realities, with a sense of opposition not to be dissolved in cheap pieties. "Perfectibilism," reasonably notes a philosopher, "is dehumanizing" in its denial of a sensibly full range of human limitations as well as possibilities. Yet to jump from that to total rejection of the utopian may be to commit a parallel dehumanization, to refuse to recognize, the philosopher continues, "that man is capable of becoming something much superior to what he now is."[63] Necessarily, he may also become much inferior.[64] Some human freedom is presumed. It is the purpose, I am arguing, of utopianizing dialectics to explore that awareness.

A further consideration. While it seems obvious to me that utopianizing awareness can take different modes, and that those loosely described as "narrative fictions" are only part of the spectrum, why need these forms be artful? Just as reporting on reality, providing a humorous stance, or exposing absurdities take the form of realism, comedy, or satire, so critical and alternative responses to social institutions take various utopian forms. Various conventions are at hand, and others possible, including (as I have previously tried to illustrate) adapting and combining the utopian impetus with the fable, the speculative essay, the fantasy projection (though I just argued that was dubious), the tract, the historical romance, and, even, the "realistic novel," among others. Included with the others (as I previously suggested) are those originating in partly nonverbal responses, architectural utopian city plans. A note on that large subject, whose record is partly in words but also partly in stone and other images, may suggest why it helps utopianizing to be concrete.

From ancient ideal cities, for man but more often for man-god rulers, through the part-ideal planning of Athens, Rome, Venice, and many other actual places, structuring a better city has been a rich utopian concern. Given the twentieth century's megalopolitan ugliness, and other problems, it is hardly surprising that diverse exceptional talents have devoted themselves at times to city utopianizing. English Ebenezer Howard's influential plans for his morally decent Garden City, Swiss-French Le Corbusier's visualizing his gigantic super-industrial Radiant City, Frank Lloyd Wright's piquant plans for recountrifying the urban in his Broadacre City, carry on long traditions of imaginative social criticism and conceptualization.[65]

As drawing, mock-up, and words (each also wrote a book about his utopian city),[66] the visualizations of the responses and concepts are interesting objects for contemplation. So more generally with utopianizing. Garden, Radiant, and Broadacre cities have never been fully built. Should we understand them, then, just as variations on the Tower of Babel? Something rather more, for the plans of Howard, Le Corbusier, and Wright have had clear influence on actual places. So, though perhaps less concretely, with utopianizing in general.

These ambitious utopian cities may also induce a certain discipline in our thinking about ideologies as well as cities. As paradigms, these plans may be said to teach awareness of the conceptual limitations of lesser "planners" and point to the hidden agendas, the covert utopias, that lie behind any planning. By planners I mean not only the professional technicians who practice that usually dubious trade, but the rulers and administrators, the businessmen and "developers," who consciously, or more often not, carry out what is usually a debased utopianism.[67] In part, all cities are planned, however confused or hypocritical or partly fortuitous their ideals may be. Cities, like other utopianizing efforts, are not just objects of nature but constructions variously imagined, chosen, willed, and made.

The utopian concepts made specific can also be informingly related to the "real world." Thus many of our suburban towns can be related (though often not decently enough) to the ideal of the cooperative community in nature enshrined in Howard's Garden City. And to its rather blandly narrow middle-class sense of culture and human behavior. Our grandiloquent urban highrise centers can be related (though usually without the rigorous coherence) to the hyperfunctional technological ideals of Le Corbusier's Radiant City. And to its hierarchical centralism and other antidemocratic tendencies. Our contradictory American responses to the urban and communal can be related (though generally without the imaginative verve) to Wright's Jeffersonian individualistic anticity Broadacre. And to its rather forced familial economics and social atomization. These utopian city plans make tangible not only major social-political dispositions but certain styles of sensibility and living.

My brief notes on three major modernist utopian city plans do not intend to suggest that their specifications allow us to choose once and for all between the genteel surburban, the technocratic centralist, and the atomized individualist possibilities. Nor does reading, say, three utopian essays or narratives lead us conclusively to eutopia or dystopia, though they may dialectically serve the process. The utopianizing process, I suggest, may be advanced by countering possibilities.

It may also lead to a critical countering of other cases. For passing examples, two more recent utopian city planners. One partly built, in the Arizona desert, is Paolo Soleri's Arcosanti. Though using, architecturally and expositorily, some of the individualist rhetoric and ideas of Wright, Soleri makes clear in his theory of *Arcology* (1969), as well as in his rather unlivable beehive city, that the role of the nonelite individual is slight.[68] Like a fictional Ayn Rand architect, he seems exploitatively disposed to impose his advantages, shapes, and mystagogueries on others. In the name of liberty, of course, under the rule of the masters. Similarly, the noted futuristic superplanner of a worldwide city, "Ecumenopolis," C. A. Doxiadis, shows in *Building Entopia* (1975) a considerable technocratic dehumanization in the styles as well as proportions of his plans.[69] The optimism of technocracy again suggests dystopia.

The utopian city plan analogues suggest several concerns emerging from utopian narrative fictions. Like the plans, the fictions may be valuable because they concretize, give the shape and feel of the utopianizing concepts. As a principle of practical criticism, it seems to me quite important to give some emphasis to the qualities and implications of the cityscape in the utopian narrative, not just the concepts and plots. After all, if one were magically transported to various nowheres, it would be good sense to pay less attention to the spokesperson for the official place than the shape and feel of things. That, too, should be part of the appropriate diatopianism.

Revtopianism:
Some Reversals in Utopianizing

Revolutionary Dystopianism

One of the striking images of *A Modern Utopia* (1905), H. G. Wells' seminal first fiction-essay directly in the utopian mode, is that of a London mostly walled in by a glass dome.[1] No specific source for this appears in the discussions of Wells, though the image is an importantly recurring one in later utopian literature. In a practical sense, no literary or other ideological source may be thought necessary: London drizzle provides sufficient encouragement for roofing in the place (and for similar treatment, say, of Moscow or New York City or Buffalo in later science fiction stories placed in frigid or polluted discomfort). Some may think it as logical as building walls around ancient towns to hold off hostile tribes. But it more than suggests a hostile view of nature (evident also in Wells' other technocratic hopes for the future, such as high-speed trains without windows). The futuristic version of the walled city becomes not only a resonant trope for the removal from natural variety into a synthetic environment but a marker for an ideology of control and a monumentalizing of purified authoritarianism. In Wells (and some others to be noted) the glass walled-in city is presented as a positive image. But given the utopianizing impetus to countering views, we might expect others strikingly to reverse its import, domed eutopia becoming damned dystopia.

So with E. M. Forster's apparent literary riposte to Wells' *A Modern Utopia,* the satiric novella "The Machine Stops" (1912).[2] Carrying the implicit logic a bit further, Forster's society-as-machine has totally walled out the brightness of the sun, the invigoration and discomfort of ordinary air, and touch, sex, free movement, and most nonmachined human variousness and richness. With proper reversal, the artificial society has so depleted the dependent humans that not only do they gag on ordinary air and become nauseous with mere human contact, but in their machine-religiosity they have finally lost the very qualities—ingeniousness, initiative, pragmatic intelligence—needed to fix the inter-dependent machines when they start to malfunction. The mechanisms become erratic, the reversals compound, and the whole machine of society fatally col-lapses. Since this is prenuclear, and therefore not quite total apocalypse, there are survivors—those neoprimitives who earlier escaped the containing city, going beyond the walled senses and thinking in a rebellious return to a simpler and more responsive pastoral life.

In many later science-fiction domed-in machine cities (like Samuel De-lany's well-known *Triton* [1976]), the ecological rationale is more incisive but there is little pastoral alternative.[3] However, as I have already suggested in discussing Lawrence and others, the dialectics of the walled-in machine-order versus the neoprimitive-beyond, technocracy versus the new pastoralism, be-comes a recurring and crucial dialectic. In several ways it provides the contem-porary ideological watershed.

Since my strategy for understanding the utopian suggests responding with several dialectics, another line of approach might be pertinent here. While I do not know the source (other than a general technological control of weather and the ancient piety to walled cities) for Wells' glass-domed London, a possible analogue, which also operates metaphorically, may be the Crystal Palace. That famous Joseph Paxton cast-iron and glass-pane domed building, the hall created in Hyde Park for the display of machines and other paraphernalia taken for worship of progress and scientism at the Great Exhibition of 1851, would obvi-ously be known to science journalist Wells (perhaps literally in its later form as a museum at Sydenham). The significant nowhere images of utopia, of course, come out of somewhere realities, though turned in abstracted time and space to larger and often somewhat different resonances. The encompassing glass wall becomes an ideological trope larger than utility, as it also has in those successors to the Crystal Palace, the sealed glass boxes that dominate contemporary cityscapes and define much of our lives in techno-submissive geometry.[4]

The Crystal Palace had also been passionately used as an antiutopian meta-phor, especially by Dostoyevsky in his manic confessional-philosophical no-vella, *Notes from Underground* (1864).[5] There it was an essential element in a triadic trope: the society as an "ant hill" of modern mass organization, the individual as reduced to a "piano key" (or "organ stop") for an arithmetically subordinated part in an imposed harmony, and the rationalistic ideal of the "Crystal Palace" of modern engineering grandiloquence. With the three-pronged trope, Dostoyevsky wished intellectually to fork away rationalistic Western eutopianism. And to replace it, of course, with his own Christian eutopianism of an even more hierarchical society, subordinated penitent individual, and divinely crystalized empyrium. The countering of utopianizing usually rests in a counterutopia, though not always admitted. While Dostoyevsky was also con-sciously countering the earnestly optimistic scientistic rationalism of a contemporary utopian novel—N. G. Chernyshevsky, *What Is to Be Done?*—he was also doing much more. (Exceptional literary works are never just to be understood in genre terms.) Besides acutely exploring a perverse character, he makes a brilliant critique of self-interest psychology and ethics, a central dogma of Western liberalism. His intellectual defense of irrationalism pits capricious man in his profound anguish against utilitarian man in his bland happiness. On the libelous premise that "suffering is the sole origin of consciousness," a most degraded personification of self-consciousness, the underground man (the masochistic marginal intellectual), must win the argument and lose all but the tenuous ultimate possibility of happiness in a divine nowhere.

Now these issues, and literary works of Wells and Dostoyevsky, provide a proper matrix for one of the best, as well as most influential (on science fiction as well as broader utopianizing), twentieth-century black utopias, Yevgeny Zamyatin's *We* (1921).[6] Zamyatin yoked Wells, whose utopias he got to know while a maritime engineer in Britain during the Great War (and the translations of which he later edited and lectured on), and Dostoyevsky, whose underground arguments (and parable of the Grand Inquisitor from *The Brothers Karamazov*) he quite consciously adapts, in creating a dystopia that counters both.[7] *We* is both antirationalist and anti-Christian. Such are the often insufficiently acknowledged dialectical counterings of literary history.

Each major building in the ruthlessly authoritarian, thirtieth-century society of *We* is a "gigantic glass beehive." This would-be ideal ordering not only serves rigid surveillance (as with Jeremy Bentham's ideal prison, the Panopticon, which can retrospectively be viewed as the forerunner of the technototalitarian) but also the pervasive sense of corporate unity, "we-ness."[8] And all of those crystal palaces, in their totally urbanized and sanitized rationality of mathematical ordering, are further purified into a bland reductiveness by the superimposition of yet another Wellsian crystal palace, one for the whole city-society, an encompassing opaque glass "Green Wall." This, with additional electronic controls (*We* 119), ironically keeps out the greenery and demarcates the ordered life of the One State (also probably a metaphor and doctrine from fervent "internationalist" Wells) and reduces most natural variety and intensity of experience. A major point here, and the thrust of Zamyatin's sensation-heightened style, is that domination depends on experience being pared down to the uniformly bland. Scientistic puritanism demands reduced sensation and its equivalent in imagination. The sunlight is muted, and much of the rest of nature excluded; all "numbers" (people) must wear grayish-blue uniforms; bright colors, sharp varieties, strong sensations, and feelings, are associated with difference, passion, rebellion.[9] The muting and confining walls, then, have become part of the denial of rich sensibility.

The large pattern of *We* is well known and has served as archetype for the more famous dystopias following it, such as *Brave New World* and *Nineteen*

Eighty-Four. (Orwell wrote about *We* prior to his dystopia; Huxley denied direct influence but acknowledged taking off negatively from Wells.)[10] The pattern includes the clever ideological-rationalizer tyrant Benefactor (the Controller, Big Brother), with his Grand Inquisitor rationale for ruthlessly imposing low-level universal happiness on all. Of course there must be a Plato-derived hierarchy of "Guardians" to enforce it. And there is the combined high technology and elaborate ritualization aimed at thought-and-feeling control. The individualist male protagonist, D-503 (John Savage, Winston Smith), somehow not fully conditioned, discovers (in literary ways) self-consciousness and the bitter truths about his society, though his rebellion is finally futile and self-destructive. His transformation depends on the female focus of his romantic passion, I-330 (Lenina, Julie), who is also connected to the socially contrary experience represented by the "Mephis beyond the wall" (Huxley's Indian "reservation" in the Southwest, Orwell's land of the "proles" partly outside the system), which is, in sum, neoprimitive life. And so with much of the rest of the paralleling development.

Dour George Orwell elected to emphasize that part of Zamyatin's pattern which insists on terroristic power, while disdainfully witty Huxley foregrounded psychobiological conditioning and reductive placating diversions. While the two emphases seem to provide alternative ways of reaching similar totalitarian ends, Zamyatin may have been wiser in stressing the fusion of both negative and positive conditionings. All three acutely emphasized the falsifications of language, though in rather different historical contexts and looking back to rather different models. (Some other differences will be noted in due course.) In sum, our archetypal dystopian pattern is a reversed romantic tale in a context of technocratized authoritarianism. But, as I will try to suggest, the romanticism of Zamyatin is richer in passional struggle and, finally, in counterutopian affirmation, than his progeny.

One reason for his superiority is that Zamyatin holds to a larger sense of selfhood than the others. D (as one might familiarly identify the protagonist of *We*) shockingly discovers, in the self-revelatory process of keeping his journal which is the novel, not only the reflexivity of modernist literature but its underlying self-consciousness—"there were two of me" (*We* 52). Rising through the "we" self of conventional corporate identity comes an "I" of forbidden individuality. With considerable wryness, that selfhood is complexly adumbrated: partly genetic regression (his hands, embarrassingly in his society, are quite hairy); partly individualizing guilt (his childhood uniform was accidentally stained at a major ritual occasion, which made him feel different, separate); and partly eccentric intellectual conditioning (deliciously, his defective teaching machine made an unusual flapping noise, thereby becoming personalized as "Plapa" [*We* 38], which affected not only him but another physical-intellectual deviant, the Pushkinian poet R-13). Furthermore, his considerable intelligence, which helps make him the chief designer-engineer of the great spaceship "Integral," which is to be used to integrate the whole universe into the One State and for whose praises he started his journal, turns up a questing self. It turns out (somewhat implausibly?) that the technocrat has a natural artistic counterintelligence of intense responsiveness and reflectiveness. Thus the protagonist is soon in radical conflict within himself as well as with the totalitarian society.

It is usually held (though not always stated) that utopian narratives are "novels of ideas," as against "novels of character" in the realistic (and other) traditions. While *We* is certainly an overtly ideological fiction, and in a number of conventions clearly utopian (futurism, synthetic society, dialogic, etc.), it also takes up an issue of character—conflict within the self. (Isn't this, in spite of genre theories, true of many of the better modern utopian fictions?) D's corporate side, which worships straight lines and the rationality of mere numbers, and acquiesces in the system premised on such sensibility, wars with his other responses. The verbal (not mathematical) play with metaphors of number (his lover's face shapes into unknown X, "irrational numbers" morally disturb him, and so on) may follow through on Dostoyevsky's mockery of reducing human consciousness to considerations of "two times two." But the perhaps excessive use of mathematical puns may also represent self-parody by the author, for many years a practicing engineer. (Self-parody, I suggest, frequently characterizes the more interesting styles because it is self-defining of the intellectual.) The divisions in D, as between the mathematical functionary and the excited sensualist, make him susceptible to overreaching passion, and to the perplexedly rebellious responsiveness that goes with it.

A technocrat who wants to believe that only "the rational and useful is beautiful," D is driven against himself and his successful social role to paradoxical love-hate romantic obsessions. His lover, I-330, a lovely sensualist and revolutionary leader, trysts with him in the museumlike House of the Ancients. Passion has led to a sense of historical alternative. He is also led from there to a tunnel that takes him beyond the Green Wall. He then briefly joins with escapees from the One State in neoprimitive freedom. One commentator reduces this to a "Rousseauistic urge towards the unspoiled primitive," but that misses the mark.[11] Those outside the wall are not only involved in a counterreligion—the Promethean sun worship of "Mephi" (Mephistopheles, in a reversal of the dark demonic)—but in revolution. Revived primitivism with such sophistication and purposes is not to be so stockly dismissed.

In sum, the protagonist has "developed a soul," which, a revolutionary doctor tells him, is an "incurable" malady (*We* 89). His illness, of course, is passion, as the romance plot becomes complicated. Three women: sweetly simple and maternal O, who, at her desire, he illegally impregnates (in a lab-birthing society) and finally spirits off to maternal freedom outside the wall; puritanic-conformist U (with sexual punning, all females are open vowels), who jealously betrays him to the state Guardians; and I, his great passion, the superior intellectual woman and exotic sensualist (rather heavily in stock 1920s fashion), who is also explicitly identified as a figure of threatening romantic mythologies, including *"la belle dame sans merci" (We* 135). Her ecstatic seduction of him, his obsessional pursuit of her, which involves him in faltering revolutionary activity and much ambiguity about her motives with him, followed by her sexual manipulation, his jealous betrayal, and her bravely literal "liquidation" by state authority, flesh the tale. It is all a bit much, which must be Zamyatin's point about the fully human.

More than the romanticism remains ambiguous, human—contrast not only *Brave New World* and *Nineteen Eighty-Four* but what we are so often advised more generally about utopian unilateral didacticism. Even the ending has, in the manner of so much modernism, a pyrrhonistic openness: What followed from the Green Wall breached and the major rebellion in the streets?[12] (And what cosmic order in the future came up with D's journal which we are reading?) Granted, the central figures (except for escaped mother O) have been destroyed by the One State. D, whose imagination has been surgically removed in a "fantisectomy" in a desperate effort by the authorities to regain total control, is once again a full participant in "we-ness" and opposes the continuing revolution. With corporate submissiveness, he concludes the story: "I am certain we shall conquer. Reason must prevail" *(We* 232).

To Zamyatin, utopian revolutionist exiled by the Czarists and later denounced for his literary vanguardism and then exiled to his death by the Stalinists, statist reason must not prevail. Nor should the rationality of scientistic domination. The countering and completing passional nature provides the fuller being, which he sexualizes much as D. H. Lawrence did.[13] As Zamyatin writes in a sardonic letter about the role of the imagination: "There are two priceless fountainheads in men: brains and sex. From the first proceeds all science, from the second—all art. And to cut off all art from yourself or to force it into your brain would mean to cut off . . . well, yes; and to remain only with a pimple."[14] The forced reduction of the erotic to squeezing pimples—of romantic poetry to "Stanzas on Sexual Hygiene" *(We* 68), of loving to rationed pink permits for sexual exchange to be used only in the unscheduled two hours of the day (a Taylorism inefficiency, we are told, on the way to time-and-motion study correction)—means the defeat of the libidinal and conflictual imagination.[15] Most moderately put, "Sexuality in *We* is identified with Zamyatin's fundamental preoccupation—freedom."[16]

In spite of such stock female types as mothering O and vengeful U, *We* does emphasize sexual egalitarianism. "Only the unsubduable can be loved" *(We* 72). Such heroic romanticism, dramatized with I (and an ambiguous strain in feminism), seems rather antithetical to the other noted dystopias. *Nineteen Eighty-Four* also has a passional woman, also betrayed by the protagonist, but in a doubly reduced way. Orwell's Julie is mostly "a rebel from the waist down," and most sexual freedom is a limited indulgence contemptuously allowed the disorderly and largely irrelevant "proles" (Orwell's confined neo-primitives in the antisexual authoritarian ordering). In Huxley's sophisticated and twisted puritanism, the erotic is an even lower-level distraction. In his reflections some years later on the sexual theme of *Brave New World,* he lumps sex with "dope and the movies and the radio," which the controllers shrewdly indulge the subjects with to distract them from more serious matters. In justification, Huxley pronounces, "As political and economic freedom diminishes, sexual freedom tends compensatingly to increase."[17] Given Huxley's historical erudition, that is indeed an odd statement. Tyrants and inquisitors in the Western traditions have usually been puritanic, at least for other people. Fascists, black or red—Franco or Stalin, Mussolini or Mao, Castro or other Latin dictators—usually enforce restrictive and punitive sexual codes. Our imaginative works often seem to recognize this historical propensity by linking social and economic authoritarianism with sexual repression. Since freedom, as the lovely Enlightenment rhetoric put it, is "indivisible," there does not seem to be much of a case to be made, in or out of utopia, for repressing the libidinal (including the equality of women, homosexuals, and others), and claiming the society to be "free." A sexually libertarian society, especially one with intensely consuming and disorienting romanticism, may, of course, be negative in other ways, such as inefficient in production, in ritualized order, in military aggression, and the like. Highly organized, controlled, and emotionally fractured sexual allowance, as in *Brave New World* and the One State of *We,* is not sensibly described as "sexual freedom." Huxley's view, then, is perverse. But this is not to suggest that the romantic passion ambiguously exalted by Zamyatin—it leads both to liberating awareness and purpose, and to obsessions, manipulation, jealousy, and betrayal—provides a full ideal of erotic liberation.

The sometimes perplexed ironies of *We* go beyond its declared didactic purposes. Zamyatin wrote of it, this "novel is a warning against the two-fold danger which threatens humanity: the hypertropic power of machines, and the hypertropic power of the state."[18] The positive utopian exaltation of the senses and passions goes beyond these satiric purposes, suggesting that the machine-state can only properly be criticized from a sufficiently countering perspective. The totalitarian technocracy of modern dystopias is no mere politics but, as *We* insists, an absolutistic religion of "all over one." An insistent theme for Zamyatin, the son of an Orthodox priest, was the origins of futuristic totalitarianism in historic Christianity. Mockingly, "We is from God, 'I' from the Devil" (*We* 128).[19] The Benefactor—a modern tyrant in his conditioning technology, a Lenin in physical appearance, and a Dostoyevskean Grand Inquisitor in his cruel salvationism—summarizes the traditional religion of love: the masses "longed for some one to tell them, once and for all, the meaning of happiness, and then

to bind them to it with a chain" (*We* 214). By totally conditioning and loboto-
mizing and controlling, after torturing and executing the dissident, the state will
achieve the "ancient dream of paradise. . . . Remember: those in paradise no
longer know desires, no longer know pity or love. There are only the blessed
with their imaginations excised (this is the only reason why they are blessed)—
angels, obedient slaves of God" (*We* 214). The salvational-authoritarian vision
of Christianity is now to be finally realized in the successor universalism of the
One State.

Individualism, seen as a community of exalted desire and imaginative
defiance, provides the counterforce to the megalomaniacal oneness. That, too,
draws on religious tradition, reversed; the revolutionaries entitle themselves
Mephis, specifically acknowledge being "anti-Christian" as well as antistate,
worship expressions of vital energy, and insist on a radically different life
beyond the wall. Atheist Zamyatin's satire aims not only at the hypertropic
technocracy but at traditional hypertropic religion, and not only rhetorically but
in elaborate parallels: the One State uniforms and rituals, the corporateness and
the scheduling, the censoring of literature and the reduction of eroticism—all
have a longer mean history.

We's heroic revolutionary witch, I, expounds the defiant metaphysic in
terms of metaphors drawn, for the sake of her scientist lover, from the Second
Law of Thermodynamics. The eternal conflict is between "entropy," which was
"worshipped as God by . . . the Christians," and "energy," which in its human
forms of feeling, desire, and imagination provides the countering life-affirma-
tion (*We* 165). (As in Blake's famous devilish aphorisms, "Energy is the only
life and is from the Body" and is "Eternal Delight.") In the dialectics of politics,
that means no lasting equilibrium, no "final revolution" any more than any
"final number" (*We* 174). Infinity rather than uniformity. The endless demand
for the eutopia of desire rejects all rigidification into, the entropy of false utopia.
The dialectic, then, is of utopianism versus utopia, with the praxis being permanent revolution.

The poet in *We* repeats the Dostoyevskean Grand Inquisitor's dualism of
choosing "happiness without freedom, or freedom without happiness." (Huxley's Savage repeats the argument, though without revolutionism.) Zamyatin's
tale bodies forth the choice of freedom, and the consciousness from suffering,
by a series of reversals. His D concludes at a crucial point, *"I did not want
salvation" (We* 186). But at issue is a denuded salvation, a reductive happiness
without rich energy of sensation, imagination, desire. While romantic defiance
may be insufficient for the generation of eutopia, it is utopian in its refusal of
much of what is and its demand for yet more.

Certainly part of my point here is not new. In one of the most elaborate
surveys, *Utopian Thought in the Western World,* the Manuels warned: "If in the
background of every utopia there is an anti-utopia, the existing world seen

through the critical eye of the utopia-composer, one might say conversely that in the background of many a dystopia there is a secret utopia."[20] (One notes the shift from "every" to "many," properly enough, since some antiutopianism is largely fear and rancor.) But in Zamyatin the positive utopianism is hardly "secret," except in the minds of conservative-twisting readers.[21]

The dystopia of *We* is backed not by conservative, entropic, distastes and fears of the utopian but by an energetic eutopianism. That countering, and resultant dialectical drive, I suggest, engenders much of its charm and power, including the quasisurreal stylistic heightening of sensation and desire. While the larger part of the fiction satirizes the forces leading to technocracy and its debased sensibility (concern with the Soviet Union by the ex-Bolshevik is rather topically secondary), it posits an antithetical view and sensibility. The libertarian alternative receives insufficient metaphoric embodiment—the Mephis and the neoprimitive life beyond the wall remain rather vague except for countering fervor (no doubt partly to be explained by Zamyatin's quite negative situation)—and Zamyatin (based on what works are in translation) never achieved equivalent art again to allow much extrapolation. But the counterutopian impetus seems central. The mockery of traditional monomaniacal religion as well as Wellsian scientism is not incidental (contrary to some of his progeny and critics), nor is the neoprimitivism beyond the wall. As Zamyatin wrote elsewhere, "The world is kept alive only by heretics."[22] Perhaps such a reversal is the most nuclear impetus to the best utopianizing.

Revised Utopianizing, and Le Guin

A commonplace charge against utopianizing emphasizes that both such ideals and such narratives are static, undramatic, therefore unliterary and boring. Expressing the stock disdain a few years ago, a well-known neoconservative literary philosopher pronounced that "the idea of utopia in any of its versions hardly inspires us any more. The prospect of life without any frictions or imperfections . . . must strike us as an empty and insipid ideal."[23] Mankind's recurrent pathological dreams of static paradises, such as soulful but otherwise empty heavens, may raise doubts about the universality of such claims. But, granted, make life quite a miserable struggle and, no doubt, static paradises have an understandable appeal. Conservative social views, understood as those maintaining current miseries, may also encourage countering static eutopias.

Certainly the Plato-More tradition may be characterized by desires for static order and harmony. Yet they were also countering the present with their images of drastic change for prevailing disorder and disharmony. When the impetus towards harmonious perfectionism became more decisively historical, as with ideas of "progress," utopianism became less fixed and absolutist. It may be plausible to argue that the emphasis on change became strong in seventeenth-century Reformation utopian images, or eighteenth-century Enlightenment images, or nineteenth-century historicist images.[24] No doubt the static perfectionist utopias belong to periods when the religion, politics, aesthetics, and morals, appeared to be fixed and absolutist, whenever that was.[25] In cultures like ours, marked by self-conscious relativism—not to mentioned conflict and contention—imperfection, change, variety, and frequently not a little ambiguity seem more probable emphases. To draw again on the germinal H. G. Wells: early in the century he insisted on the incomplete and speculative pattern of his *A Modern Utopia,* which held that appropriate ideal places must be construed as "stages" in a "kinetic" process, changing, time-limited, and evolving.[26] In *The Time Machine* he insists that "there is no intelligence where there is no change."[27] He may have confirmed his principle less in his particular utopias (burdened with classical expectations?) than in writing of different, alternative, future places.

Post-Wellseans have sometimes made the alternatives more concurrent. Herbert Read in *The Green Child* (1935) presented as simultaneous in time two contrasting utopias (one progressive materialist, one neo-Platonic).[28] Aldous Huxley, as previously mentioned, used similar materials for dystopianism and eutopianism (*Brave New World* and *Island*), not to mention some variety of partial utopianizing in between. In more discursive form, Paul Goodman (who also wrote rather bad utopian fiction—*The Empire City* [1964]) presented in his book on utopian thinking about cities, *Communitas* (1947, 1960), three utopian "Community Paradigms."[29] One might be characterized as supercentralized capitalism, one as decentralized communalism (obviously the most positive), and one as a double-ordering of aggrandizing consumerism and Blanquist work-welfarism. No claim was made that they were the only, or unchanging, or conflictless possibilities. That seems more characteristic than not of utopianizing for at least a couple of generations.

However, it may well be true that some utopianizing shows an insufficient sense of change, as do many nonutopian social, political, and moral thinkers and fictionists. Certainly many utopian narratives are bland and insipid, as are many romances, allegories, comedies, and other types of fiction. There would seem to be nothing inherent in the notion of a socially critical imaginary world which requires that it be boring, static, or stupid. Rather more specific, nongenre, discriminations seem necessary, again. If one insists on generalizing the impetus, most utopian narratives assume a rather drastic change from the present, which may be what the pseudogenre objections are really against.

Zamyatin's *We,* which I suggested as germane for many that were to come, revealed a utopianism based in endless change—permanent revolution. His announced heresy of never-ending libertarian defiance has contemporary as well as earlier analogues. Indeed, it may be said to be a utopianizing tradition (and one to which I will several times return). For a partial contemporary case in point, we might consider one of the best-known (and frequently discussed) utopian-dystopian fictions, Ursula Le Guin's *The Dispossessed* (1974).[30] More than half a century later than *We,* and out of a considerably different context, this work also interestingly emphasizes a dialectic of countering and conflict, though one more modulated, less romantic. Its protagonist also decides, at a crucial point, that "his society, properly conceived, was a revolution, a permanent one" (*Dis.* 142). Le Guin, not surprisingly, has been an enthusiastic admirer of Zamyatin: "*We* is a dystopia which contains a hidden or implied Utopia; a subtle, brilliant, and powerful book; emotionally stunning and technically . . . still far in advance of most books written since."[31]

That radical spirit, I argue, has become its own countering tradition. Change, both from the present, which after all is assumed in most utopianizing, but also within eutopia, any utopia, is an accepted principle. And why not? Rigid and insipid, indeed, must be the person who cannot entertain images of a more ideal education, more gratifying erotic arrangements, more beautiful communities, and more just social institutions. Are we to take seriously a sensibility so unidimensional as not to sometimes expand awareness with nowhere but recognizably human possibilities?

Before and after *The Dispossessed,* Le Guin has published a variety of science fiction and fantasy (I am not particularly an admirer of much of it), but this fiction seems most appropriately discussed in utopian modes. Unlike much of fantasy (including some of Le Guin's), the characters' physical and mental attributes remain within our generally recognizable range—no elves, no demigods, no psychic transmission, no immortality. There is little in the way of miraculous forces and events, given a possible (though improbable) technoscientific extension two centuries ahead. But those projections are largely secondary to contemporaneous social issues. Thus the narrative takes up such matters as gender equality and bisexual freedom, shared rotation of jobs and other communal goods, decentralizing organizations and depowering authorities, and the like, in ways that alternatively reflect our realities. Fancy, we might say, is subordinated in the utopian imagination proper to social-moral dialectics, which means to argue with what is.

But the work is partly within the conventions of science fiction developing out of H. G. Wells, and that raises several problems. *We* also came partly out of Wells, but note that Zamyatin treated the advanced technology (a characteristic sci-fi decor) negatively, that is, as primarily serving the One State and its repressions. Not so with Le Guin, who treats much of the futuristic technology in positive ways. A large portion, of course, is simply decor: thus in *The Dispossessed* space travel and new substances largely give an exotic heightening to old journeys and equipage rather than a qualitative change in the social order. Problems of communication and distribution, however interplanetarily expanded, retain their difficulties, and the new technotropes still have the logic of old concerns. Within these limits, sci-fi conventions may be viewed as useful mythology, simplifying and dramatizing, in the sense that, say, Tudor history provided mythic conventions for Shakespeare in the *Henry IV* plays. To take the science fiction mythology too literally would be to miss the social dialectics, just as too earnest attention to Tudor mythology overrides the more interesting and pertinent Falstaffian comedy.

But on one major issue in *The Dispossessed* science fiction mythology and social dialectics come together. Shevek, Le Guin's physicist hero and central focus for the whole narrative, has gone further with theorems of "indeterminacy which old Ainsetain [read: Einstein, though the reason for the verbal twist escapes me] had refused to accept," and so with a physics metaphysically expanded has arrived at his "Theory of Simultaneity," which allows the development of an instrument, the "ansible," for instant interstellar communication (*Dis.* 224). At the level of novelistic pattern, this is simply a game with the sci-fi conventions since instant communication puts interplanetary messages into approximately our traditional region-bound time frame; calling another planet is like calling another town in the same state, thus making neighborly relationships possible. But why one would want cosmic neighborliness is an unexplained megalomania, though common in sci-fi.

Le Guin has several portentous purposes with her Theory of Simultaneity (such as, apparently, fusing linear and cyclic theories of time), only one of which I am going to pursue a bit. Her scientist's home planet, Anarres—actually our moon, modified (but sci-fi conventions call for rococo renaming)—rejects his scientific initiative. The main contrasting society, A-Io on Urras (a rather caricatured number-one future U. S. on Earth), which is the mother society of the utopia two centuries from now, honors and aids his science, but, like contemporary America, would exploit it for profit and state-military dominance. When his theory becomes operational during his stay in A-Io, he resolves his ethical dilemma by not giving his "invention" to his own society, which would suppress it, or to the mother-society, which would dangerously exploit it. Instead, he broadcasts it throughout the universe from neutral ground, thus making it available to all. In effect, this is a reaffirmation of the Enlightenment ideal of universalizing "natural philosophy" as part of "natural liberty" for all mankind. (But cosmically extended, any definition of humankind seems no longer as sensible.)

While affirming the Enlightenment ethical ideal of science seems admirable, it becomes in the circumstances more than a little problematic. Perhaps glancing at a source will highlight part of the problem. Le Guin, it has been widely reported, based her scientist hero on her positive image of Robert Oppenheimer.[32] Ironically, Oppenheimer, in fact, often took an amoralist view of science, hard to distinguish from opportunism. Note, for example, his explanation for developing the atomic bomb, which was certainly dubious on the grounds of his moral and political views. "When you see something that is technically sweet, you go ahead and do it and you argue about what to do about it only after you have had your technical success."[33] Shevek, then, is implicitly an Oppenheimer who (improbably) kept his technical success secret until he had the opportunity to apply his enlightened ethic. With more irony than intended, his ethical universalizing may be taken as a partial corrective to the actual scientist on whom he is based.

The issue is several ways fudged in the fiction. For Shevek's considerably libertarian society, Anarres, has on the face of it a good case—its own precarious libertarian order, given the current technology and exploitative mother planet—for not advancing drastically transforming technoscience. Its fragile economy and separatism—it is a satellite in several senses of Urras—may depend on very restrained technological change. The issue is not really considered. Wells gave sci-fi a dependence not only on technological gimmicks but on internationalism extended to the cosmos, and Le Guin has followed, perhaps partly victimized intellectually by the sci-fi conventions.[34]

She does at several points dramatize, with others as well as Shevek (including Tirin, a dissident and persecuted artist), an argument which might be summarized as "ideas must out": "It is the nature of ideas to be communicated. . . . The idea is like grass. It craves light . . . thrives on crossbreeding, grows better for being stepped on" *(Dis.* 56). The homey metaphors, characteristic of Le Guin's most effective style, rather greenly cover a strong issue without, I suggest, adequately responding to the destructive egoism and moral vacuousness of modern technoscience. Thus where a modern sci-fi devotee criticizes *The Dispossessed* for subordinating science to "humanist idealism," I am criticizing it for partly following sci-fi conventions into the techno-gimmick-and-cosmic-megalomania which often make it a dubious utopianizing.[35]

One could also argue—more "humanist idealism"?—that the conventions of fantastically changed conditions, ornate apparatus, synthetic nomenclature, and such, which are endemic to much technoscientized fiction, depersonalize and thus weaken a subtle sense of human relationships. Certainly the "partnerships"—the egalitarian and relatively open but enduring pairings that for some (apparently a minority) have replaced our conventionally coercive marriage on the utopian Anarres—come out, as with Shevek and Takver (a woman marine biologist pursuing her own career, but who acts rather wifely), somewhat thin, inadequately explored, and sentimental. But in addition to the sci-fi limitations, Le Guin tends to the sentimental in her fictions. And perhaps the utopian more generally thins relationships because of its expository burden, hence abstraction, in redefining things, conditions, places, and people.

Certainly Le Guin does better in much of her utopian social delineation. She dialectically presents, in alternating chapters, two societies: the libertarian (Anarres) and the "propertarian" (A-Io on Urras). The libertarians, a large dissident community exiled from the propertarian society seven generations earlier, had arduously colonized the sparse and periodically drought-ravaged moon, and remain ardently separatist (though dependent on limited trade). The revolutionary community had been ideologically founded by an admirable odd woman anarchist leader, Odo (partly based on Emma Goldman), whose legacy provides a partial substitute for the ethical dialogue in traditional utopias.[36] The emphasized conflicts between the propertarian and libertarian worlds are not the planetary warfare of vulgar science fiction but dialectics in the mind, and contrasting stays, of the protagonist.

However, the issues do not reduce to simple antithesis. The ostensible libertarian community has partly turned its egalitarian and cooperative order into quasibureaucracy and petrifying conformity. Still, it remains far more decent than the future U.S. (A-Io), whose statist capitalism has produced an advanced and lavish order for its elite but repressive misery for the rest, thus inducing a new wave of utopian rebellion. Hence eutopia is partly dystopia, and antiutopia recurrently creates utopian movements.

The novel is properly subtitled "An Ambiguous Utopia," and it is so in multiple ways, partly realized in the consciousness of the first person, scientist Shevek, to live in the advanced stages of both societies. The dialectics, of course, are less relativist than purposive, and the protagonist finally chooses to return as a radical activist to his uncertainly libertarian society because it suggests more possibilities for improvement. Even the unsuccessful revolt in the propertarian society during Shevek's visit relates back to the earlier Odonian movement which founded the utopian society. Revolution is properly a returning to primal values. The libertarian-utopian purpose is less a set form or doctrine than a radical commitment to the always dissident possibilities for equality and freedom.[37]

At the end of the novel, the gradually radicalized Shevek (after all, he was a scientist, a slow learner in social wisdom) is on his way back to Anarres to recall the community to its libertarian heritage. He is joined by a visitor from another planet (Ketho, a link to the multinovel pattern of Le Guin's science fiction), suggesting the continuation of the wanderer-rebel who tests and defines liberty, equality, and spirit. But, as one dissident warns the other, "Freedom is never very safe" (*Dis*. 310). And, as opening and closing metaphors of the fiction indicate, freedom requires that the "dispossessed" (empty-handed outsiders) transgress the walls of the society and the mind.

The libertarian ideal presented in *The Dispossessed* is heroic (perhaps too much so for good communist-anarchism), with the superior ethical scientist as saintly dissident. While some critics make much of Le Guin's partial Taoism, the highly Western concept of heroism is one of the stronger quasireligious emphases in the fiction.[38] Probably the Taoist sympathy, as so often with Westerners, derives from libertarian motives, rather than the other way around.[39] An essentially religious argument, also more Western than Taoist, focuses on the hero's compassion. He discovers as a youth that the basis of community must reside in a metapsychological "solidarity," a transcendent ideal of "brother-hood" which depends on a recognition of suffering. "Suffering is the condition. . . . We can't prevent suffering. This pain and that pain, yes, but not Pain. A society can only relieve social suffering, unnecessary suffering" (*Dis.* 48). Disparity, grief, pain, death—the consciousness of them defines the human condition. Some contrary views receive dialogic acknowledgment, such as pain as functional (a commonplace reductive view), pain as dissolved by the commitment to mutual aid (Kropotkin's optimistic-anarchist view), and pain as transcendent exaltation (the socially destructive traditional Christian view). But the intense young hero concludes with the commandment: "I'm trying to say what I think brotherhood really is. It begins—it begins in shared pain" (*Dis.* 50).

Anarchism, then, may be viewed as tragically profound, as Le Guin reasonably presents it. But, of course, such tragic faith certainly does not include acquiescence in the pains of social injustice. While her scientist does not bother to directly dispute a Urrastian's "tautological argument" that no women work on space ships because "running a space freighter was not women's work," he does question the assumption of different "social status" for women: "*Status* is the same as *class?*" (*Dis.* 13). The other "tried to explain status" but failed— apparently Le Guin's riposte to that dominant American political sociology which obscures American class orderings and denies the reality of social conflict in American status quo dominations. The social arguments, then, show considerable sophistication.

Further miring himself in obtuseness, the male-dominance apologist insists that the lesser work-status of women is due to their lesser physical strength. The libertarian counters that such strength is mostly irrelevant in a technological society and, besides, women have greater endurance. The male bigot falls back on sex-role fear ("masculine self-respect") and the information that the leading scientists are naturally male, though granting that he has "known highly intelligent women, women who could think just like a man." Shevek, trained and inspired by women scientists, wonders at the nature of self-respect that requires one to "consider half the human race as inferior," and about the strange sexual twistings (including conceiving of marriage and other prostitution as "copulation in the economic mode") that must result from such prejudice (*Dis.* 14). Various dramatizations, as with his female "partner," scientist Takver, and with his abortive affair with Vea, a manipulative sex-teasing-withholding upper-class woman in the propertarian society, underline the "status" contrasts and the psychological costs of male domination. Still, the feminist arguments seem partly vitiated by the fiction's quasimarriage relationships and male heroism.

Conventions other than just the sci-fi mar the libertarianism. But, reasonably enough (and an issue I will further pursue in the next chapter), feminism is part rather than parcel of a larger egalitarianism.

Le Guin draws less satirically but more thoroughly on the libertarian traditions in her descriptions of community, work, and economic equality. Walking through the main town of the libertarian society, one sees "a bare city, bright, the colors light and hard, the air pure. It was quiet. You could see it all, laid out as plain as spilt salt." And so are the rest of the aesthetic eutopian concepts of community:

> Nothing was hidden.
> The squares, the austere streets, the low buildings, the unwalled workyards, were charged with vitality and activity. As Shevek walked he was constantly aware of other people walking, working, talking, faces passing, voices calling, gossiping, singing. . . . Workshops and factories fronted on squares or on their open yards, and their doors were open. He passed a glassworks, the workman dipping up a great molten blob as casually as a cook serves soup. Next to it was a busy yard where foamstone was cast for construction. The gang foreman, a big woman in a smock white with dust, was supervising the pouring of a cast with a loud and splendid flow of language. After that came a small wire factory, a district laundry, a luthier's where musical instruments were made and repaired, the district smallgoods distributory, a theater, a tile works. The activity going on in each place was fascinating, and mostly out in full view. Children were around, some involved in the work with adults, some underfoot making mudpies, some busy with games in the street, one sitting perched up on the roof of the learning center with her nose in a book. The wire-maker had decorated the shopfront with patterns of vines worked in painted wire, cheerful and ornate. The blast of steam from the wide-open doors of the laundry was overwhelming. No doors were locked, few shut. There were no disguises and no advertisements. It was all there, all the work, all the life of the city, open to the eye and to the hand. (*Dis.* 80–81)

This neomedieval cityscape, with its squares, decorations, and decentralized emphasis on crafts, belongs to the tradition partly propounded by Peter Kropotkin and William Morris. It also may revisualize American anarchist Paul Goodman's "integrated community."[40] In addition, it quietly illustrates major points of the libertarian decentralist ethos: habitation, production, trade, and culture are *not* separated but united. Children are educated by partaking continuously in the adult world.[41] There is no segregation by age, sex, or activity. The aesthetic is also largely "neofunctional"; that is, form follows function, but the modernist principle is modified to openly express the ethos of an egalitarian organic community within moderately ascetic (scarcity) limits. Socially as well as aesthetically, Le Guin's imaginary town poses a radical alternative to our schizophrenic urban environments with their fragmentation and alienation of much of life. In the counterscenes (the megalopolis of A-Io on Urras) she displays the pattern of our urban dementia—grid, suburb, superstores, industry, culture, and power center all ghettoized—expressing class segregations, fractured functions, hierarchical controls, and the rest of the competitive-statist ordering in its inequalities and unfreedoms—the nasty paradigm of the contemporary American city.

Yet some of the advantages of the propertarian order of Urras also appeal to the protagonist. Not the least of these are the aesthetic gratifications not usually noted by our apologists for statist-capitalist society: the variety as well as the lavishness, the involuted sensualism as well as in the intriguingly perverse formalization, the high polishing of roles and specialties, and the expansiveness and monumentalizing that can only emerge from power-ridden societies. They are granted strong human appeal though obviously also exploitative, which is part of the reason for their existence. The perceptive utopian recognizes that societies, actual as well as ideal, partly exist for aesthetic reasons.

The advantages and disadvantages of propertarian society can be briefly glimpsed through the students at the elite university (Iou Eun), who impress the libertarian visiting scientist with their polite high competence. Even beyond the absurdities of tests, grades, and certifications, they are rationalized into narrow concerns—free not to be free. For "what they were free to do, however, was another question . . . their freedom from obligation was in exact proportion to their lack of freedom of initiative" (*Dis.* 108). Careerists, they lack most passionate disinterest and "denied the importance" of any larger sense of things. The society that supposedly exalts individual initiative essentially undermines it. As in classical liberal thought, the conception of liberty even at its best remains mostly negative: a selfish "freedom from" rather than a positive "freedom for" individual desire, understanding, and community.

But does even the libertarian provide adequate redress of positive and negative freedom? The scientist has fled his own hardening eutopia partly because of its denial of individual initiative, his science, and partly because he feels excluded. Yet his situation seems inevitable even in a communitarian-anarchist order. For such an order may increase freedom but it does so by replacing the rule of law and coercion with the rule of community and custom. For the deviant, that power can become drastic ostracism and meanness. Not only scientist Shevek but a dissident artist (Tirin) and Shevek-Takver's young daughter are unjustified victims of it. The artist is driven almost insane by the mistreatment. With admirable candor, Le Guin has exposed a central problem in the libertarianism she broadly affirms.

While one might argue that it is far better to be sent to Coventry than to prison, some strongly disagree. For example, a noted historian, drawing on 1930s Spanish anarchist cases, recently concluded that if he grievously violated accepted community standards, "I would prefer to be fined or imprisoned rather than to be cold-shouldered by my neighbors. Far better to be left to the tortures of individual conscience or the ministrations of a psychiatrist than to receive the blows of the 'fist of public opinion.' "[42] (After enduring several of the alternatives, I would certainly make the other choice.) Curiously, such rejections of anarchism confirm the potency of its claims to provide an alternative means of order. However, the issue is not simply resolvable. Freedom is never total, society never fully uncoercive. Le Guin's libertarianism, especially in its simultaneous commitment to communal solidarity (based not only on an ethos of cooperation but on the brotherhood of human suffering) and to individual initiative (based on the exceptional culture-hero, scientist or artist) is here truly ambiguous, and perhaps necessarily so.

But Le Guin does emphatically dramatize that her values of individuality as well as community require an essentially egalitarian ordering. Her protagonist has become a strong and independent scientific thinker because of an early proclivity to paradoxical formulations. (Social thinking, too, requires this in order to respond to human contradictions.) He had the encouragement of a remarkable woman teacher (Mitis) and the sanctification of her example. But that, too, demanded egalitarian circumstances: "the absence of all enhancement of authority left the real thing plain. There are people of inherent authority; some emperors actually have new clothes" (*Dis.* 45). They will be more visible when not disguised by the false costuming of institutional role; then the authority is not expressed as status, power, and control but as the primal legitimacy of knowing, doing, and being.

For society to minimize the inevitable falsity of power relations, a radical alleviation of common welfare is required. In the communitarianism of Anarres such basics as housing and clothing are distributed with impersonal equality by simply drawing them from public service centers and depositories. The concept here seems akin to Engels' famous one of replacing the "rule of people" with the "administration of things." Some persuasive arrangements are sketched, and, as if in reply to a doubter, Le Guin also presents a selfish character (Desar) who pack-rats an endless, even inconvenient, number of unneeded things. The overall arrangements impose an obvious practical limit on accumulation. Other than that, moral and other social disapproval may be applied to such unbalanced acquisitiveness, but no directly coercive measures. In the libertarian society, social behavior but not all of human nature has been modified by its conditioning. People have a right, as it were, to selfishness—to "egoize," as it is disapprovingly labeled in Odonian morality—and a right, at the cost of disapproval, to stupidity, waywardness, sin, which are also crucial human freedoms.

Freedom, of course, is always partly defined by its literal, physical context. Le Guin chose as the conditions for her semieutopia a technologically sophisticated community on an inhospitable planet. Very limited natural resources, aridity, recurrent grave droughts, and other scarcity conditions demand parsimonious social economics. Full pastoral alternatives are hardly viable here.[43] Is the underlying attitude ascetic? Only moderately, I suggest. It is commonplace in cultural anthropology that communitarian equality is usually linked with relative nonabundance.[44] Therefore the distribution of essentials that periodically fall in short supply must be organized so that threatening degrees of acquisitiveness and competition may be limited. The serving of most meals in communal dining rooms discourages the Odonian evils of inequality and waste, though also providing (not emphasized) a mode for social communion.

It has been argued that anarchism functions less as a political doctrine than as a theory of social organization.[45] Given the scarcity conditions Le Guin has set, including a sophisticated society rather than a hunting-and-gathering tribe, arduous work seems necessary, and there is an obvious bias towards a kind of Protestant work ethic. Her protagonist is dutifully entrapped for long periods of time in emergency menial labors. Also given the conditions, there is a built-in tendency towards invidiously complex social structures. Sure enough, hierarchical control (as with scientist Sabul over Shevek) develops and undercuts libertarian values.

Not surprisingly, then, a central dispute in the narrative becomes the control of intellectual activity by the usual cliques of mediocrities via covert bureaucratic power (as in most American universities). Midway, as it were, in this process, the protagonist unites with other discontented people to form a Syndicate of Initiative, which rightly requires public support for their sciences and arts. The suggestive notion is that alternative, counterculture, possibilities in the form of counterinstitutions have been built into the system. This, we may take it, is a practical metaphor.[46] Still, even given this and the premises (anarchist traditions for two centuries, a committed large group with a charismatic founder, cosmic isolation, communal reenforcement by cyclic natural adversities, a cooperative ethos with considerable rigor), the libertarian utopia is in trouble. Seven generations of success have also produced antiintellectual censoring, covert bureaucratization, punitive treatment of dissidence, and the pervasive domination of individuals by the social ethic, though not yet, fortunately, a State. As Zamyatin's heroine had it, never make the mistake of thinking there is a final revolution, or ordering, or any ultimate intellectual allegiance except heresy to what is.

Le Guin's utopianizing shows a healthy skepticism, which is not to be confused with mere cynicism or passivity. For her protagonist, after some experience with a propertarian society, anarchist principles still look good. Shevek discusses the cast of his society with a propertarian functionary, who suddenly bursts out, "what keeps people in order? Why don't they rob and murder each other?" This traditional fear of the repressed gets the traditional anarchist answer: robbery is not common where there is little need for it. There remains, of course, some selfishness, advantage taking, anger, fisticuffs. But, Shevek replies, "As for violence, well . . . would you murder me, ordinarily? And if you felt like it, would a law against it stop you? Coercion is the least efficient means of obtaining order" (*Dis.* 120). Or, in Proudhon's lovely aphorism: "Freedom is the mother, not the daughter, of order."[47]

Counterargument is also applied to the test social issue of "dirty work." How in a truly free ordering does one get done such jobs as "garbage collecting," "grave digging," "shit processing," and "dangerous mining"? In the American-style ordering, it gets done by class and caste indoctrination into submissive roles, by economic compulsion, and finally by coercion. In the libertarian order such things get voluntarily done by such procedures as neighborhood rotation. It is admitted that volunteerism and lottery-choice do not create experienced competence; "It's not efficient" is the accurate enough propertarian objection. But in disagreeable or dangerous activity, the fairness of rotation and random duty must prevail over efficiency. Nothing else would be decent.

As for the motivations for voluntarily doing the dirty work, Le Guin typically presents multiple ones. These include a communal ethic drawing on the natural—Kropotkin's propensity for "mutual aid." This is the widely recognized but still undervalued cooperative side of evolutionary development.[48] Rotation duties for communally needed labor are also encouraged, especially in a naturally limited environment, by the common human desire for a bit of variety in activity, and one limited to a brief interlude. Then, too, some people desire at certain stages in life to try the difficult and exceptional.[49] And, of course, there is the strong social ethic in a cooperative society, especially in austere conditions. And yet even a more basic motive: "After all, work is done for the work's sake. It is the lasting pleasure of life" (*Dis.* 211).[50] It may be objected that this is a covert dependence again on a secularized Protestant work ethic. There is, of course, an old cultural matrix for Le Guin's society, with its clean community design, its antiwaste ethic, its earnest individualism and communalism, its austerity, its absence of many common vices—a secularized puritanism without Christian antisexual obsessions. In a yet further utopianizing, one might well emphasize a less puritanic work motive, notable for its absence in Le Guin: the fusion of work and play, which characterizes so much that is well done, from games to art, gardening to literary criticism.

The positive play of various motives would no doubt appear in a work-democracy where the commonality of tasks is confirmed by ethos and mythos, social conscience and its rituals. Yet, again, what of those who resist such cooperation? The question, one might suspect, is itself based in a compulsively totalistic utopianism, which this is not. Le Guin's answers range from mild disapproval to fairly drastic social outcasting. But dramatized as they are against a futuristic linear projection of American dire economic compulsions and statist coercions, the libertarian principles make a plausible case. Which is what good utopianizing is about. There are better ways than our prevalent ones for doing things, including her scientist's commitment to his vocation, a right to work appropriately at a self-chosen and self-defining activity that is reasonably supported and shared by the community, which is much of "being human." Not likely to be perfect? Of course, but the objection may be viewed as an antiutopianism rooted in an unadmitted absolutist utopianism.

I am emphasizing these usually not much discussed aspects of *The Dispossessed* not only because they are often well done but also because they are a substantial part of what the utopian imagination works on. Le Guin's dramatic crux follows from the work issue. Her protagonist has, out of ill-understood personal motives (some perhaps self-punitive in his mother's rejection and his scientist's oddity), given up his scientific work for long periods to do common labor. Perhaps some of this might be implicitly understood, though I doubt that Le Guin does, as the proper professional guilt of the modern scientist (recall that Einstein, after the atomic bomb was dropped, wished that he had been an ordinary plumber instead of a theoretical physicist). Countering his abnegation of his vocation leads Shevek to his voluntary exile, and then his militant return to radicalize his society. In its semidecadence, "the social conscience completely dominates the individual conscience, instead of striking the balance with it. We don't cooperate—we *obey*" (*Dis.* 265). That violates the libertarian, regardless of other consequences, and blocks its dialectic and development. One cannot, to note again Le Guin's heavy metaphor, retain full humanity while accepting such "walls" in society and the mind.

My reasons for belaboring these aspects of the utopian novel include the sense that literary criticism often does poorly by such work because it downplays, if not ignores, such substance. It also tends to ignore the "nonliterary" context, such as the continuing libertarian-utopian tradition that gives dialectical point to many of the particulars. Instead, literary discussion gets hung up on secondary matters, such as the sci-fi conventions (which I suggested were part of the weakness of the work) or abstruse parallelisms (such as Taoism, though much, such as the cosmic internationalism, is anything but Taoist) which substitute for the substance, No doubt as a social-political libertarian, I have a countering bias. But after all, this seems to be primarily a utopianizing work, not primarily a space adventure or a religious parable. Utopianizing is what utopianizing does.

In an essay around another fiction, Le Guin suggests that the utopian is characterized by posing a *"practicable* alternative to contemporary society." This, I take it, does not mean a literal plan but a response applicable to its conceptual specifics (as I have tried to indicate with work, cityscape, social order, etc.). Fantasy, on the quite different literary hand, she notes, is "based on an imaginary, radical change in human anatomy."[51] (Often, on this premise, what I describe throughout as technotopianism is more fantasy than utopian.) Further speaking of her most famous fantasy fiction (*The Left Hand of Dark-*

ness), she notes that the anatomically different (literally androgynous) figures
there are not something that she was "recommending" but a "heuristic device, a
thought experiment."[52] The anarchism of the utopian *The Dispossessed* is, then,
not the conceptual dallying of fantasy but something recommended.

The recommendation may not only be marked by intentional ambiguity but
by considerable skepticism. We may also note that in the end the propertarian
society is not significantly changed and the libertarian society has yet to be
revitalized. One bland critic makes this lack of resolution into a reading-test
virtue: "The absence of utopian synthesis" is part of a "strategy to involve the
reader in the very dialectical process of utopian production."[53] While that may
play nicely as classroom exercise, the lack of closure, of course, is frequently
characteristic of the open, pyrrhonistic endings of modernist fictions, and expresses a highly critical (and self-critical) perspective, not a mere pedagogical
device.

In contrast, a quite unbland critic, heavy with dogma (and thick with
jargon), makes a political test of Le Guin's skeptical ending. According to his
sustained attack on Le Guin's lack of feminist-activist dogma—her dependence
on male intellectual heroism ("a privileging of male heterosexual superiority"),
and her un-neo-Marxist acceptance of "scarcity" ("she ends up opposing morality to post-industrial post-scarcity materiality and does not give us emancipatory
utopian interaction with nature")—she has no sufficiently radical conclusion.
For "in the final analysis she remains ambiguously within present boundaries of
the status quo."[54] This more-radical-than-thou posturing highlights some obvious problems (included with those previously discussed here), and it ignores the
larger part of what is actually in the book (the libertarian specifics cited above).
But perhaps what is really at issue is discomfort with Le Guin's earnestness, her
"straightness" of sensibility amongst exacerbated contemporary utopianizers.
Identifying with the latter, the critic counterdefends patently more poorly done
literary sticks which can be glued to a political platform based on leftist cliches
and an unexamined faith in history as a "revolutionary spiral."[55]

The Dispossessed will no more pass as reified political manifesto than as
great realistic novel. It is a probing novel of considerable intelligence with a
special tendency, utopianizing, whose weaknesses are less "political" (anarchism, of course, is considerably an anti-politics) than literary. The psychology
is obviously thin, not only in the too conventional relationships (which many
note) but in the rather sentimental goodness (which results in many being un-
happy with the protagonist). I have noted the questionable jargonish and ideological sci-fi dependence, resulting in partial entrapment in the technotopian.
The emphasis on the imagery of walls and circles, which many (including Le
Guin) make much of, provide a rather mechanical shaping, as do the alternate
societies in alternate chapters. Present America may be too easily caricatured
(and so I have largely ignored it). But the strength of *The Dispossessed* lies

elsewhere, especially in the didacticism about social alternatives, in the set-up dialogues which display social intelligence and imagination. To object to them would be to apply a dramatistic principle that would deny utopian purpose. Of the few positive generalizable characteristics of utopian narratives, argumentative dialogue is one, social intelligence is another.

The Dispossessed interestingly combines thoughtful libertarian arguments with some of the verisimilitude and density of the "realistic" novel, just as *We* combines satire and romance in the heightened manner Zamyatin called "neorealism." Both depend on an intellectual literary agility which gives us striking reversals: Zamyatin posits an extreme dystopia in order to present his extreme radical utopianism of the endless heresy; Le Guin posits a complex and pertinent version of an anarchist eutopia (one of the few in our authentic, that is, non-Marxist, radical social-political heritage) and yet treats it with a critical skepticism. Both cases result in lively and provocative utopianizing. From a perspective emphasizing utopian dialectics, both deserve considerable reverence.

3

Femtopianism:
Some Gendered Utopianizing

The Revenge Problem

With a certain reluctance, appropriate to a feminist fellow-traveler, I suggest considering some genderized contemporary issues first from a bigoted perspective, femtopianism.[1] This should not be confused (though sometimes seems to be) with more open kinds of feminism, which are important but inseparable parts of a fuller egalitarianism. This minor literature of *ressentiment* may have a bit more than symptomatic interest because it also highlights some limitations to utopianizing.

A couple of current political theorists, arguing for the positive values of utopian thought, seem earnestly constrained to admitting some large limits: "We need some criterion to disallow bizarre inventions from counting as utopian political theory."[2] While they do not specify such criteria, it is easy to come up with some, which usually turn out to be methods of exclusion. All utopias as well as dystopias tend to be "purified" societies, which exclude the troublesome, or the merely problematic. Plato wanted to eliminate the irrational poets, H. G. Wells the stupid. Most Western eutopias tend to be racially or ethnically homogeneous, an obvious bias. While I am not aware of any that eliminate "whites," it would seem that a case is waiting to be made. Eliminating us would not only reduce skin cancers (reportedly increasing) but partly correct, at least briefly, some imbalances in world economic and political power. Also, given a more uniform physical type, it would seem easier to move towards a more uniform psychological type, thus coming closer to a universal niceness.

Admittedly, that would still leave gender differences. If one considers them to be major, one could remove some conflict, and also reduce overpopulation, by getting rid of one sex, as soon as we get the now conceivable technology in place. Eliminate the group frequently thought of as on the dumb side, as well as physically inferior and increasingly disruptive? But given the historical record and the current state of science, it might be morally and technologically easier to exclude the men. After all, it would just be eliminating a half-race of rather ugly and violent mental defectives. With sex-selective abortion, large-scale sperm storage (until cloning is further advanced), and changes in rituals (replacing circumcision with castration), a nonmurderous femtopian process would be in place. Surely such menicide would be more decent than genocide. Still, the logic of it does retain an irrational specie prejudice. Why not go with the real living majority? Insectopia. We may be on the ecological and nuclear-war progression to it anyway.

But short of eutopia for beetles, who do not seem to need us, are there any rather necessary limiting premises to utopianizing? The political theorists previously cited fall back on human "universalism," i.e., all must be eligible to meet the theoretical requirement of a good *human* society. That may be hard in itself to justify, a mere Enlightenment prejudice, an unexamined secularization of some anthropomorphic religious fanaticism.

Still, if we dogmatically assume human society, there are difficulties with the arguments for eliminating large groups from it. While *roles* might reasonably be eliminated, such as those of politician or poet (or literary critic), to eliminate the white or dumb or male (if I am not being redundant), runs into difficulties of discrimination and fairness. We might, of course, not eliminate but institutionalize gender conflict. Anthony Burgess suggested a meliorative effort to meet it, and overpopulation as well, in his *The Wanting Seed* (1962), with systematic and permanent warfare between men and women, lightly mystified and with balanced high-kill ratios.[3] It can be organized as a major protein source, too, though Swift's more parsimoniously arranging the slaughter for an earlier age may still have some modest advantages.

It seems that a feminist objection to such arrangements is not only that men, given their history, would not long fight fairly, but that the issue should be male aggression versus female nurturance. This dubious dichotomy, imbedded in some feminist theorizing, defies the commonsensical evidence that both aggression and nurturance go beyond gender. After all, much that passes for nurturance must be aggression by other means. Who in traditional gender societies nurtured all those bellicose, power-mad, rapist males?[4]

Much utopianizing (but not that of Manichean Anthony Burgess) holds that aggression can be considerably reduced, whether by social control or human transformation.[5] A libertarian approach, such as the one dramatized in Le Guin's *The Dispossessed,* merely posits limited aggression; arguments, fist-fights, riots (including one that causes a death), as well as more indirect forms of hostility, continue in the anarchist society. But aggression is limited by deinstitutionalization (no State, military, or other coercive ordering), by removing major social causes (large inequalities and other injustices), and by a full-scale ethos of cooperation rather than competition. It also helps to have a rather homogeneous and isolated society. It may further help that children are raised communally rather than in intense bonding to mothers. Hence all, including mothers, tend to be equal in nurturance and aggression. While similarity violates a radical feminist principle of women's superiority, the libertarian has a bias towards equalizing differences.

Not surprisingly, some feminists do object to Le Guin's utopianizing. No doubt male critics contribute to the problem by discussing *The Dispossessed* in terms of continuity as well as equality with male utopianizing (as I did in the preceding chapter). But isn't Le Guin to blame for organizing the fiction in terms of a questing male protagonist? And are not the values presented (to use a current coterie cant term) phallocentric?[6] No wonder we male critics admire its feminism. Even when Le Guin presents a more thoroughly androgynous view of sexuality—in the fantasy *The Left Hand of Darkness*—she is falling into a man-trap which reveals that "her own social conditioning skews the tale until a preference for the male point of view is established."[7] The critic, apparently raised in a world of only women, did not have such conditioning in a male viewpoint, whatever that reification means. Another woman coldly indicts "Le Guin's biases for monogamy and heterosexuality," even though they are at most only partial, and dominantly associated (often on quasievolutionary grounds) with traditional women rather than with men.[8] But the trouble with these claims is also a more general one. They assume not only that there is no nongendered truth but that all realities are discreet. By similar logic, there can be little common ground not only between men and women but between, say, black and white, old and young, intellectual and dumb, and other exclusionist reductions of the human.

Another feminist scholar generally concludes that after wide-ranging "research on utopian fiction I have not found or even heard of a single utopia by a man that posited a society composed entirely of men. But there are quite a few feminist utopias in which societies composed exclusively of women are envisioned."[9] Certainly there have been some of the latter since Charlotte P. Gilman's rather narrow and repressive *Herland* (1915).[10] But the denial of all-male places seems to be a victimization mostly by literary definition, again—a narrow view of the utopian impetus which excludes Robinson Crusoe's island and Thoreau's Walden Woods as well as the vast old literature of mostly masculine society in exotic voyages, and the like. Genderized utopianizing has been around for some time.

No doubt some men have created utopias with women mostly for their own pleasure or domination. But "the women, in envisioning a society without men, are merely giving up their roles of victims and becoming persons."[11] This femtopian assumption seems to be that women are inferior in their ability to imagine societies with men for women's pleasure or domination. If victims are not persons, and being is defined as gender exclusiveness, and women are so fearfully weak that they cannot even propose living in a society which has men (with whatever conceivable arrangements), such femtopianism may be more pathetic than persuasive.

So, too, with the previously cited Joanna Russ in her explanation of all-female eutopias: "if men are kept out of these societies, it is because men are dangerous. They also hog the good things of this world."[12] While such crass overgeneralization hardly merits counterargument, it does sadly reveal that some ostensible feminists see women as fearfully incompetent, even in hoggery and utopian imagination. The reason they are weak, this argument continues, is that they have been deprived, as their eutopias confirm, of "family/communal" life and the fullest relations with other women. This view tends to confirm patriarchal definitions of women, adding only that they are innately and exclusively good in their weakness.

At least one noted male critic of the metaphysics of fiction appears to agree. "It is plain to me," writes Robert Scholes, "that if we have a niceness Olympics, the women's records would far exceed the men's."[13] Only, as he must know, such femtopians as those cited would not deign to compete with men—and isn't it typical maleness to grasp, even in defending women, for a metaphor of ruthless competition? But anyway, "Women are better than men." For it is self-evident that "they are kinder, less violent, and quicker to learn the lessons of ecology—as a group." If so—though there is not much of a case that I can find, except for the "less violent" (but from Euripides on, many women-sympathizing men have doubted even that)—their goodness may be attributed less to femaleness than to powerlessness. Hence, to keep them nice, to whatever degree they are, would be to keep them powerless. But maybe, the self-abasing male gesture concludes, "an all female world is the only hope for the human race."[14] Since about half the human race has been eliminated (and the women who might want men deprived), the "niceness" at issue here can only be gross parody.

Certainly we may view some femtopianism as nicely feminine in the old-fashioned way. As a contemporary feminist scholar concludes about the literary utopias by feminists of the late nineteenth century, they "dominantly sentimentalize motherhood and assert women's moral superiority."[15] Some (male) utopias gave women even broader superiority: Zee in Edward Bulwer-Lytton's *The Coming Race* (1871) has greater physical and intellectual powers than usual males, as well as greater compassion, though of course she sacrifices for love of a male. The ladies even in feminist bellicosity continue to emphasize nurturance, in spite of its antiegalitarian results.[16] However, more thoughtful women's utopias, parallel to many male ones, will necessarily argue for a reordering of the conditions of nurturance, much of which must have been misnurturance to produce such horrible maleness. One may have to dewomanize nurturance (as has interestingly been argued) to better feminize it, and the males.[17]

But such femtopians as Russ are less concerned with future possibilities than present retaliations. Her announced literary premise is that "utopias are not embodiments of universal human values but are reactive; that is, they supply in fiction what their authors believe society . . . and/or women, lack in the here and now."[18] One of the universal human values claimed for utopianizing has usually been that it criticizes the utopianist's society, though not as a mere "lack." But the "reactive" half-human values in some apparently representative femtopian works no doubt deserve some brief consideration.

According to Russ' own femtopian, though badly underdeveloped, sketch "When it Changed," what women in the here-and-now most lack is the abolition of men.[19] In the future "Whileaway" society—also the fragmentarily presented eutopia of the collection of not very acute (indeed, rather dishonest if one examines many of the announced issues) diatribes entitled *The Female Man* (1975)—all males have died off some generations earlier.[20] The all-female society (apparently continued by parthenogenesis) is organized in quite conventional (on the simple side) twentieth-century American ways, of a rather imitative male style which includes violence and cops, though stock marriage is just between women. The women in this society are totally threatened when a few innocuous-appearing Earth men arrive. No matter the reality, men must be assumed to be inherently nasty. With a surprising, and quite unprepared, total collapse of morale, a supposedly brave and violent female cop decides that the women's utopia will be "completely turned around" by the mere proximity of men. Despairingly, she and the story conclude, "Take away my life but don't take away the meaning of my life." The meaning of life for women, in this poorly done utopianizing which may, however, be of sad symptomatic interest, is the fearful rejection of all men.

Surely a better case can be made for feminist separatism, such as all-female communities, so long as approximately equal allowance were to be made for all-male communities. Perhaps a decently responsive utopianizing might even make provision for quaintly archaic mixed-gender communities. Otherwise some of the fearfully weak sisters may enslave themselves in transvestite costuming in male pornotopias. But a really decent utopianizing might dissolve much of the issue by a more egalitarian—genderless or androgynous—ordering.

Gynocentrism

We are obviously not considering eutopian equality for women in looking at much contemporary femtopianism, though that is one of the oldest utopian themes. Plato, one dryly recalls, proposed in *The Republic* conditions for making women equal. He held that reproduction was the only significant difference, "We shall continue to think it proper for our Guardians and their wives to share in the same pursuits."[21] Women were to exercise nude with the men for physical equality. They were to turn over their children for nurturance by the State (breast-feeding apparently was to be random). Since local wisdom included infanticide, they were not to be confined and defined by procreative and nurturing functions. Plato even, Iris Murdoch reminds us, thought women could "do philosophy," the ultimate activity of the best men.[22] Women, then, can be fully equal even within an authoritarian class society, however repulsive in other ways that order may be, though one may suspect contrary tendencies to develop in a hierarchical ordering.

Some contemporary femtopians have something in mind other than equality, something far more "reactive." Perhaps some of that can be detailed from a frequently cited example (including by Russ), Sally Miller Gearhart's *Wanderground* (1980).[23] In the not too distant future, some enterprising women have defensively withdrawn from the male-dominated walled City to live a simple physical and communal life in the hills. They dedicate themselves to cultivating "nonviolent psychic powers" (*Wander* 179), and an antiman ideology as part of the witchery. Rather vaguely described, a "Revolt of the Earth" has caused not only women but other parts of nature to reject males. (In an early sign of the revolt, all the animals at a rodeo insisted on throwing off the men, but not the women, riders.) The male City retaliated with violent persecution, "witch hunts" of "liberated women," who were defined as those who wouldn't wear skirts, preferred the company of women only, and tried to resist the specified roles of "whore or housewife" (*Wander* 89). The escaped Hill Women maintain a marginally subversive role in the City, apparently to recruit new members for the femtopia and to testingly strengthen their resistance magic. The male/female, city/country, aggression/nurturance conflicts seem mostly at a stand-off during the fragmented and often murky narrative.[24]

The men from the City, which is a bit more advanced technological ordering (decaying mid-twentieth century), still sometimes pursue the simple-living Hill Women. One of the few even partially developed episodes is a *"Cunt Hunt"* (*Wander* 160 ff.) in which three stock redneck types go into the woods to rape, torture, and shoot stray women. But up against collective witchery, their guns won't fire, their penises won't erect, and even their pickup won't start. They are contemptuously driven off by a tribe of tough, booted, but smugly restrained females. As long as the women's movement keeps distantly active, men apparently can still rape in the city but are mostly impotent outside it (*Wander* 128).

There is one other somewhat vague countermovement by the small minority of "unmanly" men called "gentles," who have forsworn the powers of raping women, and the rest of nature. Refugees from "when the men owned all things," they are the "men who knew that the outlaw women were the only hope for the earth's survival. Men who, knowing that maleness touched women only with the accumulated hatred of centuries, touched no women at all. Ever" (*Wander* 2). But when they came (in one of the childish revenge episodes) gravely ill to the hills and "cried for the ministrations of the women," they were refused and left to die. After all, they were still male, though "unable to sustain their own man-ness . . . unable to grasp their own woman-ness." The women insist on seeing them, even repentant and dying, as power-mad, driven to "destroy themselves and us and any living thing." The merest maleness is irredeemably evil, except when practiced by women.

Toward the end of the patchwork narrative, some other weary old male "gentles" meet with the reluctant Hill Women (*Wander* 169 ff.). Even though these gentlemen have become partly psychic, imitating the women, their version is not really feminine enough, not a "Circle" but a hard and straight psyche, "another fancy prick to invade the world with." They beg the women to help them by increasing their witch-powerful covert action in the City, thus further disempowering maleness, and they vaguely promise to become more like women. But it is left unlikely that mere men can become roundly decent, or that true women will give them much aid and succor.

Mostly in *Wanderground* the male badness is more assumed than developed (coterie writing). Rather than justify this view, most of the little sketches sentimentally burble around stock though hyperbolic feminine powers, such as "mindstretch" (intuition) and "enfoldings" (empathy), made literal, and applied only to female things. This suggests not any meaningful society but the rituals of syncretistic religiosity—orgiastic moon worship, nature pietism, and a melange of supposed female magics. The outlaw women rub up against responsive trees and mawkishly commune with dogs, cats, ponies, and their "sisters."[25] Neither their orgasmic nor their maudlin activities go much beyond mysticopornography to image forth alternative social arrangements, however feminoid. (But the splattering of neologisms may be contagious.)

Style? Much of it seems crude burlesque, but consider an example of the recurrent deeper manner centering on paired women engaging in orgasmic breathing:

> "Soon, Alaka."
> "Or deep, Evona," chanted Alaka.
> "Soon."
> "And deep."
> "Red waters."
> "Deep."
> "Deep."
> "Deep."
> They spoke together: "Deep. Soon." (*Wander* 9)

A woman scholar, uncritically vibrating deeply to the passage, suggests "its references to menstruation and other natural currents and its association of those elemental experiences with intensity of experience and immediacy of involvement. . . . "[26] The nonbleeding countercritic can only note its profound verbal limitation. However, it may well be consistent with an ideology in which "feminist literary historians are now defining the contribution of women to modernism, concentrating on the fluidity and interiority. . . . "[27] The flow may also be that of traditional female repression, now inverted into smug superiority. But perhaps the exterior fixity of literature, this side of a femtopian total culture, is inadequate for the experience.

With some basic similarities to *The Wanderground,* Suzy McKee Charnas' *Motherlines* (1978), also serves as a commonly cited femtopia.[28] Though generally pedestrian and often stilted in style, the Charnas is at least more narratively competent than the Gearhart. It sketches a feminist future society with some variety of women's motives, beyond revulsion to rapist males (redundant phrase in this context). Apparently for several generations in an indefinite future time, women have been escaping to a semiarid wilderness from a degenerating male-dominated city, Holdfast. Refusing to hold fast to male ordering, two partly hostile and overlapping female societies have developed in the wilderness. The less organized consists of "free fems," escapees from male enslavement who nonetheless still partly hold to traditional "feminine" roles. They still display considerable dependency, conniving, limited physicality, vestigial romanticism, heavy personal decoration, obsession with revenge against the males, and in several senses, a sterile order. In effect, the fiction's treatment of the nonreproducing refugee free fems—who make their marginal living by feminine stereotypical handicrafts (which they trade to a more autonomous women's society)—mockingly exposes a feminism which is mostly reactive and has not gone far in creating an independent femtopia.

The more elaborated "Riding Women" society, a fully established nomadic order centered on horses, has contrastingly developed ornate female kin-structures (hence "motherlines").[29] Arduous horsewomen, they also practice forms of aggression usually considered macho male, such as rough games, animal slaughtering, and even warfare (though that violence is supposedly confined by strict ritualization). Unlike the free fem encampment, the horsy society claims to be egalitarian and democratic, though the emphasis on physical prowess, kin orderings, and (already!) insistent traditionalism rather drastically undercuts most freedom. Much more than the equality seems ambiguous. The tribal "Mares," as the free fems denigratingly call them, are separatist and exclusivist in more than feminist ways. Theirs is also insistently an ecologically balanced way of life. Supposedly far better than any society with men, it is, however, explicitly not a complete eutopia, as the discontented character who joins it after escaping the male world sadly discovers.

The Riding Women society does reproduce, by a vaguely described form of parasexuality (one of the few sci-fi gimmicks). But that has to be induced by the women's full sexual intercourse, trained for and ritualized, with young stallions (*Mother* 172 ff.). This take-off on what is usually thought of as male pornography shows, shall we say, rather unfeminist proportions.[30] It also yokes rather incongruously with the woman-on-woman sexuality, and the supposedly nurturing ideology of diverse-group parenting with ritually elaborate "share-mothers." That form of parenting seems mostly decorative anyway since the little girls are raised less by mothers than in removed groups of peers, "child-packs." This collective peer-nurturance, and its consequent generational auton-omy, seems incoherent in relation to the hyped system of "motherlines." But reactive gestures rather than rigor seem to control the material.

The main narrative development traces the growth of the primary protago-nist—escaped slave Alldera, one of the few to integrate into both free fem and Riding Women societies—over a decade into the kind of woman who raises other fems to the level of horsy women. By the end, mere free fems become nearly extinct, though the converts still retain an uncertain allegiance to sex-warfare and the hope of attacking the reportedly collapsing male city. That feminist dystopia was the subject of an earlier Charnas diatribe-fiction, *Walk to the End of the World,* and the narrative continuation in *Motherlines* ends on a note of incompletion, though with a vague hope that the male world will com-plete its own inherent destruction.

Not much seems needed. The rejection of the male, except in the form of slavering stallions and imitative females, seems fairly complete. From the memories and stories presented, men are universally enslaving exploiters and raping brutes. They also seem to be incompetent at most things, including taking care of themselves. Nor does this incompetence result from merely bad condi-tioning or wrong social arrangements. We are repeatedly reminded that males are essentially bad, "torturers and thieves by nature" (*Mother* 17). It is not so much rebellion that brings them down as it is their very essence as "world killers," raping all, including the female environment and each other. In the narrative, however, the popular tales of males are hardly developed beyond simple contemptuous venom.

The main "reactive" motive for this fiction, then, is resentful hatred of men, as in the other femtopias so far considered (and yet others, which it would seem merely tiresome to detail). I am reluctant to attribute their obvious literary and intellectual failings just to their negative motives. (Indeed, I have repeatedly argued elsewhere—on Lawrence, Céline, Wright, Melville, Nietzsche, Mur-doch, Mailer, et al.—that literary criticism has undervalued the power of the negative as vital incitement to awareness, understanding, and beauty, but most of my examples were male.) Perhaps yet another limitation male-dominated culture has imposed upon many women is inadequate development of the power-ful negative responses. Clearly, these literary women resent and hate much, but they perform it rather poorly.

Perhaps, I half grant, obsessive resentment works out to be an inadequate literary motive, especially unpersuasive when arbitrarily genderized. These femtopias not only indict traditional maleness (though little such discrimination is made); they also implicitly indict some feminism as self-bathetic revenge. Resentment does seem to stunt social imagination, and even appropriate retaliations against us awful males.

Resentful rule by women can, of course, be utopianized in other ways. Since I see no sufficiently good reason to make gender exclusions on any subject at all, even femtopianism, I might briefly note here an example from an easily identifiable "male point of view." Burlesque novelist Thomas Berger's *Regiment of Women* (1973) takes place in a twenty-first-century eastern America where sex roles have long been systematically reversed.[31] Females, with what by 1970s conventions would be male garb and mannerisms, are the rulers, bosses, soldiers, and professionals. Males, obsessed with cosmetics, pantyhose, breast implants, and the like, are the secretaries, mistresses (only called "mattresses"), and other social underlings. Reproduction takes place in laboratories, with eggs furnished by honored females, and sperm by forced extraction from young male conscripts (a quite unpersuasive detailing). Licit sex is by anal penetration of males by females wielding monstrously large dildoes. Pandemic gender exploitation includes psychoanalysts (all women) financially, sexually, and psychologically abusing pathetic male clients. Many of the mid-twentieth-century uses and abuses of women, especially all the inculcated varieties of self-denigration, including breast fashions, are now imposed by manish women on feminized males. Tat-for-tit.

The first person narrative is that of a twenty-nine-year-old submissive male office underling (in an incidental satire of commercial publishing) who in spite of his/her intentions becomes a rebel against the womanized regimentations. Taken up, after a jail escape (the crime was cross-dressing as a manly woman), by a revolutionary male-liberation movement, Georgie is indoctrinated in pseudo-radical ideology, including the rewriting of history so that "men had once had power but lost it through pity for women" (*Regiment* 175). Berger has a polished cleverness at detail and scene but the parody of early-1970s "Women's Liberation" is so gross as to be simply contemptuous. All group efforts at change are treated as silliness. So, undercutting the fiction's premises, is almost everything in the female establishment. The femtopia is near not only social disintegration but ecological collapse. The dominant women are messily incompetent in most things, even including the repression of ostensible males. In tone, the joke often does not like itself.

The jokey ironies cut both ways, but not equally. While the detailed sympathies for the restrictive and denigrating roles traditionally imposed on women might seem acute, especially in the rather lavish concern for synthetic appearance, their displacement onto men in a femtopia renders them absurd. The caricatures of manish women display jejune authorial nastiness.

The resolution takes clichéd form in those refuges of individualism, neo-primitivism and romance. Running off to the Maine woods (in a Rolls stolen from an incompetent rich woman senator) with a defecting FBI woman, Georgie has to learn he-manly things, such as driving, camping, robbing, and raping, all of which he rather messes up. He not only discovers that she is sometimes a better man than he is, but realizes the basis of passion: "I need you, and I hate you because I need you" (*Regiment* 346). Thus gender war is forever.

But he will learn to do his manly part in life in the woods, confirmed by her erotic and reproductive needs. The ameliorative parody ends, "he could be boss once in a while." Why? After all, "he was the one with the protuberant organ" (*Regiment* 349). Mere reversal, followed by a pat reversing of the reversal, lacks utopian imagination and thought in the crass reconfirming of cliché.

Rather less rancorous is a woman feminist's double reversal, a femtopia with a mentopian movement, Gerd Brantenberg's *Egalia's Daughters* (1977).[32] This matriarchy in the indefinite future is supposedly an egalitarian (and parliamentary) society in which the menwim (males) "know instinctively that their only purpose is decorative and ornamental," except for menial jobs and the housebound condition of raising children. The menwim must wear pehoes (cod-pieces), in fashionable styles, outside their skirts, take monthly contraceptive pills, let women be sexually dominant in spite of their clitoral practices not leading to male orgasm, celebrate wim's menstrual power, and worship "the Great Allmother." While conditions have improved since the old days when "prick-scissors" were used on useless menwim, and now some spinster-males are allowed (though at less pay) some variety of jobs, a masculist liberation movement develops. With some sympathy, the narrative follows the struggles of several menwim in the Masculine League. They counterargue the prevailing justifications for their degradation in the animal queendom and seek to raise their roles to full equality in the huwom race.

The menwim burn their pehoes,and engage in other outrageous protest, in spite of having their vision of equality denounced by traditionalists as an outrageous Utopia, the "perverted dream of frustrated menwim." After all, the matriarchy has created not only an ecologically balanced order but an international nonaggressive world State of Pax. Few believe the weird myths that there was once a patriarchal order, or that menwim are by nature other than essentially passive, frivolous, sexually erratic, unadventuresome, incompetent, overly emotional, unsuited to the maritime (the genesis is Norwegian), smelly, fashion-obsessed, unintellectual, and generally, in spite of their size and strength, inferior. Rather relentlessly, Brantenberg has run the mirror-changes on most of the 1970s feminist counterings. The ending is inconclusive, with the menwim still struggling for equality. A leading daughter of Egalia has the last word: "In a society where menwim were allowed to rule, all terrestrial life would die out. If menwim weren't kept down, if they weren't restrained, if they weren't civilized, if they weren't *kept in their place*, life would perish." Does not the irony finally cut itself? The obsessive reduction to gender issues leaves virtually no place to go, neither utopia nor dystopia.

Femtopias do suggest several larger than life issues. Women tend to be credited with two insuperable advantages (besides internalized genitalia): "mystery" and "nature," which often merge. Since aggressive-exploitative males have long viewed women as witches, and even contemporary macho-seducer heroes make a big point of rediscovering that "God is a woman," the religious "mystery" of women may be the last desperate male imposition, comically agreed to by some pseudo-radical feminists.[33] The exalted identification of women with nature may seem more problematic, given the obvious female nature-nurturance metaphors. But the male rape-of-nature now seems to be an overwhipped companion trope that rides off in all directions, and thus in none very clearly. One direction is the trite old sentimentalism of the feminine towards flora and fauna and being nice to animals, which appears in all of these fictions. It may be viewed, in this version, as trivially displaced nurturance.

Another direction is religiosity merged with the matriarchal, which includes the worship of Mother Earth, or variations on such figures as the classical Greek earth goddess, Gaea. All sorts of environmental programs as well as more exalted pieties are yoked with such "natural religion." This religiosity is treated as ecologically positive, especially in contrast to the inhuman technological and toxic poisoning of the male-style (even when woman-run) cities. Since, however, no major religion has been, however woman oriented, ecologically sound, this treatment must strike the knowledgeable reader as arbitrary and forced.[34] Perhaps the theological claims values within nature which simply are not, and cannot be, there. The worship of Gaea, and similar ladies, did not discourage the classical Greeks from damaging their ecosystem to a degree not adequately corrected, or correctable, more than two millennia later. Goddesses are not especially pertinent in saving the scene, and femtopianism that pretends otherwise is best read as cult fantasy (its communing function).[35] As one of the sharper feminists (Angela Carter) rightly notes, "Mother goddesses are just as silly a notion as father gods." And as unjust and unfree.

More interestingly, femtopianism seems to be insistently neoprimitive (as in most of the examples discussed). The constricted city is alienating and exploitative, and dominantly male, while the open, simple rural life is feminine and communal.[36] This is not just literary, for in discussing actual rural communes a feminist seems to typically praise them as places "to which women can come to cleanse themselves of male, negative, and city energies."[37] Such sentiments, of course, link to long traditions of more-or-less male utopianizing, our deep heritage of "soft primitivism," the loving pastoral (further discussed in the next chapter, below). Prophets of "deep ecology," that is, revolutionary change from present exploitative attitudes towards the natural environment, and the "holistic consciousness" of widespread "New Age" ideologies, identify feminism as an essential part of the nature-nurturance responses. It may seem puzzling that feminism, historically in good part a sophisticated urban movement towards an advanced society's social-political equality—and equalities and freedoms often dependent on advanced technology and organization—should be identified with the rural, communal, "simple and natural" living.[38] It can only be understood in terms of the dominance of the pastoral in the critical utopianizing traditions. To the degree that women are not ideologically identified (whatever the practical realities) with socioeconomic power, including control of the inherently expansive-destructive technocracy, they may seem countering to the environmental rape so easily identified as male. To the degree that the women's societies of the future are envisioned as limited in technology, relatively low in population, decentralized in organization, nonhierarchical in power, and scarcity-bound in development—and with a relatively ascetic ethos—they tend to be ecologically positive. Gender, in spite of some bombastic femtopian rhetoric, has little essential role in such a social vision, though I suppose that in time the insistence upon it could make it integral. Nor do the tribal metaphors thickly employed in some of these fictions and arguments need to be taken very seriously. (Many of the Native Americans, who since the 1960s have provided radical metaphors for reorganization in tribal ways, also did ruthless ecological damage, regardless of their sacral views, though more slowly than their more numerous and technologically elaborate successors.)[39] Surely there are positive values as well as resentments in these femtopias. However, those values seem not to be gender-dependent, and may be poorly presented because of gynocentric bigotries. But perhaps what these women (and even the ones in female disguise) really need is a good . . . writer.

Piercy's Protests

Some better utopian fictions by feminist writers might, happily, suggest additional perspectives. One of the best known is Marge Piercy's *Woman on the Edge of Time* (1976), a combined eutopian, dystopian, and naturalistic fiction focusing on feminist themes.[40] Much of Piercy's perspective and manner come out of what may be best described as the naturalistic-protest literary traditions. That includes the emphasis on seeing socially marginal characters as representative victims of "the system"; gritty realistic details of environment and class; tendentious leftist rhetoric about injustice, capitalism, and other exploitation; satiric, caricatured treatment of the prevailing manipulative cultural symbols; and a pervasive radical moral indignation. (Richard Wright is a major example.) Piercy has elaborated her version of these in a number of topical fictions in the last two decades. In two she has adapted utopian scenes and issues.

Adapted-utopianism would seem the right emphasis because the futuristic places are always dramatically as well as conceptually imbedded in, and subordinated to, current social scenes and issues. Thus her earlier use of the utopian, *Dance the Eagle to Sleep* (1970), is about an only slightly futuristic society in which she redeploys the "Youth Revolution" of the late 1960s.[41] Mainstream America, it holds, has become increasingly repressive and adopted a favorite pseudoliberal panacea (a proposal still ominously bantered around) of universal service conscription, here called the Nineteenth Year of Servitude. Other forms of repression have also become more highly organized and violent. The several years of fighting-the-system covered by the narrative are told from the approximate points of view of half a dozen highly rebellious late adolescents, including an American Indian dropout who becomes a revolutionary tribal leader, a black teenage guerrilla, a radicalized rock musician, and two uncertainly liberated, runaway young women. In a literal attempt at eutopianism these leaders develop a countering tribal "nation," with thousands of the young engaged in a movement with both urban and rural communes (only briefly described), drawing on some of the obvious intentional communities of the time. The movement is noted for its ecstatic rituals of naked dancing to rock music, aimed (as the title awkwardly suggests) at overcoming the "eagle" of American exploitative aggrandizement.

As with the radical "Movement" of the late 1960s, that of the fiction is a confusing mixture of various educational, political, cultural, and cultist efforts.[42] "They could learn the good ways of being in harmony, of cooperating, of sane bravery in defense of each other, to be one with their bodies and their tribe and each other and the land" (*Dance* 32). The social counterculture is presented with didactic positiveness (at times a bit heavy on the more extremist SDS factional rhetoric).[43] The personal relations, varyingly promiscuous and possessive, are presented somewhat more complexly. More briefly developed is the rising left-feminist issue of supposedly radical males in fact reproducing the "same old division of labor" with subordinate roles for women (*Dance* 145)—a major historical impetus to the revival of American feminism. This, and a neatly cutting satire on American psychiatry and its conformist-adjustment ethic (*Dance* 217 ff.), till the literary field for the later utopian planting in *Woman on the Edge of Time*.

Eutopianizing efforts suffer a grim defeat at the hands of the future U.S. military, turning the narrative into an absurd guerrilla war (an enlargement of the Weather Underground of SDS of the time). Those not taken over by psychiatry or otherwise coopted are brutally destroyed (the suicidal Indian leader in a scene adapted from the famous early tractor one in *Grapes of Wrath*). But there is a saving remnant of scarred movement organizers prepared to go on agitating. "We were right and wrong, but the system is all wrong" (*Dance* 231). The too patent upbeat ending includes loving and childbirth, similar to some social protest fictions of the 1930s. This is "agit-prop" literature, in not the worst sense, with left-utopianizing politics adapted to a mildly utopian manner.

The feminist concern, responding to the historical effulgence of the early 1970s, becomes far more dominant in *Woman*. Here there is a single central figure, a thirty-seven-year-old abused Chicana, Connie. The main narrative, set in the America of the mid-1970s, is a naturalistic account of this woman's victimization by welfare poverty and psychiatric institutionalization. Such reality seems dystopia enough—"the life like an open sore" (*Woman* 279). Connie has been forcibly hospitalized several times, but the current incarceration, for assaulting her compliant sister's abusive pimp, seems especially unjust. She has also been the victim of various other males, lovers and employers. Not the least of these is her crass and embourgeoised brother, whom she visits on hospital leave for Thanksgiving, only to be unthankfully exploited as a prisoner-servant. In spite of various attempts at manipulatively confirming to or naively resisting the male-dominated institution, including a pathetic abortive flight, she always loses. The culmination comes with imposed psychosurgery, which she unsuccessfully resists by poisoning the doctors' coffee. The homicides apparently make her a permanent institutional case. The persuasively vivid detailing of institutional life, as well as the grim melodrama, concludes in a bitterly ironic epilogue document—obtuse pages from her clinical record which confirm the ongoing nasty reality of the totalitarian institution.

Before turning to the counterpointing eutopian narrative, several characteristics of the naturalistic narrative should be noted. As an indictment of psychiatric totalitarianism, *Woman* might be viewed as a partly inverted parallel to Ken Kesey's *One Flew over the Cuckoo's Nest* (1962), to which it is probably indebted.[44] Piercy's inversion lies not only in taking a pathetic woman instead of an heroic rogue-becoming-saint as protagonist, but in a feminist insistence throughout. Kesey, with crass obsession, made all his males (whether innocent, intellectual, doctor, or hero) victims of manipulative, guilt-twisting, castrating females, culminating in the controller of the ward, a Big Brother with boobs, Big Nurse. He also deployed a dystopian subplot: in the paranoid mind of the giant Indian patient, Chief Bromden, Big Nurse works for a conspiratorial "Combine" (probably adapted from the fragmented futuristic criminal-police-syndicate in William Burroughs' *Naked Lunch* [1959]) which seeks to control everyone. Though Piercy's less hyperbolic (and humorless) treatment of characters lacks Kesey's comic and satiric flamboyance, the gender obsession is nearly as insistent. In hers, all of the men are the vicious ones, especially men in authority, such as the doctors. While the reader is no more inclined to regret their poisoning than the defiance and semirape of Big Nurse, the single-gender-as-evil leaves a bad taste in more than the melodramatically poisoned coffee. Piercy does allow an exception, a sympathetic male (Skip), but he is a not very successfully rebellious homosexual who is early lobotomized into withdrawal. Kesey, too, allowed minor variations—a couple of good-hearted whores and the aslant (Oriental) nurse in the Disturbed Ward, but those are just the confirming exceptions allowed for in the rule of misogynistic American he-man mythology. In both *Cuckoo's Nest* and *Woman,* Manichean gender obsessions partly undercut the powerful anger at totalitarian institutions. Psychiatric authoritarians, of course, the Big Nurses and the exploitatively conformist doctors, come in all sizes and sexes. When they do not, the reader should feel imposed upon.

Many fictions in the naturalistic mode suffer from the same congenital weakness (besides often heavy-handed prose and politics): the inadequacy of their main characters. Predefined as representative social victims, their responsiveness is unimaginative, intellectually narrow, generally thin. So with Piercy's defeated Chicana, Connie. But by bringing in another world of experience, a eutopian vision, she much increases the range and dialectics.[45] Piercy utilized a couple of sci-fi devices that result in the character's intermittent psychic removal to the future. In effect, these are alternating dream-visits to eutopia by way of an alter ego of the future, Luciente, which provides the only light in her miserable life. The reality/utopia double-play does pose ideological as well as formal problems. As one responsive commentator puts it, the doubling "privileges, even glamorizes, the most intensely oppressed victims of capitalism as visionaries with special access to the future." While I doubt the judgment that the reality and utopia "cancel each other," they do certainly elicit that "ambivalence [which] is the essential feeling in utopian writing."[46]

Still, the utopianizing is an interesting effort at enlarging the naturalistic mode, as well as interesting in its own right. Developed with some didactic thoroughness, the eutopia is primarily the community of Mattapoisett (in present-day Massachusetts) in 2137. The good society is technologically advanced in some areas—biological sciences and deep-ecology—but neoprimitive in decentralized organization, nonaffluence, tribalist rituals, and communalist qualities.

However, traditional sex roles have largely been overcome in twenty-second-century America. This crucially includes female nurturance. Babies, in a positive feminist take-off on *Brave New World,* are created in the laboratory. They are cared for by breast-feeding (by way of hormones) males and mixed-gender parenting. As one of the twenty-second-century women explains:

> It was part of women's long revolution. When we were breaking all the old hierarchies. Finally there was that one thing we had to give up too, the only power we ever had, in return for no more power for anyone. The original production: the power to give birth. Cause as long as we were biologically enchained, we'd never be equal. And males never would be humanized to be loving and tender. So we all became mothers. Every child has three. To break the nuclear bonding. (*Woman* 105)

Since racial variety has also been consciously incorporated, this is a society essentially "without the stigmata of race and sex" (*Woman* 106).

Some reactionary feminists object. As one puts it, women giving up exclusive motherhood are allowing male power the control of reproduction which "has been the goal of men for centuries."[47] But this seems willfully to miss Piercy's point (just quoted) that real equality must depend on both disempowering any gender and despecializing all nurturance. Supposed feminist arguments against this direct themselves less towards equality, except as a rhetorical cover, than towards power. Power relations, so evident in the resentment-and-revenge femtopias (such as those discussed above), do not allow equality. To exclude males from childrearing is a power play. Another feminist critic more appropriately points out that Piercy's utopianism "makes the future work for women."[48]

Not that Piercy's counterings of present sexism avoid all resentment. She rather ostentatiously makes female soldiers—a peripheral war is going on between eutopian Mattapoisett and the future unreconstructed elements of exploitative America (to keep the hand of revolutionary ideology in the narrative)—and the women are as tough and violent as the men. And still in the future good society those who twice commit the rare crime of rape (or similar violence) are executed as incorrigibles (*Woman* 208). These institutionalizations of total violence certainly qualify the libertarianism of much of the rest. Even in literary terms, such mixtures, including high-tech warfare and neoprimitive mutualism, sci-fi manipulation and organicist sensitivity, seem incongruous to the point of fictional and ideological instability. Morally and aesthetically the hostilities are sometimes too crude.

With perhaps better directed hostility, Piercy also briefly provides an alternative dystopia. Connie slips in consciousness into the wrong future in New York City. It is a horribly polluted, superautomated, class-divided, corporate structure, and totally control-conditioned society. This nasty *Brave New World* (from which it partly derives) is represented by a female caricature who looks and responds like a contemporary TV ad. Almost totally synthetic, and drug and diversion compliant, she is a contract whore of vacuously prettified ugliness (*Woman* 287–300). Piercy, then, in partly presenting with some acuteness two futuristic as well as presentday Americas, deploys some of the imaginative range and critical social speculation that characterizes the better utopian fiction.

"We can only know what we can truly imagine" (*Woman* 328). That includes radical resistance to the dystopian possibilities rooted in the present by breaking "allegiance" to exploitative institutions. Or ideologies. Part of the resistance to sexism comes from attempting to truly imagine the fullest alternatives, androgynous personality types, and the consequent reordering of daily life. Some of the refusal of our vicious competition comes from tangibly imaging forth cooperative and mutualist possibilities.

And better ways of work. The dehumanizing division of labor, whose overcoming is probably the most powerful and profound utopian principle in the leftist traditions (anarchist and Marxist, though the latter lost this emphasis), requires reconceptualizing work and labor.[49] Piercy, drawing on this, attempts to show all work—art and science included—as essentially equal and significant, without male and female distinctions. All work also exists within the humanizing context of everyone accepting fair proportions of "family duties, political duties, social duties" (*Woman* 267). It is the projection of nonalienating work that provides the nexus of a just society. This is not the abstract and elitist humanistic ideal of the "well-rounded man" but tangible and shared daily activity. The grotesque specialisms of politician or scientist or artist, as well as the more obviously deforming roles of menial laborer, service worker, hierarchical technician, require drastic reconceiving for a humane order. This her fiction also attempts (though I will not pursue the details here).

For, as Piercy seems well aware, the powers that press us down are not just the pyramids of economics and the State, hierarchies of money and coercion, but the self-alienating compacting in roles, in nursery or studio, laboratory or bed, shop or book. Arbitrary work role and sex role and cultural role reenforce each other. To be really against sexism is to be against all hierarchical divisions of laboring as well as loving since they create each other.

That is a large order. Piercy attempts to make it tangible by interspersing the naturalistic and utopian narratives. For example, near the end of the fiction her Connie fights the doctors of the world in a total-institution while she is simultaneously fighting a sci-fi war in eutopic Mattapoisett. The hard-pushed analogy is that both battles engage essentially the same institutional forces and ideologies—"and all the other flacks of power" (*Woman* 267). Conceiving eutopic possibilities, then, is less a collection of fantasies than a consciousness-heightening handbook of ways of passionately thoughtful resistance to things as they badly are in this world. To utopianize may even improve the odds.

Granted, some of Piercy's emphasis is rather on the quaint side. There is, for example, quite a bit of earnest reworking of language to combat sexism, such as "per" (from person) to replace him/her.[50] That may be one of the better neologisms in what has become an insistent but awkward effort at new coinages. Not just a manner of radical feminism—many offended by our manipulated and debated language have a go at it—it seems generally widespread in this generation's utopianizing. Perhaps some of it is, and has long been, integral to the very perspective of utopianizing. But the forced argots do come at a stylistic cost.

Also, as in so many femtopias, Piercy displays a disproportionate emphasis on ritual, and yet more ritual, with an often soddenly synthetic poeticizing. I must suppose that this, too, is "reactive" to the imposed and exploitative mass-media ritualism of our society.[51] But individually artificed counterrituals, not the creation of a community and history, are perhaps bound to seem arbitrary and tiresome. The ritualism seems more homeopathic than persuasive, and may be better read for such pathos than for the ostensible poetry. So, too, with her too naive protagonist, whose pathos takes over even in her eutopic discoveries, be they participatory politics or cunnilingus (or even the surprisingly sympathetic portrait of a compulsive seducer, Jackrabbit). This interesting fiction is much flawed.

Not surprisingly, *Woman on the Edge of Time* has been characterized as a "hybrid feminist vision."[52] Really, most utopias might well be described as hybrids. While in this context the phrase may also suggest some reservations about Piercy's feminism, it does apply to the mixed modes of the fiction, with the crossing of eutopia, dystopia, and social naturalism. Hybrids, of course, as with mules, can be a problem. But so with speculative feminism which, to the degree that it would counter contemporaneous society, needs to break out of mere social realism. Thus hybrid gender and nurturance, in such forms as androgyny and truly egalitarian childrearing, for eutopia. That requires radical breaks with the restrictive social conventions, which are also the conventions of genre. The utopian, then, functions less as a set form than as a convention-breaking possibility. But isn't that much of what utopianizing has always been about?

Antifemtopian Feminism and Atwood

From my perspective, women's roles and equality are not the only important issues of utopianizing but are sufficiently pertinent to be considered almost everywhere (and I repeatedly touch on them in every chapter). But the pertinence rather confirms that the issues are problematic. An appropriate instance might be Margaret Atwood's feminist dystopian novel, *The Handmaid's Tale* (1985).[53] Except for a brief academic parody of an epilogue in the twenty-second century, this is a skillful first-person account by a thirty-three-year-old "handmaid" (concubine) in the 1990s. During the 1980s the United States, now called Gilead, had become a terroristic theocracy, taken over in a bloody conspiracy by a fundamentalist religious fascism espousing "traditional family values," antisex and antiabortion, and spectacular prayer services. The society combines the commonplace techniques of totalitarianism with antique religiosity and social customs.

Atwood, well-known as a Canadian cultural nationalist, takes a harshly distant view of the neighboring madness.[54] But the cruxes may be seen as less topical satire than as ambiguous feminism. Ambiguous not least in that Atwood's near-future America of patriarchal repression casts women as just as much the enemy of women as are men. Though often responded to as a feminist fictionist, no doubt partly because of her cutting portrayals of males as well as her emphasis on quests for women's self-discovery and autonomy in such novels as *Life before Man* and *Bodily Harm*, Atwood also treats women sardonically, especially for their deceptiveness.[55] Strikingly, in her feminist dystopia a female utopia is explicitly rejected. The protagonist handmaid has opposed, in her earlier life, her radical feminist friend's separatism: if she "thought she could create Utopia by shutting herself up in a woman-only world enclave she was sadly mistaken. Men were not just going to go away" (*Tale* 223). The narrative reports, including the destruction of the women's commune and male revenge, confirm the ugliness as well as the improbability of any such gender politics.

The narrating handmaid, Offred (property of Fred, though perhaps also a pun on her rejection of the identifying cover-all red costumes imposed on hand-maids), is a self-acknowledged "wimp" as a too-mild feminist.[56] She is the daughter of a 1960s militant feminist, presented with sympathetic irony. Her best friend since college (Moira) is a militant lesbian and a rebel in Gilead. There are, very briefly, other positive women, part of the "Mayday" rebel conspiracy (which includes men), and apparently in the related "Underground Femaleroad" where men and women help trapped women escape to Canada. But the nastiest characters in the tale are women, such as the official wives of the ruling Commanders, and the vicious controllers-indoctrinators of captive women, the "Aunts." Commonsensically, as in much of contemporary society, women show themselves the most virulent antagonists of feminism, as of other types of equality and freedom. (The simpler femtopians quite miss the point with their indiscriminate "sisterhood.") As a pedantic commentator notes in the epi-logue, "Gilead was, although undoubtedly patriarchal in form, occasionally matriarchal in content" (*Tale* 390). For essential parts of the narrative, "occa-sionally" is pedantic understatement. As male-exploited Offred counters, in her reflections, her feminist mother: "You wanted a women's culture. Well now there is one" (*Tale* 164). And it is as nasty as can be. Not only have the patriarchal Commanders given their resentfully sterile wives near-absolute con-trol of their sex lives and all nurturance, but the women also set the ambience for the religious authoritarianism. Matriarchy and patriarchy, then, are less oppo-sites than variant and correlative forms of control, systems of oppression. (There is little reason to believe that a matriarchal ordering would be much better than a patriarchal one, and both deserve similar responses.)

Atwood's perceptivity and intelligence do not, of course, stop her from playing out her dystopian ironies with bizarre twists of rather gothic proportions. As in the overwhelming majority of serious contemporary utopianizings, the natural world is in a bad way. Because of the "infamous AIDS epidemic," "nuclear plant accidents," "leakages from chemical-and-biological warfare stockpiles," and the pervasive spread of toxic wastes (*Tale* 386), a large major-ity of women are sterile. And the larger number of what pregnancies there are miscarry or result in deformation. Consequently, in Atwood's theocracy, women who might be fertile are terroristically indoctrinated in "Rachel and Leah Re-education Centers" (typically combining allusions to totalitarian techniques and one of the nasty Old Testament stories). These are controlled by "Aunts," who use group therapy, military-style order, and cattle prods to prepare the women for concubinage to the ruling caste of Commanders. In grotesque conformity with fundamentalist Christian "traditional family values," the Commander is only supposed to have sexual intercourse with the assigned handmaiden while she is held between the legs of the proper (permanent) wife, without pleasurable signs of sexual play or affection on anyone's part. The official wives get any resulting children, the handmaidens get reassigned or otherwise disposed of. While these bizarre arrangements strain plausibility (and a rebellious male wonders, with the reader, why they don't just pour in the semen from a bottle), it does serve as mockery of the Christian doctrine of purely reproductive sex. It is, of course, also a form of pornography (in literature as in practice), religio-politicized to go along with the gratifications of brutally executing pornographers and abortionists and of having regular rituals in which frenzied handmaidens literally tear apart (as in *The Bacchae*) dissidents accused of rape.

What is rather more fictionally perverse, I suggest, is that Atwood has elaborated such a drastically counterfactual premise as, in effect, underpopulation. While that may not totally strain social plausibility, given the accelerating destructiveness of our technocracy, it may strain moral sensitivity. Most contemporary utopianizing quite sensibly assumes that ever greater overpopulation is one of the horrors of the future. The simplest definition of the contemporary premise of dystopia might be "a place that is overcrowded." With good reason on a five-billion peopled earth. Eutopia probably must assume much less peopled circumstances. (Every utopia considered in this chapter, and most of the positive ones considered in other chapters, posit far less than contemporary population conditions.) There is a callously manipulative quality about Atwood's premises, as there is an arch coldness in her pervasive tone.

While Atwood's themes in *The Handmaid's Tale* (as in the preceding nonutopian fictions) may be taken as strongly feminist in emphasis and values, she is a sardonic stylist and deflating ironist, and those qualities tend to dominate. With an exactness in describing minute sensations (indebted to the woman's novel of sensibility) and a precisely laconic dramatization of relationships (indebted to the novel of manners), her novel illustrates the fact that utopianizing can take form in ways identified with the well-made novel. (So much again for the usual genre distinctions.) However, her fictional crafting is so sparse that her dystopian society at times lacks the exposition that would make it logically coherent.

Fudging such issues a bit, her wimpy Offred goes femininely out of the way not to ask about who rules, and just how. She is, instead, preoccupied with bits of her former, 1980s, life as loving wife (what happened to her husband is unknown), sweet mother (her young daughter was given to some Commander), and accepting daughter (her wryly heroic feminist mother was forcibly made an

"Unwoman" dying in labor in some toxic-poisoned colony). Offred had also been a somewhat independent woman, until the early actions of the repressive society eliminated her librarian job, her credit and money, and other contemporary signs of personal autonomy. These reminiscent counterings to dystopia (and I am again looking for the eutopia underlying dystopia) become a bit sentimental in implicitly suggesting pre-1980s America as something of a positive utopia. Witty, no doubt, but the ironies may again rather destabilize the dialectics of the utopianizing.

For this is a quite self-reflexive fiction. Of the submissively self-punishing handmaids, we have the acute comment: " . . . people will do anything rather than admit that their lives have no meaning. No use, that is. No plot" (*Tale* 279). The plot-meaning ironies flow quick and hard in the tale. For example, the narrator's Commander, a powerful exploitative leader though controlled by his wife, the grim Serena Joy, wants something more from his handmaid. She expects that his demands will be "kinky sex"; what he actually wants is play, including games of scrabble, and a "real kiss" and genuine "intimacy." That last, within terms of the "equivocal" power characteristic of any gender relationship, she is not about to grant.

The ironies that take over the narrative are pyrrhic. We never learn (except in the few bits of mocked pedantic obtuseness in the epilogue) what happened to the narrating woman whose journal has been found, or to her husband, her child, her friends, her lover, or to the Gilead dystopia, except that it has eventually disappeared and become a set of puzzles for historical archeology. No less ambiguously, in the final parts of the narrative an ancient plot has equivocally taken over the feminism—a romance. Offred has a passionate, and dangerously illicit, erotic affair—ecstatic orgasms, trembling devoutness, and all—with the Commander's chauffeur, Nick. Though parodying the tough and taciturn he-man (he may also be a "Guardian" spy and a "Mayday" revolutionary conspirator), he is yet her true love as well as her savior, leading her to the Underground Femaleroad by which she escapes. How seriously are we to take this obvious Lady Chatterley's-servant-lover plot twist?

While much of the novel is carefully unresolved, the feminism does rather dissolve in the ambiguities of the romance, with its undeniable female fulfillment in submission.[57] This may be taken as liberation, but not in the contemporary feminist sense. Much else remains ambiguous. The hidden words scratched by Offred's predecessor as handmaid in her cell, her Victorian-style bedroom in the Commander's house, *"Nolite te bastardes carborundorum"* (*Tale* 69, and repeatedly) become her mysterious talisman. When she learns that it means "Don't let the bastards grind you down," it becomes her hope of resistance. But then she also learns that it is burlesque Latin which her predecessor got illicitly from the Commander and that the predecessor ended in despair and suicide. So utopian hope in an impossible world becomes but a multiple travesty. Or is it, altogether? A residue of heroic resistance may be taken as one of the ironies.

When the handmaid is clasped tightly between the legs of the resentful wife Serena Joy, and the fully dressed Commander is mechanically penetrating her, the grotesqueness becomes bitter comedy:

> My arms are raised; she holds my hands, each of mine in each of hers. This is supposed to signify that we are one flesh, one being. What it really means is that she is in control, of the process and thus of the product. If any. The rings of her left hand cut into my fingers. it may or may not be revenge.
>
> My red skirt is hitched up to my waist, though not higher. Below it the Commander is fucking. What he is fucking is the lower part of my body. I do not say making love because this is not what he's doing. Copulating too would be inaccurate because it would imply two people and only one is involved. Nor does rape cover it; nothing is going on here that I haven't signed up for. (*Tale* 121)

"Signed up for" because she accepted, however reluctantly, the handmaid role— as women have long accepted feminine role-playing—since the alternative was to be sent off to miserable slavery and early death as an "Unwoman"—meta-phorically, the fate of women who do not play the role. The reflectiveness, indeed, linguistic pedantry, of the passage has its grim hilarity. "One detaches oneself. One describes" (*Tale* 123). This tough, cool manner is vintage Atwood (some readers find it altogether too masculine). It is also a style of the all-genders contemporary intellectual's protective irony, and what this feminist ironizes includes feminist utopianism.

This antifemtopianism, much in the manner of well-made fiction, uses the utopian as a mode for critical intelligence. That is what it is there for. While I have pointed out some drastic limitations of *The Handmaid's Tale,* I think it may be granted that it suggests its case. Conveniently for my argument, it was written from a considerably feminist point of view by a feminist woman. But quite possibly it (and more than the cool style) could have been written by a man. Granted, he could not directly experience, say, menstruation or childbirth or some of the paradoxes of feminine role-playing, but he could experience analo-gous abuse, weakness, parenting, semirape, exploitation, inequality, suffering, and mechanical sex.

After all, certainly the utopian, but also much of literature more generally, depends on intense analogous experience. There is not, then, really any femtopi-anism—just the arbitrary pretense of it—except as part of a larger utopian dialectic. Quite likely, too, there is not a separate *weltanschauung* for women, feminist or other, except as part of the larger process of man-woman, human, relationships. But certainly those literarily costumed as femtopians are right in insisting that those relations can be considerably changed, hopefully improved, perhaps even radically androgynized, which seems the most likely way to real equality.[58] And the literature is not adequately responded to without that context.

4

Primatopianism:
Some Pastoral Eutopianizing

The Golden Age Social Aesthetic, and *News from Nowhere*

One can sensibly posit that beyond the walls of the cities of unfreedom might be founded the simple, "natural," good life. For men as well as for women. Society would be small, artful, golden. The relation of the human with the rest of the physical environment would be characterized not only by restraint but by harmonious balance. This is what (in earlier chapters) I have often abbreviated as "neoprimitivism," noting its significant role in a wide range of utopianizing (with Zamyatin, Lawrence, Huxley, many of the femtopians, and others along the way). It is, of course, what we broadly recognize—mythically, historically, morally—as the *pastoral*. Its metaphors and meanings, I think, can be seen as providing the major traditions of utopianizing, including, of course, various counter uses. Pastoral provides the prime eutopia. Perhaps (though I will not directly elaborate the explanation here) that is because it is also primal in several other senses, including not only our basic mythologies (hence sensibility) but our tangible sense of community. Even Western humankind is only a couple hundred generations (not much in evolutionary terms) from neolithic orderings of life. Neopastoralism recapitulates our more enduring past; pastoral utopianizing is fundamental.

Granted, pastoral is a loose cluster of tropes and tendencies not suited to a simple yet general definition. But similar directions and responses do seem obvious. Much modern and contemporary pastoral might be characterized as related to older pastoral but edgier, tougher-minded, harsher, rather more primitivistic—since self-consciously so, neoprimitivistic. Given modern contexts, the dialectics of the pastoral tend to antiindustrialism. Given the dominant contemporary ideologies, neoprimitivism counters the technocratic. The green and golden order now defines itself against technocracy.

Those aware of earlier pastoral utopianizing should recognize that such a view of the good place can hardly be the result of the present "ecology move-ment," though mythically and morally consonant with much of it. Indeed, it might be put the other way around: modern ecology exhibits more anxious manifestations of certain long traditions of the eutopian. The Green Party, as well as other green thoughts in a green shade, has long been with us. Its neoprimitive cast seems to provide a radical response not only to horrendous overpopulation and environmental destruction but to certain forms of ugliness. The artfully cultivated versions of the simple life in nature almost always empha-size the aesthetic, a bit paradoxically understood as a subtly cultivated sensibil-ity, not just in the individual but in the entire social experience. So large is the demand for a different social aesthetic that it often becomes revolutionary, not least in revolving back to some obscured fundamentals, not just primitive but primary, of human existence. The return to the neolithic is often a radical transcendence.

It will not do to dismiss such visions as primarily nostalgic or otherwise irrational. Recall that several generations ago intolerantly optimistic social scien-tists categorized such rearward allegiances as "cultural lag," mores not keeping up with supposedly rational progress. But in a self-conscious culture it has often seemed reasonable to look back in looking forward. Most vehicles of sensibility contain rearview mirrors. That does not mean that they are always being driven in reverse.

Whether neolithic life was really mean, brutish, and short, or warm, coop-erative, and long, seems hardly to the point. Hobbesean or Rousseauist (or Lévi-Straussean) ideology is not the only way of yoking up pastoral values.[1] The utopian, of course, is responding not to a literal but to a mythologized past which it freely remythologizes. A heaven on earth? No doubt some obviously, and others indirectly, display the secularizations of otherworldly paradises. But they often may be understood the other way around, with heavenly paradises the etherealization of secular utopian impetuses. As the great utopian social psy-chologist William Blake noted, many "abstract the mental deities" in order to create an enslaving "system"; "Thus men forget that all deities reside in the human breast." Even in more moderate views, precedence may not always be certain between alternate this-worldly or otherworldly images, be it with the happy Isle of Para in a Greek Cynic tale or in the revolutionary Third Kingdom under the aegis of the Holy Ghost in the long millenarian prophetic tradition linked to Joachim of Fiore.[2] Separation of transcendental and earthly felicities is rarely as clear as the apologists of orthodoxies (that is, of control) pretend. Granted that some good places have been abstracted into religious nonplaces; still, the desires for better places on earth are at least as fundamental.

Whatever neolithic realities were, their transformation apparently produced such legends as the Greek ones of the Golden Age declining into the Iron Age, as in Hesiod's *Works and Days* (eighth century B.C.). That tale became twisted in Plato's *Republic* into a vision of classes of men and duties for ordering the just State. Thus metaphors of the past were fixed into absolutistic orderings for the future, at least as mental models. Yet the repeated return to the primal images suggests that they continued to carry other connotations.[3] Pastoral past richness fuses with future possibility. The tropes of Happy Isles to be found or refound seem so recurrent in our traditions as to be basic to at least the Western imagination. The geographic discoveries and demographic closures of the recent past have, of course, made some alternatives, and some fantasies, seem less usable, except as displaced into superior technocratic islands in outer galaxies. Science fiction, as I see much of it, less replaces the older utopianizing than continues it. The sci-fi gain in alternatives is counterbalanced by their experimental, and therefore more arbitrary, cast. But the more limited, primitivistic, sense of good places also continues, with or without the high-tech conventions. I take it that the neolithic became the Arcadian, the idealized pastoral world that takes some of its characteristics from Theocritus, Vergil, and other poetic exaltations of Mediterranean ruralism. As I understand this, such pastoralism carried a covert paganism as well as a cultivated literary tradition through the high Christian period. The Renaissance effulgence of pastoralism as well as other utopianism was more than artistic. The poetic forms carried an ideology exalting mild nature and amorous social relations, countering much of the social reality.[4] Social class was partly undercut, or disguised, by tropes of a small-scale harmonious social order.[5] The pastoralism may be primitivistic in its distant origins and in exalting the simple and natural, but it is highly "civilized" in its cultivated scene, ritualistic relations, and elaborately urbane tonalities. The odd combination of the simple and sophisticated, "soft primitivism" (as it has been called for some time), continued to characterize pastoral utopianism in the following centuries.

Certainly I am much simplifying a complex history. Other considerations might well include, for example, the pastoral as a vehicle for the English idealization of the good life and place as rural (certainly antiurban), though in rather class-gardened senses.[6] Such loving rusticity no doubt combined a variety of imperatives, including certain agricultural traditions as well as pagan and, later, romantic views of human nature. Ruralism, romanticism, and paganism certainly are major parts of the pastoral utopianizing of D. H. Lawrence (as discussed in chapter 1). His aggressive countering of industrialism had, of course, other lineages as well, such as Samuel Butler's Victorian mirror nowhere, *Erewhon* (1872), whose pastoral elaborately mocked industrial-technological values.[7] But he emphasized a skeptical reversal (crime is but illness, though poor health is a crime, etc.).

William Morris, the pivotal pastoral utopian between Butler and Lawrence, claims much more. His *News from Nowhere* (1890) requires fuller consideration to gain a sense of modern Arcadian eutopia.[8] The narrative presents a late-fiftyish man, William Guest (sufficiently inappropriate to be an obvious surrogate for the author), whose "dream" visit to the twenty-first century is insistently a social "vision." The fiction overtly combines rather pallid utopian "romance" and revolutionary socialist tract. Its oddity includes a claim for the future condition of England as "pure Communism" (*News* 129) which is yet in totality "now a garden" (*News* 91).

Morris' Marxist politics and Golden Age pastoral are indeed a curious combination. The most tendentious, central, section of the story—the often heavy-handed dialogue of the narrating William with the historically minded Old Hammond—emphasizes an economic class analysis of nineteenth-century Britain.[9] In this political climate an increasingly pauperized working-class (a central Marxian dogma now generally recognized as dubious) turns to accelerating protest, General Strike, and revolutionary solidarity, which results in the total overthrow of the class order. Although praised by doctrinaire Marxist critics, this aspect of the work is quite discrepant in tone and perspective from the rest of the pastoral narrative.

Instead of allowing a "State Socialism" (*News* 132) to take over the means of production, which would be mainstream socialist ideology of the time, Morris opts for ultimate communism, with the abolition of the State. Not only the State but urban-industrial ordering quickly withers, following a great "exodus of the people from the town to the country" (*News* 217). While there are significant bits of utopianism in Marx and Engels (though they emphatically rejected it in favor of "scientific socialism," a dogmatic scientistic counter to their competitors), a political philosopher aptly characterizes it as a "kind of anti-utopian utopianism" which has "weakened and subverted its utopianism to the considerable detriment of Marxism itself, both in theory and practice."[10] This antiutopianism includes not only the religiosity of historical process centering on nineteenth-century industrial production but a temperamental distaste for the pastoral, as in Marx's notorious scorn for "the idiocy of rural life."[11]

In important senses it is that very "idiocy" which Morris most admires. The central positive actions of his narrative focus on a party, which the narrator joins, traveling up the Thames to the mindless labor of haying in Oxfordshire. The project is presented as a communal ritual and high pleasure (though, probably with artistic misfortune, we are not shown the experience, as with the communion during hay-cutting of Tolstoy's Levin in *Anna Karenina*). The haying is no incidental metaphor but part of the insistent "antiintellectualism." Morris' eutopic England has heavily gone in for deschooling, not only in putting down the mean public schools and snobbish universities (and apparently most other schools as well) but also in limiting scientific "invention"—a point repeatedly insisted on. Literature is also limited and "bookishness" discouraged (*News* 41). Morris fervently favors what in America was later to be thought of as "progressive education"—learning by doing—but with a dominant antiindustrial aesthetic. Writing against the grain of Victorian commercial and class ideology,

Morris also makes, sensibly enough, a good many disparaging remarks about what passes for literary and artistic culture. But, in his intellectual antiintellectualism, he hardly posits sufficient alternative. The life of the mind is indeed thin and static in Nowhere, as is often the case with pastoral utopianizing.

The traditional artisan skills in handicrafts, the main organized learning in twenty-first century garden-England, may also be understood as Morris' answer to the Marxist diagnosis of the "alienation of labor." Delineation comes from treating much of the work as group communion and ritual. We are shown communal affection and festival but no hay cutting and stacking. Such work as supposedly gets done is not for wages, much less profits, but for the "conscious and sensuous pleasure in the work itself" (*News* 114). With such aesthetic motives fully called upon in a communal context, people will naturally do the other needed and desired work. But the objects of desire have decisively changed: "many of the things which used to be produced—slave wares for the poor and mere wealth-wasting wares for the rich—ceased to be made. The remedy was, in short, the production of what used to be called art" (*News* 161). The dominant motive in the good society is "art or work-pleasure" based on the "craving for beauty" (*News* 165). This social aesthetic, the exaltation of everyday applied art (not "high art"), provides the conclusive purpose for the society after the demands of justice have been met. The artsy-craftsy, a mocker might say, has become a terminal condition.

But there is a larger affirmation here: "Pleasure begets pleasure" (*News* 79). Though hardly carried out in a drastic way by Morris, the hedonic ethos, which goes beyond countering the puritanic, may be taken as the metapsychology of pastoral utopianizing. Pleasure becomes the one conditioning, ordered by the social aesthetic. It is all rather undialectical, with dissent from garden-England shown as mostly just quaint, as with a curmudgeonly character who longs for the more diverse, conflictual, old days. The communal arts-crafts are, in what we may take as an inverted echo of Plato, mostly of praise (though not, of course, of the State). That does seem static and dull. While the "artisanship" is quite emphatically not class or gender defined, it exalts decoration. Is thick ornamentation the literalization of praise? Considerable emphasis is put upon the elaborate patterning we know in Morris' handmade tapestry, stained glass, wallpapers, book designs, etc. However reactive against his ugly times, Morris, at least to a more modernist taste, displays a wearying insistence on overelaborated decoration, including embroidered clothes for all. This creates a disturbing claustrophobic quality, in contradiction to the emphasized "natural." Guest, the narrator, sometimes seems aware of this, more tastefully emphasizing the "simple and plain" in homebaked bread, loose women's dress, and country homes. Such an emphasis better makes the case against Victorian bourgeois fussiness and overstuffing as the expression of domination.

Morris' rage against his contemporary commercial-industrial debasement tends to override other considerations. Thus the cast-iron bridges over the Thames have all been replaced with stonework or solid oak. The horrible factories have been replaced with "banded-workshops" for collective handcrafting (*News* 59). But the sources of power (which must be other than dirty coal) and the organization of nonartistic production and other dirty work seem fudged.[12] Building is literally medieval, and so is the size of the towns that have replaced the cities of "the time of the Degradation" (*News* 198). In the fusion of country and city life, metropolitan London and other large conglomerates have essentially disappeared, as must a considerable part of the population, though the issue is not raised. The deindustrialization and decentralization patently demand it. Most pastoral utopianizing, it should be granted, assumes a radical demographic change.

Morris' presentation of gender roles appears to be radically unmedieval. "The men no longer have any opportunity of tyrannizing over the women, or the women over the men. . . . The women do what they can do best, and what they like best, and the men are neither jealous of it or injured by it" (*News* 75–76). This transformation has eliminated considerable conflict in the twenty-first century, for much of the earlier tension was based on "the idea (a law-made idea) of the woman being the property of the man." That, along with many other forms of viciousness, "vanished with private property" (*News* 102).[13] But how convenient, then, that what many women "do best" and "like best" are the traditional domestic roles concerning food, clothing, cleaning, and similar services. While an older woman who is a leading decorative woodcarver dramatizes the countering point that women engage in a range of activities by free choice, such a point seems rather pyrrhic in context. The drastic reduction in the level of technology, including domestic machinery and the dependence on handwork in construction, farming, and manufacture, are hardly compensated for by the physical freedom of females to engage in crafts, rowing, traveling, and other anti-Victorian gestures. The unexamined division of labor must incline to strong gender roles in spite of egalitarian rhetoric. Those dressed-stone bridges and oak-beamed houses are not built by quasiladies.

However fervent about women's equality, and, rather covertly, about sexual freedom, and however appalled with the style of tightly laced and upholstered nineteenth-century ladies, Morris has hardly confronted the conditions for gender equality. His groping for it in *News from Nowhere* may now seem poignant. Not incidentally, his late-fiftyish Guest, another yearning William, has an erotic eye for the women, but his romantic inclination for a physically and intellectually sprightly woman (Ellen) remains unconsummated, skittish. And the dream abruptly fades.

Rather skittish, too, are the politics of the future. Revolutionary socialist Morris has eliminated most administration with the State (not the same thing). The council forms suggested really seem to be Kropotkinesque anarchism.[14]

"The whole people is our parliament" (*News* 94), but more by consensus than by majoritarian tyranny (in close "division" no action is taken). The coercions of "gallows and prison" as well as exploitative private property are no more. But how things are ordered instead is mostly left vague, not even sufficiently noted to be suggestive to the sympathetic reader. nor are the details given for maintaining the most fundamental of principles, the "aspiration after complete equality which we now recognize as the bond of all happy human society" (*News* 219). The issues all tend to dissolve in the simplest responses around the "passionate love of the earth" (*News* 253). It helps, of course, that the nineteenth-century narrator's visit to eutopia takes place solely in a lovely, golden June.

There are some odd undertones in the revivified Golden Age emphasis of Morris' garden-England of medievalized socialism, along with some acute criticisms of late Victorian commercial-industrial society for its sheer ugliness as well as cruelty and falsity—after all, the book's main didactic purpose. In spite of the elimination of the coercive State and exploitative private property, character has not been much reconceived.[15] The equality achieved, as repeated details suggest, is rather childlike. That seems more than incidental. From the subtitle—"An Epoch at Rest"—on, there is an insistent flight from anxiety, struggle, even intellectual engagement. While people wear colorful embroidered clothes and seem almost universally affable, the sense of yearningly youthful charade seems inescapable. In a frequently quoted passage, Guest's lovely young woman leads him to a stately old house (obviously Morris' beloved home, Kelmscott Manor): "She led me up close to the house and laid her shapely sun-browned arm on the lichened wall as if to embrace it, and cried out, 'O me. O me! How I love the earth, and the seasons, and weather, and all the things that deal with it, and all that grows out of it—as this has done!'" (*News* 247). Too tan and too responsive to be a lady, she is a pastoral nymph narcissistically projecting natural piety to resolve the human problems. Dream, indeed.

It may seem unkind to season the responses to Morris' rather charming but vaguely developed *News from Nowhere* with sardonic dialectics.[16] It has some of the virtues, and many of the weaknesses, of the continuing pastoral traditions. His eutopian news, whatever its fictional and intellectual flatness, does seem to reverberate interestingly for a century.[17] But that may suggest that the matrix he draws upon is rather more significant than the literary work itself. (Admittedly, I am frequently driven to such responses by undramatic and undialectical pastoral utopianizing). Not only the denuding of propertarianism and statism, but the deschooling, decentralizing, and demasculinizing to project a society of insistently humane and egalitarian communal arts, in a benign natural order, are still importantly with us.

Countering Backward and Forward

The pastoral social aesthetic of *News from Nowhere* may represent part of a larger and continuing utopian dialectics. But Morris' more direct impetuses were countering not only late Victorian England but an immediately preceding utopian fiction which, according to its author, "was written in the belief that the Golden Age lies before us."[18] So Edward Bellamy optimistically asserted of his *Looking Backward* (1888), reportedly the most popular of all modern utopian fictions.[19] As a novel, traditionally understood—that is, as a narrative description and dramatization of characters in a recognizable life—*Backward* is quite paltry. Thirty-year-old, upper-middle-class Bostonian Julian West accidentally sleeps for a hundred and thirteen years, to wake up unchanged in 2,000 A.D. The doctor who wakes him spends a few days explaining the new social organization. West is easily convinced to become part of it, and to marry the doctor's daughter, Edith, who in a tricky plot revelation turns out to be the great granddaughter namesake of his fiance of 1887, a similar simperingly dull and blushingly proper Boston lady.

Most of Bellamy's future Boston is equally stock. One of the more exact descriptions: "Every quarter contained large open squares filled with trees, along which statues glistened and fountains flashed in the late afternoon sun" (*Backward* 43). Kinds of trees, statues, and surroundings are never specified except that most things are ponderously and vaguely "colossal."

The rhetoric of impassioned socioeconomic argument is somewhat more persuasive, and, indeed, constitutes most of the book. However, on one of its avowed major premises—what has happened is "a process of industrial revolution which could not have terminated otherwise" (*Backward* 49)—the rhetoric should be deterministically irrelevant. On the contrary assumption, the book is a sermon for what Morris scorned as "State socialism," which Bellamy fervently avows. Indeed, one of the longest sustained scenes in the fiction is literally a Sunday sermon against free enterprise competition (*Backward* 183–94). What is advocated passes as socialism (certainly the most fashionable utopian doctrine of the period) because it is state capitalism with equality. (Grant Bellamy a partial appropriateness: most applied socialism in the following century turned out to be state capitalism, though without much equality.) Capital has been totally consolidated and the State "organized as the one great business corporation" (*Backward* 53). All production and distribution are centralized and rationally planned. So, to a considerable degree, is consumption, with lavish department stores, restaurants, public laundries, etc., replacing domestic arts with a premium on mass efficiency. Bellamy counters earlier American competitive free enterprise ideology:

Their system of unorganized and antagonistic industries was as absurd economically as it was morally abominable. Selfishness was their only science, and in industrial production selfishness is suicide. Competition, which is the instinct of selfishness, is another word for dissipation of energy, while combination is the secret of efficient production. . . . Even if the principle of share-and-share-alike for all men were not the only humane and rational basis for a society, we should still enforce it as economically expedient, seeing that until the disintegrating influence of self-seeking is suppressed no true concert of industry is possible. (*Backward* 165–66)

The combination of industrial rationalization and secularized Christian compassion gives the argument its force, and the rhetoric its highs; the energy of the earlier period "had mistaken the throbbing of an abcess for the beating of the heart" (*Backward* 211).

What is pustulant about Bellamy's rationalized system for answering not only capitalist inefficiency—"four-fifths of the labor of man was utterly wasted" (*Backward* 216)—but an intense sense of misery and injustice, is that so much of his countering is conceived in terms of military bureaucracy. Military analogies run through the account. All questions of work, for example, are resolved since the authorities "simply applied the principle of universal military service . . . to the labor question" (*Backward* 57). Everyone is compelled to uniform schooling from six to twenty-one (studies, including an apparent emphasis on sports, left vague), then to work from twenty-one to forty-five. Only post-forty-five retirees can elect the "generals" who run the professions, the economy, and the government. All get the same income but hierarchy is maintained by elaborate differences in schedules, perks, ranks, grades, and military-style honors (including different colors of coveted ribbons). This benevolent authoritarianism is a perverse fusion of equality with meritocracy in a technomilitary hierarchy. The faith in rationalized bureaucracy may now seem astonishing, not least in systematizing the supposedly rejected competition.

This is all to come about through persuasion to rational reform (and indeed Bellamy engendered a considerable quasipolitical movement). Unlike Marx and Morris, Bellamy rejects class conflict, and the resulting revolution. He even attacks the left-radicals of the late nineteenth century not only as irrelevant but as engaging in "inconceivable folly" consisting of strikes and protests (*Backward* 170). His is extremist reformism.

A few issues of the time Bellamy does attempt to answer rather than merely dismiss. Women's "emancipation," for example, is accomplished technocratically, with domestic enslavement replaced by more efficient public services. And by separate-but-equal roles (that favorite pseudoanswer to inequalities in the period, such as race).[20] Women have their own, apparently lesser, industrial occupations with their own quasimilitary structures and female "generals." But, after all, women are so different from men that "we have given them a world of their own, with its emulations, ambitions, and careers, and I assure you they are very happy with it" instead of being in "unnatural rivalry with men" (*Backwards*

174). Clearly, Bellamy pities the poor women of his time and even senses the need for more autonomy from men on the part of other women. Nonetheless, he ends with an ideology of hierarchical inferiority and control. We may be reminded that sympathetic awareness of an issue, such as the abused roles for women (or, in another period, what was sometimes described as "consciousness raising") does not guarantee even nice, much less more just, answers. Indeed, it may inhibit them by seeming to respond.

Apparently Bellamy also had little consciousness of what was to bother Morris about such utopianism, including the totalitarian dangers of complete centralization (Bellamy even abolished all lesser political forms, such as the states); the replacement of ruthless competition with an apparently more bland, but hardly less coercive, elaborate technomilitary hierarchy; or the subordination of culture (Bellamy allows it a tritely pompous inspirational role at most) to industrial rationalization. Not incidentally, where Morris fantasized people happily singing and dancing, Bellamy fantasized an efficiently expert equivalent of Muzak piped into every dwelling. Bellamy's futurists are quite beyond cutting hay, carving wood and stone, embroidering blouses, responding to nature (except in a conventional flower garden), or struggling with love. No wonder Morris was incensed at what also claimed to be a socialist eutopia. Bellamyism, with its hyperefficient producers-consumers, actually did little to counter late nineteenth-century sentiments (except for the ostensible egalitarianism), or mainstream styles of a century later.

Contemporaneous Morris and Bellamy were both egalitarian socialists, but the fundamental differences in their sensibilities, and thus in their social aesthetics (including their taste in buildings and the tangible qualities of life), seem of far more account. And there lies a continuing crux. If I read the utopian record rightly, the difference is not only still with us but has become more exacerbated. An exemplary case might be the utopianism of counterculture "ecotopia" versus the "high frontier" of technocracy. The works at issue here are awkwardly semifictionalized tracts of little literary merit: Ernest Callenbach's *Ecotopia* (1975) and *Ecotopia Emerging* (1981), and Gerard K. O'Neill's *The High Frontier: Human Colonies in Space* (1977) and *2081: A Hopeful View of the Future* (1981).[21] To the degree that one can informally reckon such matters by mass paperback reprintings, citation, and anecdotal evidence, both authors have been influential and respected, though not in the same quarters. The differences between the two are not of literary sensibility, since neither seems to have much, nor of good intentions, since both seem to be knowledgeable, earnest, and positive in their utopianizing. Rather, the difference seems to lie in what I have pointed to as social aesthetics. And part of that must be a difference in cultural (not just social) class. Not least, as I will note, they and their characters take their pleasures in different ways. And that may be one of the most crucial things utopianizing accounts tell us, the dialectics, as it were, of desire. A century later than Bellamy and Morris, Callenbach and O'Neill may offer a parallel contrast of countering utopianisms.

An apparently reputable physical scientist, O'Neill has been a leading spokesman for the pragmatic colonization of near space—placing permanently habitable machine-stations in the asteroid belt—in the near future. Whatever the technological issues (not my concern), he also sees such a development as explicitly utopian in large senses. His American space colonization plans, he advises us, are far superior to "classical Utopian concepts," however murky he may be about what those were (*High* 198 ff.). His vast organizational effort towards the eutopian space frontier justifies itself, as he posits it, as a disproportionate answer to what would seem a somewhat smaller scale problem—cleaning up the polluted and overpopulated earth.[22] There are two eutopias at issue, then: a radically refurbished earth, and a radically new space frontier. They would supposedly reenforce each other. Curiously, the cleansed society left behind will become a soft primitivism, a smaller population, "industry-free pastoral earth" (*High* 225).

It is striking that even cosmic technofanaticism has a positive place for pastoral utopianizing. Earth will become pastoral by having transferred its production as well as its surplus population to the space colonies, in an updating of an old Western imperial pathology. But it does seem merely fantastic to propose that not only will the earth not have transferred its toxic and demographic dilemmas to the colonies but that somehow high-tech transfer planning will have automatically produced better government and a better social system (*High* 232). There appears to be a holy ghost in the machine of such high-tech planning which mystically transforms people and their institutions.

People and other waste pollution, which Bellamy had no sense of (though Morris seems to have had it in his revulsion to sooty, crowded London), have replaced competition and poverty as the overriding problem. But if the problem has been redefined, the answer has not and remains similar to Bellamy's: it is to be found in supertech bureaucracy. In a century of linear development under its "Drivers of Change"—those wisely developing computers for everything, and robotics, space-colonization, massive solar energy structures, and hyperelectronic communications—all will be wisely reordered by 2081. In the mixed essay-narrative exercise of that title, O'Neill projects his naivete to the cosmos, such as declaring with "certainty" that there will be large space colonization within a few decades (*2081* 75). But in spite of the optimistic tone, the real push for space colonies seems to rest on the need for human dispersal—we are unlikely to blow up the whole solar system, just our world—in response to the 1980s revival of fear of nuclear holocaust (*2081* 102, 202, 242, etc.). Underneath, technotopianism now seems as much driven by fear of what it has wrought—nuclear, toxic, demographic—as by hope of what it can resolve. It must take a special kind of obtuseness to make a vicious circle into a pious program.

The technocracy of the future, of course, is presented as free of bad side effects to the technofixes. In quasidramatized accounts of future travel to earth by the blandly nice space-colony inhabitants, we get rather vulgar updatings of old eutopianisms. Earth may be a pastoral vacation home for the progressives from space, but the visited American city is, of course, glass-walled-in (vide Wells, et al.), ostensibly to control the inclement weather. What else is controlled in the crystal suburban palaces is not considered. Thrilling cultural life includes advanced robots for everyman servants, backyard barbecues with house-sized South Sea living holographs for thrilling ambience, computer-laser automated motor homes for carefree programmed touring, and a general fatuousness which makes servant-robots look like the last depositories of passionate intelligence (will they, like Karl Capek's robots, take over?). Even Bellamy's jejune West still read (bad) books and listened to (sentimental) classical music and argued (reductively) social-moral issues. Does high-tech faith such as O'Neill's now require an even lower level of petite bourgeois sensibility?

O'Neill now and again displays some reflective concern. Unlike some of the technotopians (discussed earlier), he doubts the virtues of drastically expanding the human lifespan. An "immortal society would be deeply conservative, and the stagnation of the human race would follow almost certainly" (*2081* 252). Not only, I take it, would technological bureaucracies become stodgy from truly eternal tenure, but compulsive change is the essence of the human. And he does variously worry about that. Even in his bland next century he fears that some earthlings will suffer technological lag, and technoretarded places such as Africa (racism?) may still be in social-political turmoil. Technocracy determines all. But generally he points the way up by going literally upward. As philosopher Hannah Arendt suggested a generation ago, the fervor for life in space seems to rest in unconscious revulsion for life on Earth.[23]

In contrast, Callenbach's environmentally concerned America of the near future—the ecologically utopian nation of Ecotopia originally formed in the 1980s from central and northern California (Bay Area parochialism)—is quite earth-bound, in several senses. Nearly everything, including the counterculture ethos of the 1960s, has been recycled. Ecotopia has achieved the balance and moderate evolution, as well as highly selective technology, appropriate to a "steady-state economy" (a key utopian concept, which is antithetical to Bellamy-O'Neill and to present dominant economic ideology).[24] The quality of life is essentially neopastoral, benignly simplified to natural norms.

An example of technological futurism might set off the contrast between O'Neill's High Frontier and Callenbach's Ecotopia. Both, drawing on a fashionable anxiety of the 1970s (and one likely to recur), propose a technological answer to the "energy problem" of declining and environmentally destructive hydrocarbon power sources. As a solution, both hold out exponential expansion of solar power, but in opposite styles. O'Neill proposes solving the issue by placing colossal solar energy production stations in space, whose efficiency would be greatly heightened by their proximity to the sun and whose power would be transmitted by laser beams to hyperefficient space factories and grids on Earth. No waste, no depletion of nonrenewable resources, no pollution. But the technotopian ignores other problems created by his vast, centralized utility structure, which would be a superbureaucratic power on which a whole solar system depends. Major old social-political issues of power and control, equity and imperial giganticism, seem not even to enter consciousness. In neat contrast, Callenbach projects a young woman (sic) inventing a new solar photovoltaic battery (*Emerging* 234 ff.). The generators and cells are distributed in do-it-yourself kits, with each household having, and controlling, its own modest energy source, sufficient for domestic needs. Dispersed windmill farms serve the larger production requirements. Decentralization and autonomy, based on technological parsimony and organizational prudence, sharply contrast with technotopian giganticism and megalomania.

The Morris ethos, as we might call it, pervades most Ecotopian activities in an ordering that attempts "to decentralize and personalize wherever possible" (*Ecotopia* 143). Appropriate to the dominance of artisan communities, the scale is small. Appropriate to an ancient social aesthetic, development is subordinated to art, relationships, community, and cultivated human feelings. Contrast the High Frontier's cosmic technological expansionism, and the scales that go with it. To the degree that there is choice about issues of technocratic order in the present, these antithetical futuristic tropes may suggest some of the dimensions. Surely a major function of utopianizing is to set off such counter views.

Ecotopia, as with much of our neopastoralism, is not antitechnological as such; it employs an intermediate level of selected, limited, balanced research and technique. But there is little place for large computer systems, robotics, and space satellites, and none for space ships and cosmic imperialism, jet planes and private cars (much less computer-laser recreational vehicles), vast bureaucracies and exploitative media, crystal palace cities, and petty bourgeoise mentalities. The Decalogue of Ecotopia's Survivalist Party includes complete economic as well as political participatory democracy (*Emerging* 35 ff.), responding to issues which High Frontier in no way acknowledges. Aggression is acted out in Ecotopia by competing in small-scale excellence, not in the cosmos, and in ritualized war games of a Native American cast.[25] Country and city have been largely merged. Population, like every other destructive expansionism, has not only been limited but is declining. Much, but not all, of domestic life is communal, with polymorphous sexuality, and neopagan rituals of nature worship (there is little acknowledged sex or religion in O'Neill). Paradoxically, such neoprimitivism is a radical redoing to reach an essentially conservative, conserving, order. Fantastically, what sociology called the "marginals," literary history called the bohemians, the American early seventies called the counterculturists, and what I suppose are now popularly thought of as radical feminists, mad environmentalists, and flakey cultists, have taken over by 1999. It is barely short of the millennial.

News from Nowhere (to which there seem to be allusions in *Ecotopia*), may be seen as a forerunner to the animal-and-tree-loving, sexy and stoned, craft-and-artist, sophisticated folkish would-be prophecies of Ecotopia. Bellamy and O'Neill are not of the same world, their aghast spirits having migrated to some cosmically removed technotopia. Their absurd one-way optimism about future technocracy is almost matched by the Ecotopian faith in bohemian ludditism. Some of Callenbach's worst vulgarities in that line lie in the revolutionary politics that transform present America into Ecotopia, including good-guy scientists secreting nuclear bombs in eastern megalopolises to blackmail the U. S. power elite into giving the new society its autonomy. (When it comes to marginals' ecology-minded subversion, as well as picaresque utopian fiction, Edward Abbey did it rather more persuasively in *The Monkey-Wrench Gang* [1975].) But the somewhat desperate new-pastoral utopianizing of Ecotopia might be understood as an awkward literary visualization of the metaphors of radical "saving remnant" ideology—it only claims to be "a small, precarious island of hope"—in the social aesthetic mind against the disasters rather more probable than technotopian or ecotopian salvations. And certainly that countering is part of what contemporary utopianizing is often about.

Fording the Golden Age

There is more than one way of coming at the simple and natural life of the Golden Age, the ever reviving artful pastoralism and sophisticated neoprimitivism, which certainly provides major continuing eutopian traditions. An angled (and admittedly idiosyncratic) light might be put on some of it by considering a "Meridional" Anglo-American pastoral between Nowhere and Ecotopia, midway between Morris and the present, by Ford Madox Ford.[26] Primarily noted (besides his influential role in cultural brokering for modernism between the world wars) as a novelist in Pre-Raphaelite, Jamesian, and Conradian modes, he is virtually ignored as a utopian because he did not write a directly utopian fiction. However, he does draw upon Arcadian scenes and metaphors in some of his novels. So with the glorified rural style of life in an extended family-farm commune in the last book of the Tietjen's tetrology, *The Last Post* (1928), the concluding volume of his Great War saga, *Parade's End*.[27] And so with the reflections on the "Meridional culture" in his melodramatic fantasy, *The Rash Act* (1933).[28] The latter work culminates metaphorically in the postsuicidal new identity the war-and-art forlorn protagonist achieves in a menage with two loving women in a lush Mediterranean garden villa, a sex and nature dream version of Ford's eutopianizing.[29] Not least, the import of these obsessional scenes might be clearer in the context of Ford's meridional-pastoral counterculture.

In a striking individual transformation, Ford Madox Hueffer legally renamed himself Ford Madox Ford (in 1919). It was more than a somewhat confusing (for a much published writer) personal whimsy, though Ford was given to such. It was also more than a rejection of the Teutonic heritage that he felt the late war had partly been about, though negation of what he took to be the Northern European sensibility was to be an obsessive part of his utopian dialectic.[30] Ford's change of identity yoked with his (and much of the modernist culture's) post-Great War disillusionment; he had crossed over to a pastoral-eutopian view of society. This became the subject of a series of potpourri volumes—combinations of quaint narrative, loose memoir, eccentric history, and social-cultural moralizing: *No Enemy* (1929), *It Was the Nightingale* (1933), *Provence* (1935), and *Great Trade Route* (1937).[31] Utopianizing, of course, like a good many other impetuses, does not confine itself to particular literary genres, forms, styles (an antireification that I am repeatedly emphasizing).

In his striking individual transformation, Ford moved from concern with the watershed experience of the Great War, in which he had earnestly played propagandist and then British officer and junior gentleman, to a fervent antithetical identification with the eutopianism of "the little garden." *No Enemy,* partly reflections on the war experience and dismeaning, opens with an emphasis on his countering dialectic of the redeeming garden. It contains the odd mixture of the visionary and the jocular that marks many of his discussions of the issue. He "proposed to save the world by intense kitchen gardening and exquisite but economical cooking" (*No* 11). He relates the tropes to exsoldiers feeling outcast and recalling the "sanctuary" images of natural, simple order which, he says, sustained them and him during the miserably grim scenes of the war front. The countering pastoral images are both psychic solace and social alternative.

In *No Enemy* the Great War provides digressions from the announced theme of the "green vision." Though Ford often casually tosses them off, the more serious considerations of the meaning of the world as "garden" are present. The war brought on the awareness that there is no longer a meaningful large social order. The potential further ravages of overpopulation—and consequent probable future food shortages—encourage the obsessive kitchen gardener in universalizing his craft. The debasements of industrial mass production and distribution, with tasteless and chemicalized food an obvious focus for his anger, demand a countering order of economic life. The loss of individual art and quality, be it in the personal vegetable garden, the romantic ballad, the well-seasoned meal, or the well-turned fiction, push one towards a whole other world

of the tasty, self-governing, aesthetic social order. Direct self-nourishing inde-
pendence, in food, art, and life generally, "is what I have gathered from the
ruins of the war" (*No* 274).

However aslant the manner of presenting his pastoral eutopianism, it becomes an encompassing response to what the Great War revealed. In perspective, the revelation lay perhaps less in combat experience, the stupidly vicious
Battle of the Somme and others, than in a large sensitivity to the loss of meaning
represented by modern war. (We can see this revelation also, of course, in
noncombatant utopianizing writers of the period admired by Ford, such as D.
H. Lawrence, in the first section of *Kangaroo,* and in Ezra Pound, especially in
the "Mauberley" poems.) The ostensible order of the world had exploded to
reveal a lunatic brutalization and an empty civilization (as it was to continue to
do through a series of wars.)

Ford is far better known for his emphasis on aesthetics, his exaltation of art,
than for his utopianizing. But it is where art meets disillusioning experience that
a countering social aesthetic grows into eutopia. Consider one of Ford's extreme
statements of art-for-artist's sake: "The world divided itself for me into those
who were artists and those who were merely the stuff to fill graveyards" (*Nightingale* 74). This is more than a survivor's ethic translated into bohemian aesthetics. For one soon realizes that Ford includes in capital-A Art not only music and
painting and literature but gardening, cooking, crafts, small production, and
even useful trade. A whole social ordering is at aesthetic issue. In this broader
sweep, it does make humane sense to say "it was only by its arts a nation could
be saved" (*Nightingale* 85).

Ford also demands a cultivated heightening in these arts, whether in the
enthusiastic and even superstitious gardening he engaged in (*Nightingale* 130),
or in his insistence that one cannot be an artist and write primarily "for money"
(*Nightingale* 146), or in his acknowledgment that, even when working a hard-
scrabble farm, "I have always dressed for dinner" (*Nightingale* 183). While Ford
makes dismissive remarks about William Morris (with whom his grandfather
had collaborated), he continues that high-moral nineteenth-century view of art
as conjoined with the true and good life.

The war had also driven Ford to that salvational social aesthetic, art as
eutopia. In the Great War disillusionment-as-rarely-before, "it had been revealed to you that beneath order Life itself was stretched, the merest film with,
beneath it, the abysses of chaos" (*Nightingale* 64). Against the very nothingness
of the accepted, ostensibly civilized, order, Ford's countering may seem small:
"I have always believed that, given a digging fork and a few seeds and tubers,
with a quarter's start, I could at any time wrest from the earth enough to keep
body and soul together" (*Nightingale* 65). But that little garden of withdrawal-
and-revival, which he literally practiced first in postwar England and then inter-
mittently in southern France in the twenties and thirties, expanded in his mind

and writings into metaphors of a greater garden of saving meridional civilization, a renewed vision of the Golden Age. What looks at first to be a bohemian-artist individual gesture, defying a false culture and destructive civilization, becomes a larger social-cultural program.

The civilization of meridional sensibility was Ford's counter to the abyss revealed by the Great War, and its past his golden prime. But: "Provence is not a country nor the home of a race but a frame of mind" (*Provence* 64). The meandering narrative and exposition of this work moves both at gut and grand levels. Since the "only way in which good humor can be secured by humanity is by habitual good eating" (*Provence* 34), it is no wonder that barbarous Northerners make world wars. Probably to start the recent one, "the German Emperor had partaken of a surfeit of underdone roast beef" (*Provence* 69). The English, with their pink-rubber beef and sodden Brussels sprouts—and generally miserable cooking and moldy climate—and the overfed and overheated Americans, weren't prepared to respond well either. Under such Northerners' domination, mankind "shall go on getting grosser and grosser" (Ford attributed his own corpulence to Germanic and British inheritance rather than his discriminating diet), and we will get "further away from Latinity and plunging deeper and deeper into mass-production, ruin . . . massacre." As an inveterate herb gardener and garlic cook, Ford holds that a "diet without spices causes indigestion," which encourages "religious and homicidal mania . . . religious war." When the conquered lose their war and spices, they, too, become "constipated, melancholic, homicidal," and engage in yet more religious warfare (*Provence* 163). They become quite dull, too.

The whimsical manner should not obscure Ford's concern with a genuine large issue of sensibility represented by Provence, continuer of ancient pastoral good life, for the utopianizing mind. He now views the twentieth century as accelerating a millennium of domination by miserable northern folk who never had a real civilization anyway since they lacked the meridional taste for good fruits, fresh vegetables, wine, seasoning, religious tolerance, moderate order, small-scale community, unfanatical politics, troubador art, direct gardening and crafting, refined eroticism, humane culture, free trade (or better, direct bartering), and open-air cafes. Without that last, without the natural "oxygen" for freewheeling intellectual responses, the "arts and civilization are impossible" (*Provence* 227). A richly simple and direct ambience is almost everything.

Our so-called civilization is now "staggering to its end," and will not be revitalized unless we "take Provence of the XIII Century for its model" (*Provence* 255). This positive provincialism should not be taken as parochialism on the part of the polyglot traveler with his catholicity of culture. And, for this counterculturist of half a century ago, the synthetic culture as well as synthetic diet of the dominant order expressed a debilitating, and accelerating, dependence on machines. Hence, "the number of machines and machine hours must be reduced to a minimum" (*Provence* 313). Otherwise (in another typical meta-phoric leap) all will succumb to machined masses, such as those of Mr. Hitler, and endless destruction.

It seems that ex-Catholic Ford would also like to revive (like D. H. Law-rence, among other prophetic contemporaries) pluralistic paganism, seen as underlying meridional culture. Taking a key from Nietzsche (one of the few German artist-thinkers he continued to admire), Ford insisted that not only is God dead but "Christianity as a faith died a few days after the 4th of August 1914" (*Provence* 297).[32] What should be the new salvational, but low-keyed and humane, faith is really a very old one: "it was to the frame of mind that was Provence . . . that is due the Latinity that today alone redeemed our northern civilization from barbarism" (*Provence* 101). We must look back to that social aesthetic in order to achieve a future "when all of humanity that is healthy and capable of innocuous pleasures shall be settled on little plots of ground on the shores of the Mediterranean—and if necessary on those of the American coasts south of the fortieth parallel" (*Provence* 297). The Great-War-countering little garden of Ford's pastoral dreams on the Western Front, which became a per-sonal and literary venue after the war, expands to the utopian world-circling and redeeming great meridional garden. It is bemused, idiosyncratic, yet also an earnest post-Armageddon faith.

This is also more or less the subject of the meandering *Great Trade Route*. This book further defines Ford's pastoral-eutopian view, still with repeated countering reference to the previous Great War, but now with a despairing sense (1937) of its coming repetition. The dutiful ex-good soldier now finally realizes that he is "in favour of pacifism" (*Route* 84), in spite of his contempt for totalitarianism and its coming "cataclysm" (*Route* 107). The British expatriot propagandist announces that we must do everything we can to make "an end at least of [national] patriotism" (*Route* 397). In contrast—and expanding his ear-lier tropes—what we have of more truly communal civilization comes from "the workings in our minds of that Chinese-Greek-Latin civilization's Mediterranean leaven," a "frame of mind to which, unless we return, our occidental civilization is doomed" (*Route* 27).

More of Ford's ruminations now take on a social-political cast, and he variously labels himself a "Quietist Anarchist" (*Route* 185—Quietest for nonmil-itant, nonterrorist, versus the popular images of the anarchist), or a totally "limited monarchist" favoring only very small countries, and other decentraliza-tion, with an order of limited officials chosen by lottery (*Route* 416). He wants a society in which the rule of custom supersedes the rule of law (*Route* 186). The Mediterranean geographical metaphor has become rather loose (now including south China), as has the decentralist anarchism (including figurehead monar-chy), but even with the eccentricities, it is recognizable as libertarian utopianism.

"I want to belong to a nation of Small Producers, with some local but no national feeling at all" (*Route* 74). He is insistent, like Morris, on the "Small, rather than Mass, Producer"; on the virtues of the little independent figure, the "Small Holder"; on the Jeffersonian "sufficiency farmer" ideal in what he takes to be the best of American traditions; on "the man who with a certain knowledge of various crafts can set his hand to most of the kinds of work that go to the maintenance of humble existences"; on the very style of "part-time" farmers, craftsmen, and artists with allegiances only to "small units" (*Route* 74, 30, 77, 151, 170, 309, 407). The beauty of self-sufficient (though freely trading on a small scale) people living directly and modestly in a decentralized communal order, preferably in the moderate outdoorsy climate epitomized by the Great Trade Route (below the fortieth parallel north—he doesn't examine other extensions of the conditions) becomes a metaesthetic for the good society. He claims no less for it than the possibility of experiencing "a return to the Golden Age" (*Route* 275).

It should be recognized that Ford's fragmentarily presented views have some strong parallels with others in his time, not only Lawrence but such American literary-social ideologues as the Southern Agrarians of the 1930s. (Part of the book's ragged travel narrative includes time spent in the American South with several of them, especially Allen Tate.) The contemporaneous Personalist Movement in France, the romantic-nature artistic libertarians in Britain (such as Herbert Read), the decentralist-ruralist movements in the United States (discussed later in this chapter), suggest the appropriate larger climate of opinion.

Not without some ambiguities, Ford's view (as some quotes have already indicated) is antitechnocratic, as most pastoralism is. In his wild swings of rhetoric: "The Medieval serf was better off than the industrial worker" of the twentieth century (*Route* 395). "The machine itself is a stupid Moloch"; and the military-political "Technocrat" is our civilization's ultimate villain (*Route* 103). These, of course, are more metaphoric than reasoned responses in the social aesthetic that yearns for a whole civilization of organic communities.

What may appear partly distinctive in Ford's version of pastoral eutopia is neither the antitechnocracy nor the libertarian decentralism (both more widespread than usually acknowledged), nor even the piety to organic vegetables and herbs (now of considerable popularity), but the linking of such with cultural tropes drawn from rather different traditions. The Nordic versus Meridional may be found, of course, in his British contemporaries, such as Forster and Lawrence, as well as the earlier Nietzsche, the earlier British and Continental Romantics, the Provençal Jean Giono and French-Algerian Albert Camus, and the later American Charles Olson, among other literary figures.[33] Partly taking off from his father's learned love of the troubadors and his own love of Provence (where he lived when he could afford to), and heightened by partly similar literary interests (such as Ezra Pound's), the attitude also more generally partook of literary-artistic modernism's opposition to social-economic modernism ("modernization"). Ford enlarged the metaphors to loosely include southern China and the American South, perhaps mostly out of literary interests. His hostile treatment of northern European sensibility and society, summarized as the Nordic, was no doubt reenforced by his anti-German propaganda in the Great War as well as his disillusionment with the British and abhorrence of the later Nazis. He constantly condemned the Nordic for their murderously aggressive statism resulting in mass wars (*Route* 107), for their puritanic rigidity of order in contrast with meridional "slacking off" (*Route* 194), and for their mass-technological, political, and religious fanaticism (though in fact none of these were really confined to the Northerners), as well as bad diet and bad taste more generally. In a decently tolerant, responsive, and vital society on a humane scale, people would live their lives "by flouting Nordic virtues" (*Route* 390). Ford, in his "irregular" personal life (for that time), certainly did. While it is no doubt unfair of Ford to so confound literal history and geography with Nordic versus Meridional metaphors, the knowing literary reader probably recognizes what he means: there is a recurrent great conflict, metaesthetic as well as practical, in our civilization between the values of expansive power and sentient humaneness. Ford, however quaintly, had enlisted again, as he rather inappropriately did in the Great War, in the good fight, the utopianizing effort.

Ford may now appear a whimsical character, given to such gestures (he repeatedly reports) as raising herbs in cracked dishes on window sills when he felt compelled to live in the city (London, Paris, New York, etc.). His utopianizing books are cracked dishes. But they do grow a bit of the sweetness and spice of a more humane vision of civilization, however insufficient in intellectual and artistic rigor. It is a vision of the richly simple and more natural life, not in a Rousseauistic sense of countering all civilization but with a cultivated garden, a pastoral eutopia, as the true civilization. It is considerably a matter of proper seasoning.

Ford is also symptomatically interesting for the self-transformation of the too-narrow literateur, the Edwardian aesthete, the imitation Jamesian and Conradian fictionist, the too-narrow British propagandist and English officer and gentleman, into the utopian gardening bohemian. This transformation pointed to a whole sense of life antithetical to established "Northern" Anglo-American society and culture. In some of its essential sense of things, his countering culture is still importantly with us. Out of the annihilation of people and values emerging from the Great War, Ford fervently reached for the encompassing perennial eutopian vision of the little garden of decent, sensitive, responsive, modest humans. The well-seasoned life. Whatever its inadequacies and quaintness, it is one of the more pleasant utopianizings.

Neopastoral Elaborations

For the sake of larger coherence, and as further corrective for the too-narrow literary approach, several other contemporary contexts for pastoral utopianizing should be at least briefly adumbrated. It is often less cultural realities than pedantic confines that lead to designating only certain narratives as utopian. If, as I hold, utopianizing is one of the most fundamental impetuses in Western culture, then the narrowing of definitions and the reduction of contexts is an arbitrary ideological imposition, often resulting from the smug dogmatisms of those who would restrict the freedoms of sensibility and society. I cannot here fully develop the reasons why belittling utopianizing may be fascism against the human spirit, but we can at least broaden the concern a bit. Which is not to suggest that utopianizing should be treated uncritically. To the contrary, it is important enough to be constantly criticized, reversed, mocked, changed, countered, as well as imagined, projected, analyzed, developed, and lived.

Such is not least the case with what I take to be that primary direction of utopianizing which can be loosely described as the pastoral. News from pastoral nowheres is all over our literature.

> You are fed up with the city and its teeming millions. The ways and means of men, as getting and lending and spending, you lay waste your inner world, are too much with you. The bus takes too long, while the subway is always crowded. So what do you do? So you buy a farm and walk behind your horse's moist behind, no collar or tie, plowing your broad swift acres. As you turn up the rich black soil, the wind carries the smell of pine across the fields and rhythm of an old, old work enters your soul. To this rhythm, you sow and reap and chivy your kine, not kin or kind, between the pregnant rows of corn and taters. Your step becomes the heavy sexual step of a dance-drunk Indian and you tread the seed down into the female earth. You plant, not dragon's teeth, but beans and greens. . . .[34]

Nathanael West's burlesque of the "return to the soil" in the simply hard and dirty rural life, with its mocking euphonious echoes of Wordsworth, Tolstoy, Hart Crane (and perhaps Louis Bromfield), and other literary expositions of pastoral eutopianism is contemporaneous (1933) with Ford's vision of the redeeming "little garden." The crude wisecracks, sexual innuendoes (and screwed-up grammar?), mock, with hysterical defensiveness (though West bought a Bucks County farm), one of the famous "escapes" for the alienated and despairing modern urbanite. Linked burlesques of romance, art, stoic hedonism, and (especially) Christian religion he saw as finishing off the now debased and impossible great "dreams" of Western culture.

Since bad jokes are also so often the good hopes in a culture above all to be characterized by masquerading and counterfeiting (West's main theme), perhaps we should take parody as one of our most essential, and indeed main, literary keys. So, in several ways, with more positive utopianizing. For example, the most central of all American literary utopias may be Henry David Thoreau's *Walden* (1855). Besides serving as model for multitudes of sabbatical dreams of the good life (and sabbatical it is, though condensing two years to one and diverting the erotic), that poetical literary eutopia in documentary guise has other reverberations. Original Waldenism, of course, was not the creation of an ideal community but the withdrawal into a narcissistically sublimating solitude in an effort to achieve transcendental highs in a semicultivated nature, a simplified barter-and craft economy, and an attenuated anarchist ethic.[35] Its version of learned soft-primitivism may be variously viewed, as, for instance, a genteel version of pioneering or a manual for marginalized pastoralism. But it may also be crassly parodied, as when B. F. Skinner named his well-known "operant conditioning" behaviorist lab community *Walden Two* (1948).

Skinner's fatuous scientism, as well as Thoreau's powerful rhetoric of transcendentalism, quite literally engendered some utopian communalism.[36] If one views *Walden* as a utopian narrative literary year of a simplified, semi-autonomous, lyrical life of ecological balance in the woods, then a good bit of other utopian accounting may also be seen as a selective report on eutopian living. So with a good bit of twentieth-century utopian narrative. Especially, though not exclusively, American, these Arcadian documentaries are almost always self-conscious counterings of industrial-urban life. Works by Thoreau, Morris, Ford, Callenbach, along with many others, can be partly viewed less as literature in its own right (whatever that is) than as literary markers in a recurrent and significant back-to-the-soil utopianizing (the emphasis I am taking here).

Self-consciously going back to life on the land to recapture an earlier and truer mode of existence, sometimes a literalization of Golden Age metaphors, has, of course, a long literary tradition in America. It often oddly fuses a politics of disillusionment about mainstream society with a frontiering or homesteading optimism about individual social autonomy and exalted self-reliance. For instance, in Helen and Scott Nearing, *Living the Good Life: How to Live Sanely and Simply in a Troubled World* (1954)—and in their less adequate epilogue, *Continuing the Good Life: Half a Century of Homesteading* (1979)—the authors' laconically utilitarian prose and presumably practical accounting never quite disguises the exemplary heroic proportions of their applied utopianizing.[37] No lesser terms seem appropriate to the images of this ninety-five-year-old ex-Marxist professor of economics (fired from an Ivy League university) and his musician-author wife, who taught a legion of young dropouts how to build stone houses and organically grow almost everything for a vegetarian diet. The combination of disciplined labor on inhospitable land, of earnest high-cultural life (classical music, theories of political economy), and of high-puritan self-reliant individualism (however at variance with the Marxism) is simply awesome.

I am, of course, only touching on a long tradition of self-conscious home-steading of utopian proportions, high-principled and encompassing, which attempts to envision an essentially pastoral ordering of the good life. In the influential writings a couple of generations ago of Ralph Borsodi—*This Ugly Civilization* (1929), *Flight from the City* (1933), and others—we find a near-apocalyptic politics, practical food preserving and diet, appropriate use of electricity, do-it-yourself pioneering knackery, and a salvational desire for a new version of an old Arcadia.[38] This vision is both more consciously literary and expertly restorative in contemporary poet Wendell Berry's combination of lyrical ruralism, individualistic family farming, and hard-nosed environmentalism. This characterizes not only his restoration of an old farm—"The Making of a Marginal Farm" (*Recollected Essays* [1981])—but the strong programmatic social-politics in his *The Unsettling of America: Culture and Agriculture* (1977), and the attempt to revitalize a whole ethos (see the ranging essays in *Home Economics* [1987]).[39]

While the Nearings recreated Vermont and Maine farms (and even a partial rural community), Borsodi modernized paradigms for simple rural living, and Berry restored a Kentucky farmstead and spirit, Gary Snyder represents a somewhat different California arcadianism in the Sierra, one more consciously communal. In *Earth Household* (1969) and *The Real Work* (1980), Snyder propounds, and reports on, a combination of Western localism, with sophisticated but limited technology, and a cosmopolitan "Bioregional Ethic" which expands ecological-organic "Right Livelihood."[40] It seeks to be an encompassing eutopic vision that fuses Buddhist mysticism with American Indian ritualism, vanguardist bohemianism with radical ecology, in what he announces as the early stages of a hundred-year back-to-the-land utopian movement to transform America.[41] No doubt it would take a redemptive century at least (and a hundred million or more reduction in population?) for the "earth household" to become the dominant American pattern of living, again. But that is hardly a sufficient argument against it.

Nor would simple technocratic arguments be a suitable counter, though they comprise the usual basis of rejection. More often than not in the past couple of generations this eutopic ruralism is not really primitivistic (though that usually appears as a polarity in the sensibility) but embraces a *Whole Earth Catalog* sophistication about practical tools (and impractical ones as well). Yet the neopastoralism is certainly antistatist, anticorporate, and antitechnocratic (the combination of high-tech and hierarchical bureaucracy). Gary Snyder, for example, explicitly rejects space colonization.[42] Jet airlines, television broadcasting networks, "developer" mentalities, and other pyramided power icons (Lewis Mumford's metaphor) seem essentially antithetical. Contemporary neopastoralism is more than a mode of life; it is a whole style of sensibility.

Perhaps one of its most crucial characteristics is the concern with the size of things, as in William Morris. While it would be a poor simplification to reduce one of the most widespread and profound utopianizings to a single overt

ideology, this concern for size may readily be yoked with the Buddhist, decentralist, limited-technology economics of the late E. F. Schumacher—*Small Is
Beautiful* (1969), *A Guide for the Perplexed* (1975), and *Good Work* (1979)—
which represents a frequently acknowledged theorizing for some of it, and a
continuing tradition of applied utopian thinking.[43] Like his teacher, Leopold
Kohr—*The Breakdown of Nations* (1957), *The Overdeveloped Nations: The
Diseconomies of Scale* (1977)—Schumacher takes a worldwide perspective to
counter the worldwide giganticism.[44] The models seek a humane size in everything from school classes to capital systems, street views to *weltanschauungs*,
as in Kirkpatrick Sale's encyclopedic *Human Scale* (1980), which concludes:

> We can go on as we are, trying to muddle through (rather more muddle than through), patching
> up disintegrating and propping up decaying states, squabbling and warring incessantly over
> depleting resources and the last few tolerable environments, and coping and groping with
> increasingly anxious and uncertain lives. Or we can hope for rescue in ever-larger and ever-
> more-complex systems and ever-stronger and more grandiose governments . . . and all the
> while moving closer to nuclear and environmental disaster. Or we can work to achieve systems
> and organizations of a size where we may regulate them, to reshape our landscape to permit
> ecologically sound and locally rooted settlements, to create for ourselves a world in which our
> societies, our economics, our politics are in the hands of those free individuals, those diverse
> communities and cities, that will be effected by them—a world, of course, at the human scale.
>   Pentagon . . . Pyramid . . . or Parthenon.[45]

Nor without irony, such encompassing eutopianism has so expanded the pastoral
values to a worldwide change of direction, and so reordered almost every developed process to classically golden proportions, that the simple, natural life has
become moot. While it may provide the underlying images—as in Murray
Bookchin's *The Ecology of Freedom* (1982), which casts all Western history as
a struggle between forms of exploitative domination and a biolibertarian teleos
of natural harmony—it claims rather much.[46] It may also require, as perhaps
Ivan Illich is most noted for arguing in the past couple of decades, the fullest
fundamental changes in the very sense of human "needs."[47] Only after
deschooling, deprofessionalizing, decorporatizing, and degiganticizing society—and descaling most travel to the speed of the bicycle, most towns to
neomedieval communitas, most technology to one-on-one artisanship—can we
achieve an authentically humane "politics of conviviality."

Such pastoral-libertarian utopianizing takes not only rural forms (which I
will return to later) but paradoxically urban ones. That is, a simpler, more
"natural," wholesome living in decentralized structures on a more humane scale
(emphasizing ecology, work as play, an open libido, etc.) may be applied to the
"city," though better understood not as the contemporary megalopolis but as the
urbane town, or at least its "neighborhoods." While not for fundamentalist
naturists, it is variously evident in Morris, Ford, Callenbach, Sale (and in Le

Guin, Goodman, and others previously noted), with a modernized pastoral cast. It might be further represented by, say, Karl Hess (a charmingly notorious ideologue who seems to have been a liberal, a conservative, a right-libertarian, then a decentralist utopian) in *Community Technology* (1979).[48] On what I take to be the undeniable principle (however widely ignored) that community "local liberty" is crucial to individual liberties, he sketches an apparently practical "argument for community participation with all of the diversity and resultant flexibility that implies" in the development of production and distribution. This aims at the local creation and control of food, energy, and services on a participatory neighborhood level, which is dramatically opposed to what we mostly have. Such local liberty includes (in one of the marks of the demise of doctrinaire socialism since Morris' time for those committed to liberty and equality) participatory capitalism: "Small business is suddenly a counter-culture phenomena." In contrast to "liberal consumerism" (perhaps represented by Ralph Nader), he restates the eutopian principle so insistent with generations of arcadian prophets, Thoreauvean or Morrisean: "the work people do is far more significant than the things they buy." This liberal heresy leads to insistence on the dominance of small business, communal-level machinery (beyond what Schumacker called "intermediate technology"), apprenticeships rather than schooling, localist economic as well as political decision making, rescaled neighborhood organizations as well as, more generally, down-scaled views and values.

While such ideology no doubt also reflects the current appearance of dispersed sophisticated technology and skills (home computers, suburban factories, etc.), the deeper imperative includes a desperate utopian countering to inhumane scale in a corporate-statist society and culture. Postcounterculture, historically speaking, there developed a utopian-reformism, which might be represented by Hazel Henderson's *Creating Alternative Futures* (1978), with the utopian purpose of disempowering large organizations, as almost all pastoral thought aims to, but directed in supposedly pragmatic economic ways.[49] More expansively, it seems that much of the utopianist counterculture of the early seventies became the "New Age" quasimovement of the following decade and more. Mark Satin's *New Age Politics: Healing Self and Society* (1979) might be viewed as a symptomatic primer for this supposedly "new culture."[50] This avows the utopianizing projects of providing "full alternatives" for the present and "extrapolations" into the far future. It shows a passing concern with eutopian communities (communes) but emphasizes a newer fashion, "networking," which means very loose, informal organizing of common sympathies towards alternative institutions. (This might be viewed as a watered down version of what earlier anarchists called "affinity groups.") While many of the values seem to be those usually brigaded with pastoral utopianizing—ecology, decentralizing, simple living, crafts, pagan rituals, and the like—it is hardly well defined. Rather, it resembles a poignantly syncretistic muddle, mixing hardnosed "intermediate technology" (Kohr, Schumacher, Hess, et al.) with burbling desires for the latest high tech (solar, pharmaceutical, etc.). Golden Age sentiments are stirred in with mush-minded occultisms (astrology, ESP, Castañeda, quasi-Orientalisms, and dozens of the shoddiest forms of psychotherapy). It promotes specific protest, such as the antinuclear, and the vaguest of religiosities, such as "planetary consciousness." Everything goes in, especially organic fertilizing. The club password is "holistic." Somehow this includes "New Age Capitalism," absurdly combined with the oldest of cooperative ethics. No doubt such an earnest flea-market muddle gives utopianizing an intellectual bad name.

The "New Age" continuation of the counterculture (and earlier bohemian and dissident movements) projects fantasy futures but aims at current applications in marginal living. Or at least marginal weekends. The more meaningful applied utopianism of the past generation would probably include more demanding efforts, such as the attempted educational communities, like Black Mountain College (actually, from the 1930s into the 1950s), which was artistically fertile (including the school of poetry centered on Charles Olson) and became a partial template for other educational innovation, as well as nurturing some interesting people.[51] More influential yet, of course, was A. S. Neill's *Summerhill* (1960), a radical libertarian boarding school on left-Freudian principles which, when translated into expansive America, became the approximate model for many hundreds of "alternate schools" and the radical educational efforts of Paul Goodman, Herbert Kohl, John Holt, and many others.[52] But eutopian schools have a long history in America, back through the Modern School of the earlier part of the century to those linked with the many hundreds of intentional communities of the preceding century.[53] Yet another explicit education-as-utopia movement was the revolutionary cooperative teaching of the exploited, most notably linked in a number of countries with Paulo Freire and his *Pedagogy of the Oppressed* (1970), and its doctrine of literacy as transformed, and transforming, social "consciousness."[54] Many of the some-place communes, as well as no-place accounts, draw on such alternatives. Educational theory and practice, of course, have been modes of utopianizing for more than several millennia.

But while such radical experiments in education may be one of the more productive as well as oldest roles for the utopian sensibility, much New Age costuming is far more grandiloquent. No mere school, community, or even society is to become the good place, but a whole "new civilization," "new planetary culture," even "new consciousness," is at issue for the New Age hierophants. The representative phrases come from William Irwin Thompson, an exacademic historian become superutopianist prophet. In *At the Edge of History* (1971), part personal narrative and part scholarly essay, he renounced mere history for participation in a "new consciousness" and "cultural transformation."[55] In *Passages about Earth* (1974) he propounded not just a new mind (or mindlessness) but a "new civilization."[56] Some of this seems to come out of a traditional American utopianism of a Jeffersonian cast, more or less antistatist and decentralist but turned to strangely hyped mystical and technological mega-lomanias. Thompson claims to explore new realms of being on the way to creating a new religion for a Wellsean one-world society. Apparently, this society is to include a high-technology infrastructure and a monastic-communal social order.[57] But it is hard to be certain since he mostly omits such paltry concerns in the hyperutopianism of which he wishes to be the mythographer.

In *The Time Falling Bodies Take to Light* (1981), Thompson discusses, with a considerable show of scholarship, some episodes of undervalued matriarchal mythology in order to return our consciousness to the centrality of the Eternal Feminine.[58] That awareness, of course, has been obscured by the false culture of a male power-oriented civilization. "Perhaps if we are blessed by the old gods in the next civilization that will follow after this one has played itself out, we will come to appreciate the ancient and forgotten wisdom." This goes beyond mere femtopianism (though I consider this mythofeminism also to be antiegalitarian) to return us to the world of the Golden Age, or anyway an androgynous myth sometimes thought to go with it. But apparently the new-old "sacrament of Eros" will also require a new man-woman suitable for the new "world-epoch." This sort of thing is grandiosely and apocalyptically vague, and therefore, I suppose, appealing and solacing to some. Wowtopianizing.

Thompson, in the more mundane meantime, had something to do with the creation of surrogate utopianizing communities, intellectual-artistic forums (Landisfarne—Thompson had been a historian of things Irish—which seems to have been variously temporal in England, New York, and Colorado). But later he rather loosely reconnected the vestiges of "new consciousness" with his native California, as in *Pacific Shift* (1985), a Sierra Club meditation that vaguely foresees California as the utopic new center of world culture because of its proclivities for combining the oldest mystical with the newest electronic.[59] The new hypetopian doctrine includes ecological Gaia worship (somewhat in the fashion I discussed with femtopianism), as well as an obsession with patterns of four (to one-up trinitarianisms?), including an appendix of colored squares for the various Ages, Modes, Meditations, etc., of mankind. The book also includes some casual splutterings against current "reactionary" politics, which are categorized as hopelessly outdated and soon to be replaced by the "politics of incarnation." Some may sense that they are reading an intellectual Oral Roberts, but I will not pursue the analogy (or the genuine but sticky subject of the substantial utopianism involved in fundamentalist movements).

Thompson disparages the New Age "alternative movement" for eschewing specific ideology and for "put[ting] forth a new list of commandments and call[ing] it New Age" (apparently meaning the likes of Satin), but he also admits: "Whether the movement from one world-system to another will involve stumbling or total collapse may well depend on the success or failure of the New Age movement." While the occasional specifics show some old, partly pastoral, utopianism—such as a classless society, work as play, sensuality instead of repression, and so on—the real place is mystic "enlightenment." But enough of the devolution of utopianizing into therapeutic religiosity.

What has all this to do with literature? Too much, perhaps, since the writing aims not only at speculative patterns but lyrical inspiration, and consciously claims other traditional literary functions, from retelling ancient myths to instruction and prophecy. Rhetorical strategies also often seem to take off on their own, as in Thompson's portentous play with tropes (no doubt borrowed from Gregory Bateson) such as "ecology of consciousness."[60] Thompson's reach also includes standard literary pretensions, such as that of science fictionist, as with his *Islands out of Time: A Memoir of the Last Days of Atlantis* (1985).[61] This novel, too, is part of the New Age, though the tritely stilted writing of the heavily decorative quest-and-sex fantasy is hardly advanced. As the "Foreword" informs the uncertain reader, this "mythical prehistory"—with usual free-floating abstraction it is also a "scientific post-history"—includes "parody of the genre of the science fiction novel." That means it unrigorously borrows from sci-fi in an apparently desperate search for a new genre since our new "informational society" requires "new forms that are not the old genre of the bourgeois novel with its attendant English Department criticism." So replace it with new English Department literary theory and call a ponderously fanciful past-futuristic narrative a "metafiction." Nothing else will adequately "embody the new electronic-aerospace culture of the American Sunbelt." While always quick with a weary cliche, Thompson is an erudite man, and therefore acknowledges he prefers *"Wissenkunst"* to "metafiction." Still, it is all the same "shift of consciousness, a movement from noia to metanoia, from travel to homecoming, from domestic habitation to cosmic astonishment," and other fancy derangements. Whatever its inconsiderable New Age charms, Thompson's writing gives sci-fi metafictionizers, Californians, English Department literary theorists, the Golden Agists, and contemporary utopianists an aura of paranoid schizophrenia. Perhaps we all a bit deserve it.

One more neoutopianizer. One of the better known utopianists of a sweeping cast is the nearly as syncretistic Theodore Roszak. In *The Making of a Counter-Culture* (1969) he rather skittishly leap-frogged together dissident "youth culture," Paul Goodman's conservative anarchism, the erotic eutopianism of Herbert Marcuse and Norman O. Brown, bits of Oriental religiosity, and antimilitarism and antiindustrialism into a romantic utopics for stolid America.[62] Also originally an academic historian (its narrowness no doubt calling forth such loose counterings), Roszak appears to have had some influence doing pop-history. But his ambitions were larger. When the shifting youth culture, and the decline of his culture heroes, left him high but still wet with easy antitheses, he extended the argument into a broader but not very insightful neoromantic attack on modernist culture in *Where the Wasteland Ends* (1973).[63] The implicit upbeat religiosity takes over from culture in the *Unfinished Animal: The Aquarian Frontier and the Evolution of Consciousness* (1975).[64] This book surveys current cultish religions and psychotherapies as developing forms of "The Hidden Wisdom" which is revealed to us through "occult evolution." Roszak should be granted some competence at conceiting together any old social radicalism and new-old mysticism, the latest in ecology and the laxest in metaphysics, admirable feminism and contemptible psycho-babble, and all with utopian purpose.

But I am unable to find much logic as to why the new true believers will reject the technocratic and join in "participatory community as the essential reality of social life." Though Roszak does not consider historical analogues, he seems to be describing what historian of classical culture Gilbert Murray long ago described as a neo-Hellenistic "failure of nerve" in intellectual matters.[65] More harshly put, in a declining and anxious technocracy his mystagogues are the more fanciful parasites of a vestigial culture. However, Roszak's arguments do struggle, rather more than the Thompson he frequently parallels, with perplexities, including those of what used to be called "social consciousness" (his pre-Ivy League origins may have been moderately deprived). So he pushes not just for "new consciousness" but for "visionary communities" to lead the utopian way to the transformation of society.

Roszak's continuation of the quasidissident mapping in *Person/Planet: The Creative Disintegration of Industrial Society* (1978) affirms the freedom and development of the person as primary over any socioeconomic institutions.[66] Though a decentralist, Roszak shows what most of those previously discussed quite fail to consider (apparently not having been raised in small towns): Small organizations, face-to-face orderings, dispersed structures can also be tyrannical. A decentralist social ethic and an antistatist political ethic are justifiable and desirable, but quite insufficient. Or as he aptly put it elsewhere, "Even the true meaning of 'human scale' may not always be a matter of size but of the character of the environment." And that is less easily definable for eutopia.

Yet Roszak's discriminations often seem quite skittish, falling back into mere "personalist" pieties and anxiously eclectic yokings of social radicalisms and religiose magics. He is given to fervent but not seriously examined utopian notions, such as the importance of a new "monastic paradigm" (as with early Thompson) for continuing eutopianizing. (But perhaps that trope can be explained as an almost automatic culture defense against the dystopian projection of such arguments as Robert Vacca's *The Coming Dark Age,* or other grim postmodern nuclear projects from the previously discussed *Canticle for Leibowitz* to the present.)[67] He is better, though rather thin, in criticizing some of the prevailing (though unadmitted) utopianism of sophisticated social scientism with its glorification of the humanly inadequate "functional rationalist" (as with

Daniel Bell's "post-industrial society"). Countering, of course, is proper utopian work.

Roszak, too, has made forays into nonrealistic fiction: *Bugs* (1981), a would-be thriller combining hip computer projections and magic, and *Dreamwatcher* (1985), a psychosexual fantasy thriller (neither of which need concern us here).[68] Like Thompson and many another ideologue these days, Roszak constructed fantasy narratives to provide an alternate outlet, which is perhaps much of what we should mean by "metafiction." But he also returned to social-cultural countering criticism, developing a critique of the "true-believing cybernetic utopian" in *The Cult of Information: The Folklore of Computers and the True Art of Thinking* (1986).[69] This book (so far as I can judge) gives a balanced popular exposition of the problems behind the "information processing model of thought" as an imposed utopianism pervading, for example, the "Hidden Curriculum" behind "computer literacy" in the schools. Though surely that is but one area of a larger antiintellectual programmed thinking in our culture.

There is also a suggestive discussion of "The Computer and the Counterculture," which divides modern utopians into the "revisionaries" (my neopastoralists), the antiindustrial tradition from Morris on, and the "technophiles" (my technotopians), the technological enthusiasts from Wells on. Naive countercultural attempts to fuse the two include Buckminster Fuller's design manias (and social obfuscation), Marshall McLuhan's electronic mystagoguery of the made-up "global village," and some "electronic populism" of people's-computer-networking.[70] I think Roszak has captured what has gone perniciously wrong with much contemporary utopianizing in its syncretistic and contradictory muddles.[71]

The muddling may also be applied to some of his own utopianizing, though he should also be credited with some appropriate counterutopianizing against totalist (if not totalitarian) technocracy, which, after all, is our dominant utopianizing, though often unadmitted. In that sense, and some other values, Roszak appears to me to continue a positive primary tradition of utopian thought. Curiously, the pastoral scene has pretty much disappeared while the utopianizing continues much of its cluster of Golden Age values of humane scale, natural harmony, the aesthetic society, and the rest. Murking up the Golden Age vision with therapeutic nostrums, syncretistic mythomatics, and technomysticism, as Thompson especially does in cosmic megalomania, seems to me contradictory and defeating. Though much of it is problematic, I am still suggesting that a libertarian legacy of utopian sensibility be taken seriously—Morris, Ford, and other aesthetic pastoralisms; Kohr, Schumacher, and other humanized economics; Illich, Sale, and other institutional descalings; and the countering educationists (really almost all of the figures). For that directs us to our authentic eutopianism.

Neopastoral Applications

Utopian narratives, I am suggesting, need to be responded to in the contexts of a wide panoply of utopianizing thought and sensibility, as well as actions. Granted, not all the contexts get directly into the fictions, or at least what we usually recognize as literature. Starting at the narrow, the orthodox literary, end of the spectrum, we might tend to equate utopianizing with a handful of literary conventions, as do the genre critics, and consequently misperceive its range, impetuses, and issues. We might even treat the ambivalences and muddles in the fictions as characteristics of difficulties of some hypostatized form rather than as contradictions in the ideologies, and as problems in the realities, as I have been arguing.

Among the possible corrective lenses for literary myopia would be glasses that allow a wider range; for example, in what constitutes utopianizing narratives. As in other areas, what may be categorized as literature may be less rather than more certain these days, what with the "novel as history, history as novel," "nonfiction fiction," and, indeed, other usurpations of self-consciously literary documentary. Otherwise put, one is unlikely, perhaps especially for this historical period, to have very adequate notions of utopianizing, and its issues and sensibilities, just by perusing novels with utopianizers as subjects, or only by reading usually recognized utopian or science fiction. After all, what utopianizing is must be in part what utopianizers do. And what they do is write a variety of works, incompletely suggested in the preceding section, which ranged from lyrical and utilitarian accounts of homesteading to scholarly and polemical mythologizing of utopian ideologies. A little variety of the literature around utopian communalism in the past generation might also be in order. There seems to be quite a bit of it. But neither the quantity nor its modes should lead to simplegeneral final conclusions about communal experiences since, among other doubts, literature, here (as elsewhere), however broadly conceived, may not proportionately or otherwise adequately reflect the realities. The literary record must often be as capricious as other orderings.

Given that disclaimer, let me proceed to generalize. It seems likely that there were (as a number of the students of the subject cited later agree), more "intentional communities" in proportion to population in mid-nineteenth-century America than in the 1960s-1970s. The earlier movement produced some literature—the most noted fiction being Hawthorne's *The Blithedale Romance* (1852), which is hardly his best, drawing on his somewhat disenchanted experiences with the Brook Farm Fourierist utopian community. There are also letters, tracts, and other accounts, including later histories (Brook Farm may also provide a case example) which point up the mixed realities.[72] But there certainly were not the self-conscious memoirs, reportage, studies, and arguments that characterize the later smaller communal effulgence. Why should that be?

One reason is that some of the communalism of the recent past was parcel as well as part of a larger movement of political radicalism (as I noted about the utopian fictions of Marge Piercy, above). It may, then, have expressed a greater degree of social-political dissatisfaction. It certainly showed more extreme variety. On one side we can find the long-lived and high-principled Catholic Worker communes, which were urban with commune farms to supply them and which catered to society's victims. While this movement continued more than a millennium of Christian caritas in holy refuges, it was also (as the autobiography of its saintly founder, Dorothy Day, makes clear) politically radical in origin and in part of its emphasis.[73] Revolutionaries were part of the cast in a good many other communes as well. But that should hardly be taken as defining. For some communes—the pathologically murderous "Manson Family" and the Reverend Jim Jones' mass-suicidal jungle town in Guyana the most notorious examples— are exemplums of human evil and the subjects of thriller narratives.[74] Between, say, Day and Manson, there is a great distance, which may remind us that with communes, as with other utopianism, considerable discrimination seems imperative.

A quite different character than either of the above marked many of the "intentional communities" of the recent past. Instead of the social autonomy and experiment, and the economic self-sufficiency and positive individualism, that characterized many of the nineteenth-century communes, in the 1960s-1970s we find the defensive marginality of the weak, the sick, the parasitic, and others of the large numbers of "losers" we engender in our often anomic society. Raymond Mungo, radical journalist, then communalist, then pretentious literary artist, might be used to illustrate the point. His *Total Loss Farm: A Year in the Life* (1970) was a melange of pseudo-Thoreauvean fragments about a youthful group on a Vermont communal farm. The book's lack of perception and style was compensated for by a more artful re-doing in *Between Two Moons: A Technicolor Travelogue* (1972).[75] We are to know that it is art because it imitates imitative cinema script mannerisms. (The original edition also had phlegm-chartreuse paper with arbitrarily varied blue print and whimsied illustrations, a variant of what was known then as "psychedelic" style.) The more-or-less linguistic part of the book burbles with clichés ("white as snow," "frost is on the pumpkin") and powerful statements of emotion, such as "Far out!" and "Wow!" The catatonic language fits the stereotyped characters, such as "junkie/saint Abraham" (holy head of the commune), adolescent little "earth mothers" (who desperately get pregnant to confirm it), and other disoriented characters in quasimythological disguise. They all pathetically hug one another for metaphysical warmth, and seek solace with heads in laps (though they keep their tongues busy mostly with non sequiturs.) Naive fragments on dubiously managed farming (a sniggering scene with a bull servicing a cow, a mawkish sketch about a lovable dog with puppies, a poorly done description of pig slaughtering), along with dull dream reports, and a running sententiousness about an uncertain world waiting to be astrologically reborn (hence the title), give a blurry sense of a "paradise seeking" utopianism. It might be better understood as lost babes in the Vermont woods. But Mungo's artsy account is hardly fair to the enduring farm commune.[76] His was an exercise in therapeutic solipsism—"there's nothing wrong out there, never has been, but only in our lousy minds"—and the mindlessness, that usually goes with sentimentality, blues through all.

As the far more intelligent (though Mungo admiring) communalist Judson Jerome pointed out, this is the ideology of protective "Edenism," utopianism as regressive sanctuary. His *Families of Eden: Communes and the New Anarchism* (1974) is a melange providing a partial apologetic for this ideology.[77] Part memoir of a poet-professor who in middle age renounced the anticommunity of scholars for full-time communalism, it is also a loose survey of the larger movement of the period (he had a research grant). Pieces of social-sciency pseudoobjectivity (questionnaires, statistics, typologies) muddle an anecdotal personal account of living on a Pennsylvania farm with a dozen or so other adults and a passel of children. It was only partly a back-to-the-soil effort—the economics included a little factory for making flower pots, and there were fees for lecturing and writing—and the emphasis was upon the social conversion experience. The extended familyism, including charmingly casual praise of nudity and mixing bed partners, was viewed as a major "social experiment" participating in "a movement toward massive cultural change." At this distance, the naïveté about the cooptive powers of American social culture may seem poignant at best.

Jerome's I-Thou apologia for the eutopia conversion experience takes a therapeutic emphasis. He grants that late-twentieth-century "communal living may be better equipped to accommodate weakness than it is to accommodate strength." Given the often ruthlessly aggrandizing ethos of American institutional life, alternate subcultures are more likely to provide protective marginality than to create autonomy. Thus an enlarged, loose domestic team replaces the anxiety-maximizing unit of the nuclear family. The more informal, presumably organic, work of farm, communal shop, and household libidinally replaces the rationalized services offered by technobureaucracies for impersonal ends. And a larger sense of commitment not only to a kinlike group but to a whole dissident way of life provides an enriching sense of purpose.

The fashionable justifications for all this—yin/yang and other more-or-less mystical metaphors, neoromantic pieties ("nature is essentially good"), "twice-born" rejection of isolating egoistic individualism for a cooperative ethos—create a religious-toned yet essentially secular-therapeutic "Edenism." This is held up as contrasting with the merely "rationalistic" traditional past utopianism. Yet, rationally enough, the Edenism, too, is linked with the libertarian pastoral—antistatist, life-simplifying and personalizing, decentralizing, "natural," oppositional—though the fuller implications are hardly examined. While Jerome shows more awareness than Mungo's pseudomystical and self-centerd sentimentalizing provides, the renegade professor of English seems unduly murky on much of the reality of his utopianizing. The result is mishmash.

Put in the context of the more purely reportorial studies of utopian communalism of the time, this Edenism partook of common inadequacies. As one study, *The New Communes* (1971), concluded, "communalists lack a coherent ideology" to give them a distinctive "orientation" and "common concern" in order to avoid "destructive chaos."[78] While I suppose that might not require as rigid a doctrine as the long-enduring religious communities (Amish, Bruderhof, Hutterite, et al.), something more than therapeutic escape and release seemed needed.[79] A large part of this communalism, argues Melville in *Communes in the Counter-Culture* (1972), was utopian only in small and temporary senses, serving a briefly rebellious middle-class youth as a "personal moratorium" from emotionally inadequate mainstream institutions.[80] A more learned comparative study of nineteenth- and twentieth-century American intentional communities, Rosabeth Moss Kanter's *Commitment and Community: Communes and Utopias in Sociological Perspective* (1972), concluded that while the utopianism was ideologically continuous, the later communities had "special problems of engagement and continuity," eventually viewing themselves as retreats—a view that provided "inadequate boundaries" for coherence and endurance.[81] A British study of somewhat parallel material, *Communes, Sociology and Society* (1976), emphasizes the paradox that the communalists fled a supposedly individualistic society yet "secular communes . . . are above all attempts to create pockets of freedom . . . sufficiently insulated from society for the ideal of possessive individualism to be realized." Thus contemporary communalism is not really utopian since it is dominated by "personal salvation, not social change."[82] But it may be rather doctrinaire not to perceive that either one often becomes the other, though probably not in weakness.

The antithesis appears as more secular-religious in Laurence Veysey's *The Communal Experience: Anarchist and Mystical Communities in Twentieth-Century America* (1978), which details a number of early and late twentieth-century communes.[83] The partly antithetical traditions of the libertarian and the religious, the latter often becoming charismatic-authoritarian, do conjoin not in politics but in the continuities of cultural radicalism. Such countering to mainstream culture not only provides options for some but would seem to have larger subversive effects, especially at times of crisis in the broader culture. And the applied utopianism keeps recurring.

A retrospective sociological analysis, Zicklin's *Countercultural Communes* (1983), sensibly notes that these communities were often the concrete applications of larger ideas of humanized scale, "environment purity," egalitarianism, mutualism, sexual liberation, and the rest of the complex that I have been describing. But, as a good sociologist, he looks less to intellectual sources than to stock social determinants. However, this bias is in part implicitly corrected by his observation that whether communes were (to use a variation on the conventional polarities) "naturalist" or "spiritualist," they all had a surprisingly similar emphasis on neoprimitive values and ways.[84] In other words, there was a pervasive neopastoral ideology.

More cleverly literate than usual, and perhaps therefore rather skittishly patronizing, the sociologist Bennett Berger does connect communalism with the larger historical culture in his *The Survival of a Counterculture* (1981).[85] According to Berger, "Rural communes are contemporary bearers of the pastoral tradition" (93), which he summarizes as "the vision of a simple and self-sufficient rural life in harmony with nature" (96). While he annotates the ideas in their "relative innocuousness" (125) as coming out of "romanticism" and American frontier ideology, at one point he does attempt a more complex ideological matrix:

> . . . contemporary pastoralism cannot be easily pigeonholed as "reactionary" or "progressive" or in terms of simple political categories anywhere in-between, because it has drawn not only (as Riesman suggested) from the anti-industrialism of the nineteenth-century British aristocracy, but also partly from the socialist critique of the wretched urban squalor created by the early stages of English industrialism that, despite Karl Marx's remark about the idiocy of rural life, might well have made the community life of peasants and artisans seem idyllic in retrospect. And, as the German youth movement made clear, pastoralism is also consistent with German conservatism (even fascism) in its emphasis on ties of blood, soil, and *Volk;* but it has drawn also from the bohemian tradition, mostly French, which, although urban, strongly emphasized Rousseau's primitivism, wilderness, exoticism, sexual expressiveness, and even mind-expanding drugs. (104)

While the cultural history (such as the short-circuiting into Rousseau) seems askew and the politics seem obtuse (anarchism is more pertinent than fascism), at least this passage explores some other dimensions. American countercultural eutopianism, then—and the conventional sociologist's central ostensible subject, a long-lived secular California rural commune—should be recognized as part of an ancient cultural pattern, pastoral utopianism.

But our applied neopastoralism shows proclivities to mire itself in other problems and contradictions. For a final example here, consider "Rajneeshpuram," an almost novel-length narrative in Frances FitzGerald's collection of four reports on "subculture" communities in contemporary America, *Cities on a Hill* (1986).[86] (The other three—the gay community in San Francisco, Jerry Falwell's Liberty Baptist Church and pseudouniversity, and the upper-middle-class retirement town of Sun City, Florida—are much less developed, and rather forcibly hooked onto the American innocent theme of "starting over" by converting to a new life, and unnecessary to consider here.) Not incidentally, this literate documentary account serves, as is so often the case in contemporary culture, the "literary" purpose of providing an intriguing "prose narrative" (as Defoe would have recognized) with striking characters in a "plot," the rise and fall of an exotic yet pertinent "nowhere."

FitzGerald's is a sharp-edged account of the notorious large rural commune in eastern Oregon in the early 1980s, Rajneeshpuram, which was the ambitious center for the religiotherapeutic alternate society under Indian charismatic cult figure Bhagwan Shree Rajneesh. The author's sophisticated (and sometimes a bit sophistical) shifting perspective emphasizes ambiguous views of one of the largest (several thousand directly involved) intentional communities of recent times. In a handful of years, it went from remarkable expansion and grandiose vision to corruption and crime, quickly ending in flight and abolition. It might also be read as a sadly paradigmatic fable of contemporary utopianizing, including the ideological incoherence I have been emphasizing in a great range of literary and quasiliterary material.

FitzGerald does not quite achieve the fabulistic with her narrative, which is muddied by an odd sense of history, including the claim that the form of the "commune was a uniquely American cooperative structure created initially for the Shakers" (*CH* 262). The Shakers' adaption of traditional communal forms to their peculiar celibate mixed-gender communities (taken up only by a very few others, such as the nineteenth-century Rappites in Indiana), hardly fits the Bhagwanites.[87] But her response is varied enough to be suggestive.

Rajneeshpuram was a ranch-commune with grandiose ambitions to become a utopian city (*CH* 249), a "Buddhafield" of religious transformation (*CH* 250), a "year-round summer camp for urban professionals" (*CH* 275), a "hybrid between an Indian ashram and the Esalen Institute" of psychotherapeutic experimentation (*CH* 277), an "alternative model of society for mankind" (*CH* quoted 278), the leader's announced refuge from the imminent nuclear holocaust (*CH* 251), the ultimate "holistic New Age Marketplace" (*CH* 292), and a syncretistic 1960s charismatic cult turning into a paranoid-patriarchal church (*CH* 314). The confusion of purposes is more than the narrator's; like the American big benevolent university, it tried to be all things on the way to being really nothing.

It was also in part a femtopia, with the prophet insisting that "women would run this commune because they were more intuitive and down to earth than men—and less involved in their own egos" (*CH* quoted 308). Not surprisingly, the women leaders were some of the best and the worst (convenient confirmation of my argument in chapter 3 of egalitarianism in evil). The dominant woman (thirty-three-year-old Indian-American Ma Anand Sheela), an aggressive manipulator, went in for electronic bugging, voter fraud, endless litigation, bombings, ornate power plays, greed, even the poisoning of intimates, and other not uniquely feminine wiles that put her in prison for a fear years.

Rather more importantly, FitzGerald effectively argues that much of

Rajneeshpuram was the utopian literalization of the "ideals of the American counterculture and the Human Potential Movement" (*CH* 300). Most specifically, the latter, combining Maslovian psychology and management techniques, and a whole panoply of Rogerean and other therapeutic nostrums, with positive religiosity (*CH* 281 ff.). A strikingly large proportion of the communards (white bourgeois) were highly schooled and credentialed, especially as therapeutic professionals, though generally they "read very little, if at all" (*CH* 267), and were for the most part antiintellectual. This description provides not only a nice annotation of contemporary American higher education but, I take it, a significant part of the explanation for the lack of critical spirit that helped further the community's arbitrary authority, exploitation of its members, and ultimate collapse.

As presented, the communards were a touchingly "high concentration of attractive, well-educated young adults with an ideology of non-possessiveness and sexual laissez-faire" (*CH* 275) who, probably not always consciously, drew on a variety of utopian notions. As with so many responsive contemporary utopians, they emphasized ecological concerns, putting into practice sophisticated water and sewage processes as well as elaborate recycling and reforestation. (The author perhaps insufficiently and unsympathetically notes only a bit of this, attributing it to Freudian "compulsiveness.") As this suggests, and other details confirm, the community was a contradictory mix of high tech—heavy construction equipment, elaborately programmed computers, an airport and private planes, legal-financial networks, etc.—and the neoprimitive notions of simple, communal living on the land. The design of the community had the same mix, ranging from the apt adaption of clustered A-frame housing to glitzy tourist developments. It could be said that the pastoral community went askew with technological as well as religiotherapeutic pathologies.

The bizarre mix of high tech and neoprimitive may be plausibly represented by the image of the exurban, exprofessionals, costumed in red oriental uniforms, laboring mightily in the fields to raise organic produce for ritualized communal meals, taking a break to gather and bow to the bejeweled guru making his daily cruise in one of his many Rolls Royce limos. It is that incoherence, that grotesque and defeating muddle of the liberating and the submissive, the naturist idealism and the mechanical servility, the egalitarian communalism and the corrupt hierarchicalism, the simple and the decadent, which may most reverberate in awareness. (This defeating mix seems to me also to apply to FitzGerald's other subcultures of electronically evangelizing imperial fundamentalists or the well-to-do old living in their emptily lavish enclaves.) Similar double binds, or perhaps more accurately, triple binds, seem pervasive: naturist, spiritualist, technocratic; egalitarian-communal, authoritarian-charismatic, manipulative-hierarchical. A good many parallels appear in other recent utopianizing, literary and applied.

Rajneeshpuram sensibly encouraged population limitation—a social as well as ecological crux—and what their prophet called the "liquid family" (*CH* 308)—antinuclear, antipossessive, shiftingly polymorphous relationships (though as power structures took over, the traditional family, of course, was increasingly emphasized). As with American communes for more than a century, and utopias for more than several millennia, children were communally raised, in kibbutzlike peer groupings. Much of the other education was learning by doing with adults. The "alternative schooling" influence of the radical reformers of the 1960s seems evident.

The work ethic was also partly in the major eutopian tradition, going back through that brilliant crank Fourier's notions of work as play. This ethic seems to have been, in both productivity and personal gratification, highly successful. But, as FitzGerald perceptively notes, from the start the laboring was suspiciously overdone, apparently as a means of control as well as typically American megalomaniac expansionism. And it was certainly suspect in that there was "no system of job rotation" (*CH* 270), an essential egalitarian test. (Even the disinterested author applies the libertarian criteria, so important in utopian literature and practice, to her subject.)

FitzGerald's ironic ending to her narrative emphasizes that in spite of the Bhagwan's indifferently selfish decamping (quick airplane getaway with mistress, servants, boxes of money and jewels, until he was arrested, jailed, and then deported), and the public exposures of crass criminal activities that destroyed the communal structure, a number of excommunards still had the spirit. Some continued to adore the "Master," and, more interestingly, justified their years of devotion and exploitation as positive therapy and education. And, in spite of the just mockery of religiotherapeutic pathology and other unholy muddles, perhaps it was.

For the countering-the-present appeal of pastoral eutopianizing—the pursuit of "more natural" sexuality, family, community, ruralism, schooling, ecology, equality, and other humane-scaled being—remains a great social-cultural legacy. We might properly look upon such utopianizing efforts as Rajneeshpuram, then, with fascinated, however critical, irony, and not a little ambivalence. As Hegel understood the work of human art as the "concrete universal" of a far larger *"geist,"* so we might understand even a rather dubious commune in relation to the spirit of utopianizing.

By sketching some of the applied side of utopianizing, I do not mean to suggest any simple cause-and-effect relationship between literature and application, utopian thought and communes. But surely there is some. (I bemusedly remember earnest communards some years ago asking me for some recommended utopian "stories," some of whose features they put on their list of "priorities"; when I later visited their semirural commune, I had the experience, not uncommon to literature teachers reading student explications, of uncertainty as to what came from where.) But I am merely suggesting that utopian narratives, fictional or reportorial, be recognized as part of a larger pattern. The pattern includes, I have been insisting, pastoral and technotopian contradictions out of the historical context, and feminist and other ideological impetuses out of the present context. I am also proposing that the literary span, which in this chapter included traditional utopian novels, essays in cultural criticism and social philosophy, poetic-prophetic statements, memoirs, sociological studies (admittedly a degraded mode), and documentary narratives (yet others, including experimental fictions and architectural townscapes, are cited elsewhere), be expanded from the usual dogmatic considerations, such as genre. It is a fallacy of misplaced concreteness to reduce the utopianizing impetus, thought, and sensibility to one, or even just a few, accidental literary modes such as formal utopian fiction, whether traditional, sci-fi, or fantastic. Utopianizing is all more or less of a piece, or antipiece, in countering what is.

By taking a ranging view, I also argue, we may better recognize the more substantial issues, such as counterutopianizings, as with the neopastoral versus the technotopian, including (as with the last example) their defeating muddle. Granted, probably my approach has still been too narrow since I did not much consider, say, cosmic pastoral (as it appears not only in some science fiction but in some technological tracts). Possibly in centering on fictional, argumentative, and descriptive literature (all somewhat reasoned images of alternate social orderings), I have omitted the most crucial cultural sources of utopias, evident, say, in religious and therapeutic tracts, technotopic and pornotopic fantasies, and others not always obscured in common discourse. But the fuller decoding (to use fashionable literary jargon) of the pervasive utopic epistemes is beyond the subject here, although the mention of these other forms is further reminder of the perplexed relations of cultural and social phenomena. While my account is partly on the side of "cultural" rather than mere "socioeconomic" determinisms, much of the relationship remains insufficiently considered. Necessarily so? In any plausible Golden Age, culture and society, utopia and its literature, would no doubt be much closer together, which may be one of the prime morals of utopianizing.

5

Entopianism:
Some Ends of Utopianizing

Metatopianizing

Since the preceding discussion of applied utopianism suggests that no-wheres are in significant part now-heres, it might be correctively appropriate to turn to more encompassing considerations. The purposes of utopianizing, once one goes beyond the too obvious filling of genre boxes, or the admittedly loose categories of "alternative societies" that I have often been using, or the summarizing of some of the things that have been called utopian, are not necessarily clear. Perhaps clarity should not be their aim, for they would then lose some speculative and imaginative functions. Still, there are larger ends that affect the ways we respond to utopias, and a few of them (again, I make no claim to thoroughness) might be briefly considered here. Since I started this present work by arguing against such simple-general theories as were rolled out on the path labeled "utopia as a genre," the opposite broad road, sometimes explicitly posted as "meta-utopia," might merit equal travel time. Granted, where genre theories obviously suffer from pedantry and pettiness, metatopianizing may suffer from grandiosity and vagueness.

So it might be best to start with a metatopia that claims to take off from applied utopianizing. Robert Nozick's "A Framework for Utopia," the detachable concluding section (he advises us) to his minimal-statist political philosophizing in *Anarchy, State, and Utopia* (1974), ostensibly defends utopianism.[1] But since (as with some of the genre theorists previously discussed) he at least sometimes assumes the Panglossian principle that we can only think about utopias as "the best world imaginable" and the "best of all possible worlds," or "the perfect society" based on notions "static and rigid," his defense seems doubtful. Whatever the merits of that Panglossian assumption in the sixteenth century, it is hardly applicable (as I hope my earlier discussions have shown) for the late twentieth century. Even in the purer realms of reason, it is quite unacceptable because quite undialectical. What, then, might be the point of such a claim? It is a trick: If utopia is a supposedly "perfect" society, then any imperfection is a disproof of its premise. In political philosophizing, as in genre theorizing, such a definition separates off utopianizing into the lands of purist fantasy, thereby reducing, trivializing, the utopian as a better social possibility.

This misleading characterization of utopian thought allows Nozick to be patronizing. Utopias are peculiar and small enough to be both indiscriminately tolerated and blandly subsumed under a special rubric, "meta-utopia: the environment in which utopian experiments may be tried out." By this odd usage, Nozick actually means metacommunalism, only, and some merely procedural rules that allow for varied little intentional communities. He summarizes the purpose: "if there is a diverse range of communities, then (putting it roughly) more persons will be able to come closer to how they wish to live than if there is only one kind of community."[2] Hence: variety, tolerance, free choice. What humane person could object? Well, there might be some nagging concern about ideal communities dedicated to, say, mass suicide (Jonestown)—the volunterrism also suspect—or to inculcating children in future terrorism or race or gender hatred, or to grossly corrupt spiritual communities (Rajneeshpuram), or quite a number of other nasty utopias in literature and history. No small set of rules, such as for opting out or against external aggression, would seem to cover enough of the situations. Nozick does not suggest any even halfway adequate protocol for his mere "experiments" in utopia. Unqualified variety (like indiscriminate reading of utopian, or sci-fi, fictions) seems inadequate in intelligence, responsiveness, and a sense of realities. Under the guise of a free-market "smorgasbord of utopian communities," one critic notes, operates many a possibility for "hidden-hand indoctrinating totalitarianism."[3]

A primarily procedural "meta-utopia" has insufficient purpose. One might propose a "framework" that would encourage, say, three or five or seven kinds of communities (and uncoercively produce yet others), but not everything goes or should be encouraged. Or, equally importantly, will be. Communities, however utopian, start in a historical society and culture, and (as I keep noting in different contexts) must considerably be understood as countering what is. "Variety" is less a purpose than a possible result of that countering. (Nozick's touting of "complexity," which he incoherently substitutes for variety—not the same thing at all—also hardly seems a meaningful purpose.)[4] In his skittish redoing of Aynrandism, Nozick seems to reduce objections to the present order down to petty variations of suburban lifestyle, called utopias, within the unquestioned "framework" of technocracy in its current capitalist form.[5]

Nozick makes no mention of subsidizing or otherwise aiding utopian efforts. In his minimal state context, public help is no doubt ruled out as an intrusion on private property "entitlements." Perhaps, though not mentioned, there could be private patronage. There have been some notable past cases of it,

such as capitalist Robert Owen, though his discriminating and specific countering of contemporaneous industrial and social organization (and advocacy of
"socialism") no doubt conceptually rules him out, too.[6] Nozick wants to minimize the state in present statist-capitalism but he does not want to minimize
unjust and otherwise false wealth, indoctrination, controlling scale, power, or
dominations. In more personalized times, this was ideologizing the barons over
the king. Now as then it seems a spurious conflict to us lesser people. Few
voluntary alternatives are to be allowed in conditions that are stacked against
them. This is antiutopianism coopting the utopian impetus. But such metatopian-
ism, however apparently open its impetus (and however revealingly unliterary,
unimaginative), is tolerance become sleight-of-hand: it reductively allows but
does not aid a small amount of countering, merely as decoration for his real
"framework"—a metautopia of a continuingly acquisitive, antiegalitarian, and
destructive society.

Countering has been the emphasis not of Anglo-American thinned-out classical liberalism, such as Nozick's, but of more grandiose cultural theorizing
from central Europe, especially in the traditions of neo-Hegelian social theology. Though sometimes called, at its own pietistic insistence, Marxism (or
neo-Marxism, or, presumptiously, "critical theory"), it also drastically counters
much of Marx's generally negative view of the utopian. It seeks to reverse the
intellectual as well as the commonplace criticism of utopianism.

> The standard critique of utopia rests on the ontological claim that the nature of things is given,
> on the regional claim that utopia is not grounded in the world at hand, and on the psychological
> claim that men depart from reality when they dream of perfection beyond the limitations which
> the reality at hand imposes. It maintains that utopia is not only unrealistic and impractical, but
> potentially dangerous; since it encourages men to give vent to totalistic, adolescent psychologi-
> cal states, and provides an illusory basis for human action. According to this critique, utopia is
> a form of unbridled subjectivism which ignores the fact that man cannot re-shape the objective
> world in his own image, make it conform to abstract plans and schemata, or base his practical
> activities on maximally preferred values. It is *irrational* in its refusal to acknowledge the
> authority of objective reality, *immature* in its inability to realize the limited nature of the
> possible, and *irresponsible* in its failure to understand the role of fallibilism in the realization
> of the good. The standard critique, summed up in the smart phrase 'That's rather utopian',
> recognizes that there are different kinds of utopians and that utopianism can adopt a scientific
> as well as Messianic guise; but it maintains that all utopians err in preferring the fulfillment of
> ideal representations to the more mundane improvements which are possible in their time.[7]

That competent summary of the antiutopian (interestingly, from someone providing a sympathetic exposition of the utopian) seems to me to provide the nexus
of what much affirmative metatopianizing wishes to counter.

A major example at hand is Ernst Bloch, a twentieth-century philosopher
who spent a large part of a long life defending utopianizing in theory (and
decades defending vicious Stalinism in practice, though he finally broke with

it). Bloch (the expositor quoted above continues) saw "utopia" as the absolute (the God term) for this century, "at a time when traditional absolutes have collapsed." Bloch pushed utopianizing for "its *cognitive function* as a mode of operation of constructive reason, its *educative function* as a mythography which instructs men to will and desire more and better, its *anticipatory function* as a futurology of possibilities which later become actual, and its *causal function* as an agent of historical change."[8]

Bloch's hyperutopianizing ranged from his *Spirit of Utopia* (1918, 1923), which emphasizes the utopian as an essential process for the emergence of the "not yet conscious," through more than half a century of adapting it to various cultural exigencies. While the utopian often claimed revisionary Marxist purposes, even one of the most affirmative expositors acknowledges that Bloch "ultimately remains a renegade" to all the Marxian dogmas except in the most abstract of commitments to historical change.[9] In the long essay, "Indications of Utopian Content," concluding *A Philosophy of the Future* (1963), Bloch treats the utopian as a transcendent but always obscurely immanent process of reaching for a future good society.[10] At least to the sympathetic, it is an abstractly appealing notion, this promise of dialectics that will reveal the utopian all around.

Curiously, when Bloch gets down to specifics, as he now and again does, actual utopias are rejected in favor of the larger spirit of utopianizing. Thus the "technical utopia"—Bacon's *New Atlantis* is the example cited—is accused of having "falsely limited" the possibilities. Neither classical utopianizing nor "its somewhat tepid extension to 'science fiction' is hardly even half-adequate." What is, then? Apparently "life as a whole is full of utopian projections, mirrored ideals, dream manufactories," and so we must find the eutopian content as best we can. The utopian should be recognized in the great overreaching (hence utopian) works such as Goethe's *Faust* and Cervantes' *Don Quixote*.[11] In less emphatic form, it should also be recognized in mythic "archetypes" (in the Jungian sense, except not just in his entrapping past but as future hope). Hence fairy tales, myths of the Golden Age and the Land of Cockaigne, and even parts of popular diversion-culture, manifest, though quite incompletely, utopian aspirations for the good society.[12]

While that utopian purpose is not much specified, it is, with Marx, assumed to point to a eutopia which is classless and realizes the fullest human potentials. But the process is also quite un-Marxist (not a cultural superstructure on a materialist class base), and vulgar Marxist literary analysis (he specifies that of George Lukács) "merely obscures the utopian perspective of every great work of art."[13] This transcendental promise should be understood as the deepest human hope, and our dialectics should concentrate on recognizing it in the "concrete-utopian" wherever it appears, for that is the highest purpose of mankind made ontologically manifest—such hope is man's nature.[14]

Utopianizing has thus been expanded until it is pervasive in culture but rarified until it is only a rather vague part of any cultural object (though more significant in the great questing works). The literary work contains, but never is (in the double sense of its being and its realization), the utopian. The intellectual reader, the literary critic (if I may draw out a small heuristic), must constantly engage in a metasocial interpretive criticism: What utopia is implied in this work?

We may agree that putting the utopian calculus to a literary work can sometimes be a good demand on it, expressing a large and perennial concern with its social dimensions and implications. But does not the same calculus apply to a building or a machine, to an organization or an activity, to a place or a person? (What an ugly society it would be if it were all such vast glass boxes in such a miserable place run by such a mean hierarchy just for making flimsy widgets. . . .) I cannot find here, except in a general romantic tendency to valorize cultural artifacts with a farreaching social dimension, and perhaps sub-cultural rebellious expressiveness, much usable critical theory, or practice.[15] It seems vague to grant the pervasiveness of the utopian impetus (even in left-intellectuals' minds). What distinguishes the utopian from the nonutopian? And I cannot find much more than hints, at most, of dialectics within utopianizing. As arguments within the more-or-less Marxist traditions, harking back with renewed emphasis to its origins prior to Marx (though some crop up in his early work), they are perhaps significant in restoring a sense of utopian vision as essential to cultural perception as well as social change.

Perhaps the currently best-known inheritor of Bloch's utopian devoutness among American academics is the acknowledged neo-Marxian follower, Fredric Jameson, who turns Bloch's notions into skittish methodological pomposities. As he "explains," with an even further reification, in the concluding chapter of *The Political Unconscious* (1981), "The Dialectic of Utopia and Ideology," "all class consciousness . . . is Utopia in so far as it expresses the unity of a collectivity."[16] Apparently trying to skirt the discredited vulgar Marxian reduction of cultural superstructure to class material base, he quickly qualifies that this is not to be taken literally but in an "allegorical" sense. The utopian (à la early Bloch) has now become unconscious, or at least unadmitted and only available to Marxist readings that understand "culture as the expression of a properly Utopian or collective impulse." Since Jameson, as has been widely recognized, shifts his grounds, reifies his arguments, and is a very arbitrary critic with a literary text, it is quite obscure how the collective class consciousness adds up to a concrete utopia, or of what kind it might be.[17] But rest assured that it is the true Marxianizer who has "restored the Utopian meaning of cultural artifacts," and who legitimizes them as part of "political" actions in a buried form of ideological struggle. Whatever the merits of this as coterie and careerist gamesmanship, it is intolerably vague and slippery. It does, however, indicate that "Utopia" has become an honorific counter where it was not before.

And so it had been for some time in the better-known Herbert Marcuse, especially his later writings, which more interestingly adapt Bloch's "concrete-utopia" to a social-cultural dialectics.[18] As a social philosopher, Marcuse was notorious not only for his polemical sloganeering (so influential in the late 1960s) and his free-wheeling abstractions (so likely to encourage some of the contradictions that any analytical reader can hardly help noting), but for his utopian insistence on a new sensibility for a new person in a new society. He might better be understood in his extreme utopianizing less as a political philosopher or revisionist-Marxist social analyst than as an ideological poet. He even has his lyric moments. Note a passage in his Conclusion to *Counterrevolution and Revolt* (1972), where he has been reversing his earlier exaltation of the utopianizing counterculture—*An Essay on Liberation* (1969)—but still wants to defend its promise of an "emancipation of sensibility," which must become far larger, and far more "a political weapon."

> The fight will be won when the obscene symbiosis of opposites is broken—the symbiosis between the erotic play of the sea (its waves rolling in as advancing males, breaking by their own grace, turning female: caressing each other, and licking the rocks) and the booming death industries at its shores, between the flight of the white birds and that of the gray air force jets, between the silence of the night and the vicious farts of the motorcycles. . . . Only then will men and women be free to resolve the conflict between the Fifth Avenues and the ghettos, between procreation and genocide. In the long range, the political dimension can no longer be divorced from the aesthetic, reason from sensibility, the gesture of the barricade from that of love. To be sure, the former spells hatred—but the hatred of all that which is inhuman, and this "gut hatred" is an essential ingredient of the cultural revolution.[19]

To the polemic that the counterculture must be revolutionary (the quaint nineteenth-century metaphor of the barricades) has been added his late hyperfeminist doctrine (the aggressive male waves liberatingly turned to loving female, caressing and licking).[20] The contradictory erotic beauty and high-tech ominousness of the southern California scene has been heightened. (From the engendering La Jolla beach, the jets/gulls trope and the "vicious farts of the motorcycles" are more literal than not, though the nearby military industries are not actually visible.) The surreal symbiosis which is contemporary reality is to be replaced by a left-Hegelian synthesis of dialectical reason and sensuous sensibility. But, the chapter concludes, that "final crisis of capitalism may take all but a century." The quote above ends with a contradictory paean (violating the naturally transforming waves?) to the hatred that justifies revolutionary violence. Utopian deformation rather than transformation.

Marcuse's dialectics are the rhetorical foaming waves around radical metaphors, such as "one-dimensional man" (coopted into a unified late capitalist culture) with "repressive desublimation" (the appearance but not the reality of freedom and expressiveness) and quite incapable of the "Great Refusal" (resistance which leads to radical change). Utopianizing allegory in the grand manner, this rhetoric intends to show all our cultural and social forces playing out the drama of "Domination" versus "Liberation."[21]

The dizzying values of such mythology (for, of course, domination, liberation, and refusals do not come in such neat personae) may be found less in the often trite "progressivism" it falls into when specifically political than in its encompassing aesthetic-erotic dimensions. In what is probably Marcuse's best sustained argument, *Eros and Civilization* (1955), he attempted dialectically to reverse Freudianism into "the idea of a non-repressive civilization."[22] But since "all liberation depends on the consciousness of servitude"—*One-Dimensional Man* (1964)—radically alternative thought is necessary. It is not the grandiosity of Marcuse's short-circuiting abstractions which is suggestive so much as the dialectical paradoxes. In our "repressive satisfactions" our counterfeiting society trumpets freedoms in self-censoring media, enlarges opportunities for manipulative fraud and exploitation, expands gratifications with consumer anxieties and distractions, accommodates development of the destructive, liberates falsification, exalts trivialization. Our institutions and their apologists liberally adapt criticisms and differences to serve their self-perpetuation and self-justification. As does the salty wet mash sometimes used in force feeding fowls, the pretenses at sating our thirst merely heighten it, leaving catatonic satisfactions and fatted emptiness. (I am using my own rhetoric to suggest the applicability of Marcusean dialectics.) This is the "insane rationality" of an exploitative technocracy in expansive decline. What is required against this one-dimension-takes-all ordering is a full-dimensioned criticism that must be "more negative and more utopian" *(Negations)*.[23] Nothing less will counter our processing and denaturing. The authentic countervision is of "society as a work of art" (a tenet of much pastoral utopianizing).

Marcuse, always rather thickly *au courant*, was disposed to find this utopian force in the rebellious impetus and styles of the 1960s counterculture, which he depicts ebulliently in *An Essay on Liberation*, holding that "the new sensibility has become a political force." According to his own dour ideological analysis of the one-dimensionality of the dominant culture, he should not have been so sanguine. And within a couple of years, as demonstrated in *Counterrevolution and Revolt*, he was not. The new antisensibility is drastically downgraded for the old modernist traditions of higher revolt (even Baudelaire for Brecht), the new messy utopianizing for the old high utopian vision.[24]

But that vision had been shifty. While the aesthetic had always been central to Marcuse (from his doctoral dissertation on artist-novels to his final little book, *The Aesthetic Dimension*), the role of seeing society as a work of art (in my arguments, but not Marcuse's, the major countering utopianizing to the technotopian) drastically revolved. One simplified example: From Hegel's division of realms (in the *Phenomenology*) into "freedom" and "necessity," we get the

Marxian application that productive labor must be in the realm of necessity, therefore unfree and humanly alienating. (Whether Marx had a final utopian vision, in a few passages, of superseding the alienation necessary to the division of labor is mostly irrelevant to the historical tradition.) In the "Phantasy and Utopia" chapter of *Eros and Civilization,* Marcuse more than a little paradoxically argued, adapting the issue to Freudian "performance" and "reality" principles, that labor must remain nonutopian alienation:

> No matter how justly and rationally the material production may be organized, it can never be a realm of freedom and gratification; but it can release time and energy for the free play of human faculties *outside* the realm of alienated labor. The more complete the alienation of labor, the greater the potential of freedom: total automation would be the optimum. It is the sphere outside labor which defines freedom and fulfillment, and it is the definition of human existence in terms of this sphere which constitutes the negation of the performance principle. This negation cancels the rationality of domination and consciously "de-realizes" the world shaped by this rationality—redefining it by the rationality of gratification. . . . it transforms the human existence in its entirety.[25]

It takes some additional rhetorical footwork to insist that this must be a radical rather than ameliorative (shorter workday, more enlightening leisure, etc.) change in order to reach the eutopian condition. The alienating realm of necessity has been minimized, even qualitatively modified, but not eliminated, with technocracy somehow possibly exempt from old dominations.

A couple of decades later in "The End of Utopia" ("end" meaning the purpose and realization of the utopian), Marcuse argues the opposite, explicitly acknowledging the "now obsolete Marxian concept" and opposing the "distinction between the realm of freedom and the realm of necessity." That distinction implied that "alienated labor" must be "organized as rationally as possible and reduced as much as possible. But it remains labor in and of the realm of necessity and thereby unfree." But now, Marcuse goes on, we can let "the realm of freedom appear within the realm of necessity—in labor and not only beyond labor."[26] As Marx put Hegel topsy-turvy (turning *geist* into material production), so Marcuse is turning Marx topsy-turvy, proceeding "from science to utopia and not from utopia to science." We are back to Fourier's utopianizing, when "play with the potentialities of human and nonhuman nature would become the content of social labor." The "aesthetic-erotic dimension" takes over, and we achieve "the convergence of technology and art and the convergence of work and play." Scientistic socialism has yielded to high utopianism, with the help of a somehow neutral technology.[27]

My concern here is not with Marcuse's inconsistency—he was hardly a rigorous thinker (the above shift probably undercuts his whole political emphasis since any aesthetic-erotic desuppression carries utopian potential, thus doing the political work). Expansively responsive to the utopianizing ambience of the

1960s, he was also providing bits of rationale for utopian applications, with a mixture of abstruse theory and sloganizing rhetoric. But his utopianizing, however limited by the Marxist mythology he sought to revise but remained bound within, has a larger suggestiveness.

For example, prior to the 1960s influence, he insisted that a good society would not only require a reduction in population but a reduction in "false needs."[28] Exploring what "needs" really are is a powerful issue (later to be provocatively taken up by Ivan Illich in his utopianizing theories, such as *Toward a History of Needs* [1977]), a quest hardly considered in most other modes of social-cultural thinking but essential (as the pastoral eutopias usually emphasize) to an aesthetic of society as a goal.[29] Beyond countering, what would man really want?

In treating part of Marcusean utopian dialectics positively, I should, no doubt, fearfully enter some disavowals (after all, resentful-rightist philosopher Eliseo Vivas demanded that professors defending Marcuseanism be "punished"!).[30] True, some ugly positions appear in his speculations. In "The Problem of Violence by the Opposition" he undialectically abstracted himself into vague justifications of violence (for a militant student audience).[31] He fatuously, I think, treats violence for social change as a universal (Leninist?) truth, though rarely discriminating among kinds, ways, and places of violent resistance. Even for the nonpacifist this must seem sloppy, and naive, rhetoric. But it is not unique. In its very sweep as well as frustration with the present, some politically activated utopianism does brigade with violence, though not always indiscriminately. And surely the reader of a range of utopian writings must recognize that terrorism has a very small role. Violence rarely qualifies as utopian, obviously.[32]

More considered, but hardly more persuasive (at least to the libertarian temperament), were Marcuse's speech-repressive arguments in the notorious "Repressive Tolerance."[33] There he begins with the apt perception that the supposedly liberal tolerance of Anglo-Americans often actually disguises and furthers ideologies of domination, and other ugliness, but he moves to dubious claims for precensorship and other forms of counterrepression. Part of his spuriousness, of course, is as old as Plato's assumption of a rational-humane elite with censoring power, when little evidence suggests such an elite has ever been in power or that even a utopia could have a coherent one. Subsidiary arguments seem equally weak; for example, that "art" is not to be censored but "pseudo-art" is, which badly begs the question (as any participant in censorship cases knows). But of course discrimination is required within, as well as between, utopian speculative theories.

A further consideration of the role of "art" (by which Marcuse almost always means literature in traditional senses, and even there almost solely Continental classics of the past two centuries) might be appropriate. Art carries utopian awareness, though not far enough to turn the "aesthetic-erotic dimension" into a "society which is a work of art."[34] In the later writings, such as his final *The Aesthetic Dimension: Toward a Critique of Marxist Aesthetics* (1977), he is countering his own (and his primary audience's) vulgar Marxist "realism" with a romantic canted formalism. "True, the aesthetic form removes art from the actuality of the class struggle—from actuality pure and simple." But that is the "autonomy of art" which produces a "counter-consciousness" (*AD* 9).[35] For "art is also the promise of liberation," not in doctrine but in experiencing the "beauty" of the ordering as against mere "established reality." "It evokes an image of the end of power, the appearance *(Schein)* of freedom" (*AD* 46). (By word play—*Schein* is also illusion—this is not to be taken with social literalism.) So what have we really experienced? The "qualities of the form negate those of the repressive society" (*AD* 53), thus producing in memory the Faustian "beautiful moment" (*AD* 65). In sum, the "utopia in great art is never the simple negation of the reality principle but its transcending preservation" (*AD* 73). Inspirational. But concrete utopia has turned within to pure sensibility.

As one of the most balanced commentators on Marcuse puts it, he quite underemphasized "those conservative-ideological elements in high culture in his eagerness to defend its subversive moments."[36] In the more developed "Art and Revolution" section of *Counterrevolution,* he more hostilely defended preservative sensibility against any counterculture.[37] For example, he condemned the latter's music as fatuous therapeutics for "pubertarian rebels" and "as "totalitarianism" in organization (did he ever reflect on the "democracy" of his beloved classical music orchestras?). His newly acquired distaste for rebelliously obscene speech (defended in *Essay on Liberation*), for the "self-defeating" qualities of "anti-art," or for any literalization of the utopian impetus, became stock pontification for more "rigorous discipline of the mind." Which might also be helpful to left-Hegelian ideologues who make no discriminations among various rebellious styles of art.[38]

Understandably, utopian and other radical qualities were in obvious decline in the 1970s, and Marcuse was somewhat desperately attempting to counter that. But his understandable self-defense of the intellectual and allegiance to high culture led to a forced emphasis on, for example, the antibourgeois element in the great bourgeois novels. Since we practicing critics partly test cultural theories on their interpretive "readings," we might note how weak Marcuse's were, claiming, for instance, that the endings of Shakespeare's tragedies were dominated by "ever-renewed hope." That is, Victorian sentimentalizing of the accession of mediocrity. He finds William Blake's radicalism in his rhetoric about the French Revolution and the formal lyrics instead of in the brilliant "antiform" of *The Marriage of Heaven and Hell*. With Kafka, I suggest, he confuses the revulsive reaction to the defeat by anxiety (the nuclear experience of the fables) with literature of "revolt." And to claim smugly the compatibility of radical responses with formalism (his illustration comes from the more conventional work of the authoritarian-revolutionist Brecht) just further sunders culture from its context. Certainly there is a utopianly radical literature in any period but it is cultural mystification to overextend it. The aesthetic, to the pleasure of all but dogmatic moralist architects, is a disordered mansion with all sorts of rooms, not to mention some weird cellars, attics, and outhouses. (That last is where the utopian is more likely to be found, in obvious contrast to the main house.)

Marcuse, though he rarely commented on actual utopian writings, probably remains significant not only for the occasional suggestiveness of his sweeping dialectics (including sweeping high modernism into utopian ends) but for bringing some overt utopianizing into the mostly sterile literary consciousness of neo-Marxism. Such metatopianizing was partly an effect—but such effects become causes themselves—of the more general utopian ambience now labeled the counterculture. Where rightist-ideologue Nozick was propounding a degree of utopian tolerance (of communalism, of varied styles of living) within the defended framework of a supposed market-economy society for the socially narrow sensibility of Randians and other fetishists of a purified capitalism, leftist-ideologue Marcuse was propounding a considerably enlarged degree of utopian aspiration (of the aesthetic-erotic dimension, of varied forms of social rebellion) within the rhetorical framework of a supposed revolutionism for the culturally narrow sensibility of Marxists and other fetishists of a purified socialism. No wonder we now tend to think, from right and left, more broadly of the utopian.

My main concern here is less to damn ideologies with which I have considerable disagreement than to suggest a utopianizing heuristic. Early on (first chapter) I quoted a utopian genre critic (Suvin) who insisted on setting aside the claims that the utopian "is identified with attempts at a radically different social system." Now having considered a number of such attempts, I can only reconclude that such exclusions are arbitrary, demeaning, and most importantly, false. We pay attention to the utopian not because of its literary masterpieces (I have praised some literary utopias, but hardly found justification to claim monumentally "great works"), and not because of special characteristics of the literary genre (I have noted a variety of conventions, many of which hardly pass as "literary"), but because of interest in "a radically different social system."

Metatopianizing not only reminds us of what is at stake in utopianizing but is part of the context in which it occurs. Granted, my examples of metatopianizers, though apparently taken as important cases in recent intellectual history, are not themselves great writers, nor, as I am compelled to evaluate them, much use in creating a more artful society. Neo-Marxism surely does not provide a proper ending to considerations of utopianizing because even at best it is a reification of utopia into the subversive recesses of the mind. But it may have its utilities in again reminding us that utopianizing is mainly countering. Utopia is also always about—to insist on the obvious—consciousness of a different society. A metaphysic of utopianizing may often dubiously deploy the impetus, but it also confirms in its abstractionism the continuing need for nowhere.

Pornotopianizing

To return to the somewhat more tangible ends of utopianizing is also to remind ourselves of yet more variety of utopian accounts. A woefully unimaginative noted philosopher, polemicizing against Marcuse, sarcastically asked about his projected "aesthetic-erotic" utopia: "What will we actually do in this sexually liberated state?"[39] Granted, Marcuse usually left rather vague the results of the removal of oppressive consciousness and "false needs," as well as the liberation of fuller human potentialities. But there is, of course, a considerable literature that attempts to answer such questions, at whatever reach of liberty, love, and obscenity.

It would be altogether too nice, and too undialectical, to ignore the fact that utopianizing may be indecent, even crassly offensive and disgusting. One of the more offensive forms, to my mind, is the popular "romance." Admittedly, stock romance fictions may be viewed (à la Bloch) as mass diversions carrying utopian elements. They aspire to the ostensibly aesthetic-erotic, with not only the resolution of sexual conflicts but a happy ordering of all life. At least for its addicts, the popular romance mode certainly counters, however tritely and reductively, ordinary reality. It is no doubt compensatory for its primarily petit bourgeois female audience. If, as one analyst argues, much of romance seeks to transform pervasive feminine fears of rape, it may even have the virtues of inculcating "courage in the adversity of overcoming men."[40] But its fantasies may also overcome any glimmerings of a truly different social ordering.

Romances provide for millions of (lower-)middle-class readers, another scholar argues, "exercises in the imaginative transformation of masculinity to conform with female standards."[41] Yet, however reductive those standards (for the childish women as well as the newly confined men), for their representative consumers "romances provide a utopian vision in which female individuality and a sense of self are shown to be compatible with nurturance and care." With a forced ponderousness, this critic even finds a radical element in romance addiction: "The utopian current running through the experiences of reading may move women in ways that conflict significantly with the more conservative push effected by the story's reaffirmation of marriage to satisfy female needs completely." Thus in their expression of "utopian longing" they are a "minimal but none the less legitimate form of protest." We should not denigrate such pathetically compensatory fantasy on the way to "creating a world where the vicarious pleasure supplied by its reading would be unnecessary." Does not that conclusion, that admission of false needs, in effect undercut the pseudoutopian argument?

Puerile romance, like the somewhat less confined macho bravery and virility-proving emphasized in adventure tales for a mostly masculine audience (confirmed in competition, violence, and quasistoic endurance) also has its vicious side. It camouflages rape in dishonest and dependent marriage, and other manners of idealized subordination. It also encourages a whole ethos of male limitation, quite beyond tenderized rape—a form of prettified domination-submission, the male master mastered by the female slave in a trivialized world. Thus I see little intellectual utility in claiming, for example, that romance-hack Barbara Cartland (reportedly the most popular of all twentieth-century fictionists), or the somewhat more directly sexual Kathleen Woodiwiss, is doing anything interesting with utopian motivations for a better society and life. (Nor would a parallel consideration of the more-or-less male equivalents, such as Louis L'Amour, be pertinent.) Commonsense observation of the readers as well as the writings can only suggest that they generally subserve a deplorable sense of society and human possibility. The bad writing of fatuous ritual fantasies (romance or adventure) may draw on something similar to utopianizing motives. But it debases them, and the very notion of literacy as liberating.

So let us turn to that which was for long largely ruled out of literacy, more hardcore obscenity, and claims for it as pornotopia.[42] De Sade's prisoner fantasies, such as *Justine* (1791) and *120 Days of Sodom,* may be of clinical and historical interest, though hardly, in their obsessional redundancy, of much specifically aesthetic interest.[43] True, they have a much larger reach than the stickily confined popular romance. By which I do not mean the callow Enlightenment philosophizing on nature and liberty with which Sade garlics the sexual meat, but that a whole world is structured, from lavish meals to ludicrous architecture, in terms of cruelly exploitative sensualism. Roland Barthes, in his published notes entitled *Sade/Fourier/Loyola* (1971), suggested that the very insistence on encompassing all produced a totalism with an "exaltation that is unknown to our societies and which constitutes the most formidable of utopias."[44]

But if the elaborately removed and serviced Sadean castle of the sexually enslaved constitutes utopia beyond compensatory fantasy, it does so only in self-defeating ways. Barthes does not note that the endless ritualization (he calls it concern with "protocol") is the substitute social ordering, and a peculiarly rigid and incoherent one (essentially dependent on outside class and money power). No Sadean attempt at gratification gratifies for long, and so it is desperately multiplied in numbers, compounded in positions and pains, repeated and repeated. The iteration provides no different, much less transforming or transcending, erotic experience. According to Barthes, "the principle of Sadean eroticism is the saturation of every part of the body." More literally, every orifice is abused. "Saturation," not transformation, is the issue of the endless quest for violation. The totalism does not work. The flow of semen, however exaggerated and even when extended to excrement and pain, runs out, and turns into the flow of blood. The attempts at erotic merging become deathly (though with the cowardly inconsistent Sade, only the death of the other). Alienated and mechanical attempts at merging become murder, which does not leave much of a utopia.[45] A recent commentator, Jane Gallop (in her annotations of the annotations of each other by modernist French Sadean annotators), rightly notes that the pornographic mode is "violently impure," incoherent, a "monstrous composite of parts," not only sexual parts for people, but essentially antithetical ideas. In their very claims to liberty, "the libertines, far from free, are confined by their subordination to 'the society'" they have mirror-created.[46] They contemptibly repeat its exploitative financial, social-class, rococo architectural, and even sentimental orderings.

Sade, in spite of the extremity and revolutionary rhetoric, is not much of a utopian. A rigorous feminist, Angela Carter (in researches more thorough than mine), concluded that "most pornography remains in the service of the status quo."[47] Granted, Sade appears more radical in a few gestures, such as "claiming rights of free sexuality for women, and in installing women as beings of power in his imaginary worlds" (but in terms of the male-imitating Juliet, not her virtuous feminine sister Justine). Of whatever gender, his libertines are finally servile. Sade's peculiar personal obsession, caprophagy, is simple the literalization of social ass-kissing and shit-eating. The elaborate structuring is not incidental but essential, as with the controlling four aged prostitutes in *120 Days of Sodom* and the regimented sexual torments in what amounts to decorative prison rooms. But is he not at least countering the hypocritical moral ordering of his time? Not really, since the obsessive profanation and sacrilege reconfirm a religious insistence. It is not even very sensual. Carter rightly concludes that "Sade is a great puritan and will disinfect of sensuality anything he can . . . ; therefore he writes about sexual relations in terms of butchery and meat." Or as I would put it, the Sadean cannot stand pleasure, and so must destroy it, turn it into ritualized pain and death. This religiousized effort to take "Utopia by force" is a drastic failure of the utopianizing imagination.

Barthes elliptically linked Sadean ritualized murderous sex with ritualized punitive prayer (Loyola), and with the more traditionally recognized utopianism of Fourier, who also, Barthes holds, designed all towards erotic ends, from sweet diet (emphasizing fruit and cakes) to the architecture of the Phalanestery (Harmony). Fourier has one parallel to Sade, his quantitative conjuration with the 1,620 human types. "Love (erotic happiness, including the sentimental *eros*) is the main business of the long Harmonian day. . . . "[48] It is certainly a broader utopian end than Sadean eroticism, and requires a far different, more varied, communal, and egalitarian, social scene. Barthes (with his usual partial distortion) has summarized the archutopian: "The motive behind all Fourierist construction . . . is not justice, equality, liberty, etc., it is pleasure." And by pleasure is primarily meant the "sensual." But Fourier's sensual is far more diffuse than the Sadean assault on orifices, and the ritual-regimented violation of meat.

And far more socially transforming. It requires "justice, equality, liberty, etc." The eroticism is integral to a free and compassionate ordering. For example, Fourier keeps returning to the need to provide erotic gratification and suitable partners for the ugly and old. True utopianizing.

Surely better arrangements for erotic gratification are a major, though not always admitted, purpose as well as motive (not quite the same thing) of utopianizing. But is pornography utopian? Possibly some, but probably not the tradition coming out of the "divine Marquis." There are of course other literary pornographies—the sardonic Rochester, the genial Casanova, the smirky Frank Harris, the bumptious Henry Miller—but they are hardly noticed by the French intellectual cultists and their American epigones. Consider briefly twentieth-century Sadean porno-progeny. Nearly a generation ago the fashion-mongering Susan Sontag pronounced that "the most accomplished" of all was Georges Bataille. His *Story of the Eye* (1928) adds some hallucinatory tones to Sadean compulsive sex degradations.[50] Bataille's exceedingly gymnastic adolescents are also often pompous—"My kind of debauchery soils not only my body and thoughts, but . . . the vast starry universe"—and ornately sacrilegious (rape-murdering and dismembering a priest, after sperming the wafers and urinating in the sacramental wine). But there isn't even much sensuality, except possibly for those fixated on pissing on people. The new fillips to the old porno-decor (isolated chateaus, the mandatory voyeur English aristocrat, stock class ordering, exceptional sexual energy and availability, etc.) include violently yoked parallel surreal metaphors, especially those of boiled eggs, "bull's balls," and severed eyes (those of a matador and a priest) all avariciously inserted in the young heroine's vulva. A brief appended memoir by Bataille to the fragmented fictional scenes somewhat confusingly links the imagery to his traumatic childhood memories of his blind and incontinent syphiletic father. The concerns, then, are less of sensuality than of guilt and its muckery. And it is from those, not any erotic passion, that one hopes to engender an "exaltation" of a religio-degradation cast.

A later much praised neo-Sadean ideal fiction is the famous *Story of O* (1954) and *Return to the Chateau: Story of O (Volume 2)* (1969) by "Pauline Reage" (pseudonym).[51] This first-person account of voluntary sexual enslavement by a contemporary professional woman ends with her, and love itself, as a cheap whore (at least in volume 2; the earlier variant is her indifferent lover's permission to commit suicide). This would seem to be (regardless of ambiguities of authorship, and formal devices such as the volume 2 preface, "A Girl in Love," which gives the genesis of the tale as a mistress's "reveries" of "frightful surrender" to please a male lover) a relatively stock sadistic male fantasy, carried out more fully than usual, and including the destruction of female selfhood.[52]

Read as moral allegory, *The Story of O* sadly confirms the incompatibility of male eroticism and the female desperation for a different kind of love, which therefore becomes self-destruction. It may be taken as a harsher variant of the now widely accepted premise that, by and large, women (whether by nature or social indoctrination) have a more tactile, nonaggressive, holistic erotic responsiveness than the visual, aggressive, atomistic sexual responses of predominant males.[53] O is the ultimate female masochist, not only in her eager surrender to almost every form of male abuse and humiliation—including whipping, chains, branding, lesbian exploitation (vol. 1), indiscriminate sexual service, commercial exploitation, and (supposedly unkindest but most exalting cut of all) abandonment (vol. 2)—but in her saintly fervor "at being surrendered to a will above and beyond her own" she reaches transcendent "perfect submissiveness." More inverse religion than sensualism.

O loves not in spite of but because of pain and humiliation. She feels metaphysical pleasure in abasement as well as "physical enjoyment" whenever anyone mistreats her (her supposed special adoration of cruel Sir Stephen therefore seems inconsistent). Her progress is, says Sontag, "ascent through degradation," and the scenes are less sex than "ritual ordeals which test the faith of someone being initiated into an ascetic spiritual discipline."[54] Sex and scene are all rather stilted, including trite descriptions of the unimaginative physical environment, monotonous subcharacterizations at the vague level of male softcore romance (all the women are attractive), and compulsive orgasm under all circumstances ("unable to prevent herself from moaning with pleasure"). (Conveniently, Sontag does not give examples of what she describes as the "elegance of the writing.") The social situations, with the chateau as a businessmen's country club, and the final subordination of the plot to current economics (Sir Stephen's dealings in international trade, the finances of prostitution for the wealthy), posit little eutopian possibility or dystopian countering. While we may tolerantly not wish to restrict the pleasures (male-imagined and hoped for?) of masochistic ladies, surely they could be more effectively, less anxiously, arranged. Even on its own premises the tritely written *The Story of O* is hardly much of a pornotopia, and may be understood as masturbatory reenforcement of negative sexuality. There is little reason to take any of this sort of literature as utopian in any positive sense, its sadomasochism confirming inequality, repression, pain, religious submission. Recall that in the Ministry of Truth in *Nineteen Eighty-Four* there was a bureau, Pornosec, to produce confirming pornography for the totalitarian victims. One suspects that the pornography produced was in the Sadean tradition. There would not seem to be much of a case to be made that punitive pornography in general is liberating, though (contra censorship) it may be that certain kinds for certain people are informing and solacing. Pain for the pained, as with the romances. But there is little countering for the present, or different possibility for the future.

That should not lead to the conclusion that sexual obscenity cannot be used in nowhere narratives. Even the humiliation of a masochistic whore can be relevant, as with Fowles' development of reactive millennial utopianism in *The Maggot* (discussed in chapter 1 above). A less harsh sexual explicitness was certainly appropriate to utopianizing D. H. Lawrence in *Lady Chatterley's Lover*. Or, for a different use, take the final novel of a noted science fiction writer, Theodore Sturgeon, *Godbody* (1986).[55] Surprisingly (for the author of the ambitiously futuristic *More than Human*) this utopianizing is placed in the historical context of present-day eastern small-town America (more likely in terms of the detailing, a generation or two ago). It consists of the skilled first-person narrations of eight caricature figures responding to the miraculous: an Episcopalian minister and his pretty wife, a crooked constable, a drastically repressed banker, a perverted antisexual female editor of a weekly newspaper, a semiimpotent town stud-rapist, an eccentric local woman vanguard artist, and a village outcast-drudge-homely girl. All are sexually turned on by the arrival of a naked redhaired messiah "with a long dong," Mr. Godbody (a sort of libidinal Mr. Goodwrench). Except for the wicked witch woman editor, all are trans-formed by Godbody's dong or hand. He heals the blind, makes women superre-sponsive ("a veritable earthquake of orgasm," which one-ups Hemingway's "the earth moved"), makes the impotent tumescent, and turns all the good to practic-ing endless lovingness. His powers are transcendent, not only in inducing sus-tained erection and multiple orgasm but in the sense during coitus of a great "Presence." (But he is hardly as libidinal, or anguished, as other sexy messiahs, such as He of Kazantsakis' *Last Temptation of Christ*.) He is also sexually unimaginative, practicing and inducing only missionary-position heterosexu-ality. Such are the restrictive ways of even an eroticized Christian deity.

Sturgeon appears to have been influenced by feminist doctrine, including the eroticism posited by one woman character, "there is only one sense, and it is the sense of touch," though for the inferior male reader he provides verbal visual approximations of ecstatic sex. He also employs some fantasy pronogra-phic conventions, including a number of women unexpectedly without under-clothing, other instant sexual availability, and exceptional male prowess. The author is also a somewhat charismatic Christian of the postsexual revolution, providing a literalization of "God is love." People are "Godstruck," and good sex follows. In this porno-Episcopalianism, "If you ever want to touch the hand and the heart of God Almighty, you can do it through the body of someone you love." But, as with the sex, the mythology turns out to be conventional. The mean, antisexual, woman editor kills Godbody with a gunshot. That is on Friday. He is secretly buried but his body magically disappears on Sunday, a miracle to be worshipped. Apparently, he doesn't take his recurring messianic crucifixion role altogether seriously since his last words before his death had been "This really is a hell of a way to make a living."

But much of the rest of the pro-Christ (however anti-Pauline) message seems earnest enough, and eutopian. The minister quits his pulpit and goes forth with a small collective of the rapturous sex-redeemed—"theolepsy seems to be a group experience" (though puzzlingly there is no directly group sex, only group nudity and a fruit-and-nuts meal in a counterculture cabin)—to live a simple life of communal Christian sexual worship.[56] Again, we have the neo-primitive ordering which I have suggested may be the most fundamental utopianism.

Earnest it may be, and no doubt a more admirable Christianity than most (from a sexual and libertarian point of view), but it is not to be taken very seriously. As with much commercial sci-fi, the pat thinness of manner of pop fiction undercuts larger intentions. It also reads like self-parody in its very conception. Grafting pornography onto otherwise conventional Christianity, and magic mythology onto otherwise stock realistic fiction, can hardly provide a persuasive literary experience, or an adequate utopianizing.

But perhaps the larger mistake is in creating a literary construct. (After all, when it comes to sado-sexual use of the eye, or other surrealist imagery, Luis Buñuel on film excelled Georges Bataille in prose.) In an intriguing, if too ingenious, argument, philosopher Alan Soble defends pornography almost solely as a visual experience (photographs and movies). That may be almost empirically justified in current conditions. I am not prepared here (or in appropriate erudition) to discuss what would be the true pornotopian cinema. But Soble's larger theoretical construct might prove useful. It is based on a eutopian question: Would there be pornography in a true communist society?[57]

> The pornography that will exist in communist society can be characterized, as I have argued, in the following way: first, it will be sexually explicit material produced to induce sexual arousal and consumed for sexual pleasure . . . ;second, it will be produced by collectives of freely associated workers, and therefore will not involve degradation in production; and, third, its content will be decided by the freely associated workers who produce it and will reflect the sexual consciousness [of the different, unexploitative, society].

Many libidinal versions of a good society assume that with repressions and exploitations gone ("false needs"), sex will find some "natural" level, and additional "arousal" will hardly be necessary or desirable. Sexual self-regulation is the implicit ideal, made explicit by such utopianizers as Wilhelm Reich, Paul Goodman, and Ursula Le Guin.[58]

But that ideal may be naive, Soble argues, if there are fundamental disparities between male and female sexuality. In that case, erotic depictions may serve to inform and adjust the differences (though Soble's adjustments seem canted in one direction; for example, he repeatedly refers to images of fellatio but not to cunnilingus). His model for such sexual materials is current highly exploitative pornography. He does not even refer to D. H. Lawrence or Tantric manuals or erotic poetry or other more discriminating uses of sexual obscenity. While the crassest pornography may serve informing and arousing functions in contemporary society, is it an appropriate model for a better society, for eutopian sensuality? Even when stripped of its more obvious exploitations for commerce and alienated work, does filmed exhibitionism provide useful, or even very interesting, informing and arousing? In a less sexually ambivalent society than ours, more openness of sexual behavior may serve some of the same functions. For highly ritualized societies (which the religious, including some Marxists, seem to prefer), one could plausibly project ceremonial sex of rather more explicitness than current "beauty pageants" and similar teasing but repressive ersatz. The accounts of a libertarian communal society might well include group sex. And so on. One hardly provides a significant countering to the present, or an imaginative utopianizing construct, by mere economic cleaning up of pornography. (Does the "socialist transition" include unionizing Sadean females, under the heroic proletarian banner of Ms. O?)

Le Guin, one recalls, dramatized arguments for early homosexual and heterosexual experimentation, but within two restraints—no direct aggression (such as rape) and full privacy. Why the latter? It could be (but was not) justified on grounds of autonomy, of removing at least direct social (performance) pressure, and perhaps of fearful vulnerability. Yet many utopians, such as Plato whose women exercise naked with men, or More whose prospective couples examine each other naked before plighting their vows, show proclivities against privacy, at least in countering obvious false modesties in their actual societies. Permanent revolutionary Zamyatin, ironically, not only allowed the shades to be drawn in the One State only during official sex hours but treated the more romantic love affair with the mixed tantalizations-restraints characteristic of that tradition. The supercinematic "feelies" in *Brave New World* suggest some pornographic content. Sturgeon combined nudity for sexual arousal and mystical Christian union. Some of the femtopianists presented quasimystical lesbian eroticism of a rather specialized appeal, and authoritarianly made it exclusive femporn. Fourier appears to have enthusiastically included lesbianism and other sexual variety in openly sensual eutopian Harmony. In sum, it seems hard to generalize the presentation of erotic materials in utopias, even on a libertarian/authoritarian dialectic. Barring Platonic censorship, pornography, then, may be a properly contentious and speculative issue for utopianizing.

However, because caught up by researches in the sexual versimilitude of tritely conventional photographic pornography (and the desire to defend it against censoring bigots), the pornotopian apologists quite miss Sadean murderous sex, truly fantastic sex (unreal super organs, for example), and other pornotopian possibilities not visualizable in standard photographic ways. Standardized suck-and-fuck imagery hardly seems a utopian art. If utopianizing is about the conditions, the society, that would allow bigger and better pornography, or would encourage its displacement (for example, by replacing its pedagogical and stimulative functions with more public sexuality), pornography cannot itself be the primary subject of the eutopianizing. Pornotopia thus seems to be a contradictory notion even for those (myself included) who would argue for a more directly libidinous society.

But perhaps the issues are being put in a too confined sexual context. If utopianizing is a countering and transforming vision of society, I would include in its sensual traditions, for example, periods of violation such as the orgies of the Saturnalia (Rome), the ribald mockeries and freedoms of the Feast of Fools and periods of "misrule" (high medieval Europe), and similar permissive excesses.[59] No social ordering is so ideal as not to need a considerable degree of disordering. No erotic pattern is so satisfying as not to need a considerable place for otherness (isn't this part of what pornography is about?), for the community and not just privileged groups. Granted, the saturnalian can never in itself be the social or literary ordering. It usually appears in myth and literature as food-wine-sex-leisure fantasies, as we know in various tales and poems of the legendary Land of Cockaigne (England), Venusberg and Lubberland (on the Continent), and the Big Rock Candy Mountain (as in the American hobo ballad of that name, bowdlerized of its booze and homosexuality into a children's folk song), and in some blues and rock lyrics. These places of immediate gluttonous gratification exalt the pleasures of the body. (Recall the sprawling bodies as well as hanging pies of Brueghel's famous painting of *Schlaraffenland*.) Concern with such immediate ecstasies often gets denigratingly tied to students, poets, and other marginals, as with the late medieval Goliards, who blasphemously made the wine bottle their *summum bonum,* or with the later bohemians, beats, et al. It would be a dully restrictive good place without such people and their license.

Where many classic eutopias encouraged indulgence in the philosopher's vices of symmetrical forms and contemplations, or the politician's obsessions with hierarchical orderings, or the scientistic's compulsion for ingenious patterns, there have always been, albeit secondarily, more delightfully "irresponsible" gratifications. Modern eutopias absorb more vulgar dreams and ritualize hallucinogenics (Huxley's *Island*) or marijuana (Callenbach's *Ecotopia*), or unnice sex (some variety of contemporary eutopianizing moments in otherwise "straight" fictions). Indecorous sensuality includes noncoercive sexual swapping, incest, pedophilia, as in that Enlightenment sexual utopia, Diderot's *Supplement to Bougainville's Voyage* (1772).[60] This dialogue about a eutopianized Tahiti includes urbane but emphatic justifications for a more various sexuality, including incest and liberal exchange of partners and children, positively countering Western prohibitions. The defense of incest and public copulation, of course, go far back, as with the reports on Diogenes and other Athenian Cynics. That might be rather more interesting, and more utopian, than watching pornographic films.

More recent sexual utopianizing, often ambivalently organized around the antiutopian sexual schemata of Freudianism, are varied and many. Wilhelm Reich's *The Sexual Revolution* (1934) demands a new sexual ethos (especially for adolescents, which has partly come about), and combines with a deviant Marxian revolutionism for a new society.[61] His later sexual ethics appear more conservative, as he moved into the messianic cosmology of "orgone energy," which could not only change sexual character structures but cure cancer. A more ornately cultivated, inward-turning, and finally mystical eroticism is that of Norman O. Brown in *Life against Death* (1959) and *Love's Body* (1965).[62] Mentally, at least, his eutopia is located in a land where a "polymorphous perverse" sexuality leads to a transcendence of traditional dualisms. Such libidinal prophets go quite beyond pastoral utopian free-and-natural sexuality to something rather more encompassing and exalted.

But that tendency, too, has a long utopian, and often millennial, heritage, be it the medieval Bogomillians and Children of Light, or the revolutionary and sexually insistent Ranters in seventeenth-century England, or William Blake's transcendent "increase in sensual enjoyment" in a new Jerusalem, or D. H. Lawrence's conversion-experience eroticism. Apparently, the antinomian side of medieval Christianity helped produce literal love sects, as a kind of social antinomianism produced the "regulated promiscuity" of John Humphrey Noyes' Oneida community in nineteenth-century America, or more contemporary sexual theorizing conjoins with sexually experimental communes.[63] Were those last merely "permissive" sexual arrangements, or was there a transformation that goes beyond what is usually considered "natural" sensuality? In some fictional-tract forms, such as the novels of Robert Rimmer, the sexual eutopianism seems secular and rational: *The Harrad Experiment* (1966) of permissive student sexuality describes itself as an "exploration of new possibilities in interpersonal relations"; a sexual futuristic fiction, *The Rebellion of Yale Marratt* (1967), revolves around bigamy; *Proposition Thirty-one* (1968) turns to more deviant familial forms.[64] Such utopianizing also might remind us how restrictive are the contexts of most pornography.

My intentionally mixed bag of examples of sexual revolutionizing leaves open the question of differences of erotic ideology. Are these differences in degree, or in kind? One theorist of sexual ideologies divides the affirmative ones into Naturalist (subdivided into prevailing-moderate and radical) and Gnostic. The extreme dualism of Gnosticism (historically rooted in such movements as the Cathars, and in earlier Manichean views) resulted in a reverse libertinism, and exaltation of sexuality to break through the usual limits of sensuality to ultimate spirituality. "Pornography is the Gnostic form of sex education," with Sade as the archmodern Gnostic.[65] In this view, Sade's modern inheritors are Norman Mailer, William Burroughs (at least in the utopianizing fragments of *Naked Lunch*), Lenny Bruce, John Rechy, and Pauline Reage, writers of transforming immersion in sexual degradation. Contrast these writers with such sexual naturalists as Henry Miller and D. H. Lawrence (surely that last is wrong for Lawrence's considerably religious, redemptive, views of the sexual). Granted, they are all sexual utopians, of a sort, in projecting libidinal nowheres that counter the more limited prevailing views of erotic possibility, but it is hardly all one sacral obscenity, and certainly not all Manichean, whose inversions may be utopianistically doubtful anyway.

In answer, then, to the philosophical question of what will we "actually do in this sexually liberated state?" much erotic utopianizing variously suggests that we will have more sex and better sex in different sexual ways. It may counter prevailing sexual limitations, whether by going beyond the mere genital (and visual) to polymorphous (and more broadly tactile) experiences, and/or by going beyond mere private and individual coitus to public and group combinations, and/or by going beyond mere singular gender, role, and taboo to more, to expanded, and to intensified bodily experience. Worth trying (though my bias is towards affectionate sex). Whether that will also entail new relations with nature or spirit or mortality may be left moot here; it certainly entails new social relations and orderings (or disorderings). Not so much the new pornography as the new Passional Person seems a proper utopianizing end. But the eutopian danger may be to suggest good sex as the reward of a good society. Perhaps it would be better to update Spinoza's lovely aphorism about "happiness": Much-good-sex is not the reward of virtue, it is virtue. And utopia has always been about virtue.

Thanatopianizing

One set of ends to speculative accounts are just that, the end of *homo sapiens* (beyond being fucked to death in a neo-Sadean place). Whether self-induced by "nuclear holocaust" (discussed earlier and below), or by some other cataclysmic process such as irreversible depletion of the environment by overpopulation or other toxicity, gross and anguished total or near-total termination seems to have many possibilities. And, what with the more than possible "ozone depletion" or "greenhouse effect" changing the world climate to encompassing flood or drought, AIDS-like incurable plagues, or just exponential expansion of double-binding technological systems, the gruesomely absurd possibilities seem to be accelerating. (I am assuming, without argument, as recent dystopian projections tend to do, that with a population over five billion and interlocked and uncontrollable dependent systems, the earth is already over the line.) Such obscenities pervade contemporary consciousness, apparently with good reason, and therefore become the conditions of much utopianizing. Pick your favorite cataclysm. (With, no doubt, a paucity of fancy, instead of projecting my several cancers, I sometimes expect to be one of millions ragingly choking in a continent-wide traffic gridlock, then the vehicles firestorm in spontaneous combustion, and then. . . .) But systematize your anxieties and rages and you may be not only futuristically but imaginatively right on as you discover new combinations and consequences, and conjurations. (Are not the curse and the incantation some of the most primal literary motives?)

Given the contemporary sense of impending doom, it might seem picayune for a commentator to suggest a few discriminations. But visions of the end have been with us for some time. Armageddon and total conflagration and apocalypse are ancient themes. Even the more scientific tropes of termination are not all that new. Mary Shelley's *The Last Man* (1826) projected the extermination of mankind by plague.[66] The end of ends could be equally indifferently induced at a cosmic level by stellar collision or solar burnout. That last is the final of many phases in Stapledon's *Last and First Men* (1930), though we become rather anesthetized by so many vast rises and falls of different mankinds before the last last. It may take a special kind of sensibility, that abstractly fascinated with astronomy and cosmology (or obsessed with Pascalean fright when viewing the heavens), to focus on that perhaps distant a certainty.

But there is something unsatisfying in the pervasiveness of easy eschatology in much contemporary fiction. One of the claims sometimes made for formula fiction such as sci-fi is its pessimism about the results of technology. However, one of its more thoughtful practitioners, Stanislaw Lem, reasonably notes the contradiction:

> Because the end of the world, the atomic Last Judgement, the epidemic provoked by technology, the freezing, drying up, crystallization, burning, sinking, the automation of the world, and so on, no longer have any meaning in science fiction today. They lost their meaning because they underwent that typical inflation that changes eschatological horror into the pleasant creeps.[67]

In pat assumptions of universal debacle, the struggle with the dialectic of meaning, the consciousness of values, has been defeated.

One can arrive at that same pyrrhonistic wisdom by less metamelodramatic considerations. It only takes some much slighter deviations in the mixture of "chance and necessity" that seems to determine our world to bring humankind to a terminal condition. But my lack of interest in sixty-five-million-year epochs (is not that the backspace to the extinction of the dinosaurs?), and longer (as some sci-fi has it), may disqualify me from considering the more cosmic modes of utopianizing. For humanly usable truths, the cosmological metaphors seem about as relevant as Revelation (or Poe's "Malestrom") or other overextended poetry in flight from human ambiguity and other actuality.

Evolutionary metaphors often seem more persuasively shorter than cosmological tropes (a couple of million years at most for something similar to the human?), with two hundred or so generations (since pervasive neolithic conditions?) the more manageable outside perspective, and cultural coherence considerably less than that. In modern utopianizing (to get really short-term) evolutionary tropes have certainly played key roles (as with the H. G. Wells touched on earlier), but actually as subordinated to a positive telos, to ever upwards notions of progress *(Men Like Gods)*. Much of that now appears to be intolerably optimistic. The contemporary temper, a sampling of its utopian fictions suggests, is more likely to see disaster patterns as providing the appropriate plots for the larger human narratives. Among other modernist liberations of the imagination has been that of Thanatos for not only the individual and the society but the world. But without an alternative world, a utopia, life-in-death has been submerged in death-in-death.

Disaster paradigms are rather uncertainly evolutionary. If I understand rightly the neo-Darwinian outline, evolution for the most part develops by interlocked mutation, adaptation, and perpetuation, but only within limits that do not include many drastic changes of the environment. Even with the "punctuated" modifications (Stephen Jay Gould, and others), the changes are in human terms slower than slow.[68] Apparently not so with the radiation, hydrocarbonization, population, and other destructive patterns technocratically engendered. Obviously evolution carries no guarantees against human extinction. Quite the contrary, given the slow specialization of adaption. And guarantees of advancement of humane sensibility?

The contrary was developed in the poetic-prose reverse utopianizing of William Golding's novel *The Inheritors* (1955).[69] That fiction mockingly takes off (as so many have) from H. G. Wells, specifically with an ironically used quote from the *Outline of History* envisioning "Neanderthal man" as the source of the "ogre." Countering Wells' rationalistic optimism, Golding sets up a dialectic with Neanderthal-like primitives versus the "new people" *(homo sapiens sapiens)* who are our forerunners. The last communal family of the earlier people are matriarchal (and goddess worshiping), mostly vegetarian, empathetic, peaceful. The coming "new people" are patriarchal, not only meat-eating but cannibalistic, guilt-tormented, aggressive, destructive. The prelapsarians (the family around Lok) are, of course, obliterated. For the rather Manichean Golding, the result is the darkness of human evil as well as literal darkness. The utopian scene (as also in the just preceding, but perhaps less persuasive because rancorously parodistic, *Lord of the Flies*) allows the exfoliation of destructive fears and forces. The Golden Age (though a considerably shadowed one) is lost again, partly by natural change, partly by nasty humanization. Evolution may actually have been devolution, especially in terms of empathetic, imaginative (especially pictorial), and moral sensibility. It can also be seen (as in sci-fi by Lem) as another undressing of the imperial pretenses of man. Such dystopianizing is implicitly an argument for the eutopics of modest decency.

While in theory contemporary utopia can as well be posthistory as prehistory, future as well as past noplaces, for more than a generation now most expansive utopias are nuclear-haunted places. All peoples, not just old or new, are at risk. In critically annotating (first chapter, above) a couple of 1950s postnuclear utopianizings—*Limbo* and *A Canticle for Leibowitz*—I only passingly noted how optimistic their very grimness now seems. While each presupposed vast destruction (only a portion of North America even left habitable) and megamass death, an all-too-ordered society lavishly, and again destructively, recreated itself (in a generation for the rather too manipulative Wolfe, in centuries for the rather more serious Miller). Later postcataclysmic fictions (even some of Ursula Le Guin's Hainish cycle) abandon Earth for far distant space.

Granted, the establishment futurist ideologues (not utopianists with alternative societies but mere linear prognosticators, quite a different cast of mind) held out fictions—formally described as "scenarios"—of a horrendous blandness. Herman Kahn, *On Thermonuclear War: Thinking about the Unthinkable* (1962), without much sensitive thinking posited half the population left "alive," and after a bit of gung-ho bureaucratic reordering to clean up the mess, American "civilization" again rocketing merrily along. While analogous to the continuing optimistic technotopian mystagoguery (described in earlier chapters), such blandness—not to mention remarkable obtuseness as to what happens to human communities, I take it from later writings in the mode (Jonathan Schell and others)—the postnuclear now seems considerably less tolerable.[70]

I do not mean to suggest that the postnuclear imagination is all one. In my "American Apocalypse: Notes on the Bomb and the Failure of Imagination" (a brief mid-1960s survey of literary responses to Hiroshima), I noted a variety of inadequate responses.[71] The novelized documentaries (such as those by John Hersey, Robert Trumbull, and others) seem both too tritely reductive (random representative figures) and too artful (fictional, genre, stylizations), leaving an after-taste of manipulated and narrow feeling. The memoirs of pained remaining *Hibak'sha* (such as those analyzed by Robert Jay Lifton, *Death in Life: Survivors of Hiroshima* [1967]) seem so burdened with "survivor's guilt" as to deny any other perspective.[72] So do the essentially sentimental literary responses to it. As with other partly parallel literature of "the self in extremity" (to borrow from Donald Gutierrez's thoughtful discussion)—such as Nazi "death camps," Stalin's Gulag, and the continuing literature of incarceration, torture, and organized murder—we are left with a most perplexed sense of the human.[73] Are we not also left with a sense of the utopianizing need for a quite different world?

Perplexed not least in our sense of the inadequacy of literature to "witness" the horrors of the twentieth century, including those of the perhaps hundred million direct victims of state violence. Obviously the limitations are not merely literary. But documentaries, memoirs, histories, theories, fictions about the bomb hardly capture even the obvious institutional evil, the primary nuclear horror, which is the purpose, development, use, and meaning of the modern technocratic state. And the predominance of that state may itself be taken as the confirmation of human devolution, as much Golden Age utopianizing seems to know.

Historians of civilizations (such as Fernand Braudel) make much of quantitative differences in population, with rises and falls changing whole orderings. What of the far more drastic and horrendous changes, even if not oblivion, from nuclear war? Utopianizing about nuclear holocaust starts, then, at a considerable disadvantage. However limited Miller and Wolfe were in their doctrinizing, their postdisaster fictions at least struggled with some of the perplexities. The same cannot be said of more popular novels, such as Nevil Shute's *On the Beach* (1957). This is a sentimentally trite and stilted portrayal of an American submarine crew and a few Australians, in the last six months of human life on earth as radiation poisoning completes its effects, which insists that nothing really changes. The usual feelings and social arrangements prevail until the retching end. Though termination seems rather due, because of irritating newspapers and a vague failure to appreciate things as they were, these suburbanites prepare for the end only by acting a bit nicer. This faith in the relentless middle-class commonplaces is, if one can ignore the stupidity and triviality, almost awesome. Pat Frank's *Alas, Babylon* (1959), a more vulgar and bouncy version of postnuclear society, has the small-town stalwarts re-creating American pseudocivilization, on their own, complete with vigilante-style hanging of the evil urban survivors, in optimistic spite of "the thousand year night."

The relentless American commonplaces do wear thin. Probably the most noted anti-Vietnam war novelist, Tim O'Brien (*Going after Cacciato* [1979]), worries the forty-year fear into middle-aged resignation in *The Nuclear Age* (1985).[74] With small utopianizing displacement, his 1995 one-time war protester (who also profited from uranium) imprisons his family while he despairingly digs a hole to escape the bomb in his suburban Montana backyard. Has he madly lost a sense of reality?

> Reality, it tends to explode.
>   . . . And because I'm sane, because I can imagine an unpeopled planet, because life is so precious, because I've seen the flashes, I am willing to recognize the facts for what they are. . . . Is it uncouth to speak plainly? Nuclear war. . . . Here, now, digging, my wife and daughter locked away, the hole egging me on, am I crazy to extrapolate doom from the evidence all around me, Minuteman and Backfire, a world stockpiled with 60,000 warheads? Are the numbers too bald, too clumsy? Am I indiscreet to say it? Nuclear war.

Apparently O'Brien is too discreet to say it in the present. Though he wishes to respond to the current nuclear madness, displacing it into the future optimistically abstracts it, a little, makes it hopefully quaint, without risking the current issue of disallegiance, or much countering.

O'Brien's antihero prepares to beat the bomb by blowing up his family in his backyard hole, but sentimentally reverses. He knows that this "world will surely end," the inescapable logic of the "terminal equation." But he wills to "believe" the "steadfast orthodoxy" of good husband-father-citizen:

> I will firm up my golf game and invest wisely and adhere to the conventions of decency and good grace. I will find forgetfulness. Happily, without hesitation, I will take my place in the procession from church to grave, believing what cannot be believed, that all things are renewable, that the human spirit is undefeated and infinite, always.

As always with fideism, faith based on despair, the ironies dissolve in affirming the commonplace that is, thus denying real utopian possibility. Utopian conventions, we are again reminded, can be used for the most paltry responses, and for the affirmation of things as they are, however inadequate.

In a recent impressively ranging survey of such material, David Dowling's *Fictions of Nuclear Disaster,* the metautopian patterns are striking.[75] Though the work is socially naive, it still indicates that a great many American and British tales of postnuclear holocaust society turn out to be essentially "pastoral." (This is also the case, incidentally but sometimes more than that, in many of the fictions whose social views he does not discuss.) This observation might be taken as further confirmation of my arguments that the pastoral (understood in part as the redoing of man's essentially neolithic nature) provides our major eutopianizing traditions, but several harsh qualifications should be noted. Even for these returns to a simple and natural society, the nuclear holocaust must be assumed to be more moderate than a good many informed analysts currently project, what with "nuclear winter," worldwide radiation, and the rest. Also, a vision of a neoprimitive future, especially in America, may be less pastoral than "survivalist," that subterranean widespread ideology of guerrilla military tactics, fascistic social hatreds, and do-it-yourself enterprise. AynRandian and similar uncompassionate and uncooperative utopianizing of aggrandizing egotism does not provide a pretty prospect under disaster conditions. Morally as well as physically, even premising improbable ameliorist possibilities, life among the radioactive ruins may well be viewed as an invasively cancerous condition.

Putting, I earlier suggested, postnuclear alternate societies in the perspective of the twentieth-century literature of holocaust and other deathly extremity may suggest an impossible demand. Not only the postnuclear projection of bland middle-class pieties of pop sentimental fictions, or of neoprimitive dreams (survivalist, femtopian, pastoral), or of science fiction flights into space supposedly to recreate a botched civilization, but any effort may be beyond persuasive literary possibility. The arts of the word can hardly do justice—one knows on one's nerves by even petty analogous experiences of war, prison, and pain—to the death camps, the Gulag, Hiroshima, and their smaller but no less bitter continuations, or their ultimate culmination in "the bomb that's slaved all human consciousness/ and made the body universe a place of fear" (Allen Ginsberg, "Witchita Vortex Sutra"). Still, utopianizing that seems oblivious to that condition, or to the order of technocratized bureaucracies that have directly created it, must seem rather trivial in its premises and in its ends. If one lives in a time when the whole world threatens to become, if it has not already become, an encompassing "death camp," perhaps we must require some of the wisdom of the survivors (as paraphrased by Des Pres): "Sanity depended on always expecting the worst. . . . "[76]

Utopianizing, I have been arguing all along, is always contingent on its context, our context. Whether revaluating the optimistic eutopias of the past, countering the dystopias of the present, or projecting utopias of the future, they require some sense of human devolution, mass destruction, and final obliteration. Otherwise we are back in dehumanized fantasy. To be richly responsive in utopianizing requires, however paradoxically, a strong sense of not only human actuality but passional possibility, which means also of its limits in absolute mortality and of its alternative in a different order. The later Tolstoy, that most utopian of moralists (in his literal rational Christian ethics) yet the least utopian of fictionists (in his insistence on the contingent) was probably right. His dying everyman concludes (in a passage late in "The Death of Ivan Ilyich," a passage marked by fervent editorial intrusion):

> "Maybe I did not live as I ought to have done," it suddenly occurred to him. "But how could that be, when I did everything properly?" he replied, and immediately dismissed from his mind this, the sole solution of the riddles of life and death. . . .[77]

The acknowledged alternative is that life is "horrible and senseless," which may be a crucial recognition but cannot be a resolution. The dialectic between how to truly live and the sense of meaninglessness (including its intrusive awareness of the inadequacy of any art) may be a true end of utopianizing. Mortality, not just of the individual but of society and the world, may be an essential awareness, the dystopia that should always be with us.

Detopianizing

It may not be quite sufficient to conclude that utopianizing is largely about love and death in the real world. Is not that rather deutopianizing? But it should be evident that in such senses I have been detopianizing all along.

My further conclusion is by way of introducing what I perhaps should have done. (After all, this is a utopianistically countering book in several senses.) To discuss utopianizing is, of course, at least implicitly to propose a utopia. The subject is sufficiently large and varied that the exclusions and emphases themselves constitute utopian choices. or at least counterchoices. We properly know our critics by the company they refuse. Those who refuse the utopian possibilities, whether by rejection of alternatives or trivializing definitions or endless relativism, in effect propose the status quo as sufficient. That fearful dogmatism may be, given the deathly impermanence of all things human, the most extreme utopianizing of all, fixating what is already nowhere. Is this study, too, properly guilty?

Skepticism shows through. If I were further to propose my own utopia, I might start with something old (I have suggested that they all really do), such as the motto that the greatly learned, humorous, and embracing Renaissance individualist, Rabelais, put on the arch of the Abbey Thélème (his inverted monastic utopia): "Do What Thou Will." But that hardly concludes the issue, for that was but the entrance to the simulacrum of a better world. And what is it we would really will? At a metatopianizing level we are left with the will to desire. And that suggests that we do not reduce the deeper impetus to its transitory utopian forms. Self-conscious utopianizing, at least, always contains major antiutopian impetuses. Thus the arches within the utopian building might contain further warnings from utopians, such as: "Freedoms made into objects become human enslavements" (Berdyaev); "What is important is the idea of utopia that overcomes utopia in its untruth and sustains it in its truth" (Tillich); and, most simply, "Anything that *triumphs,* perishes" (Lawrence).[78] It is not incidental that so many moderns kept rewriting their eutopias/dystopias. Even counterdesiring is not to be so simply resolved.

If utopianizing, then, is by and large a dialectical, a countering and self-countering, process, then this incomplete and inadequate survey from contemporary contexts might well conclude with some deutopianizing. In that spirit, I offer some partial counterings to my own emphases. Otherwise put: If I were to further pursue utopianizing, what would I be after?

A bit more substantial treatment of several of the recurring issues might be desirable. For example, about most of the works, past and present, I raised some "feminist issues," that is, gender questions, concern with the role of women, criticisms of femtopias as well as male-bigoted utopias, and the like. While at least as old as Plato, that is surely an especially contemporary context of consideration. No apology, I think, is due for my utopianistic emphasis on gender equality (held, though, as meaningful only as part of a more general egalitarianism) and on a more androgynous character and style. But I did not come up with any adequate example of a truer androgynous ordering. Androgyny as an ideal for human change does not, of course, settle all the gender issues, or, I insist against my brother feminists, many other social issues.

All through, also, I have suggested that neopastoral utopianizing in several senses provides prime traditions of ideal society, and continues to do so. It certainly is a far more pervasive context of utopian values than is usually acknowledged. But I avoided, partly through ignorance, more fully justifying why our continuing sense of community and humane order must be of the relatively primitive sort that underlies our neopastoral aesthetic. It may be that the literature, even when extended a bit beyond the usual categories (as I attempted to do), does not adequately explain the necessary appeal of the green and golden places.

And there lies another problem: the broad inadequacy of utopian literature. For my extension beyond the genres must presuppose that the usually accepted senses of what constitutes the literature are insufficient. However apt my objections to the narrow views, was it not rather disingenuous of me to insist that the subject was not any specifiable body of literature but a larger utopianizing impetus? Perhaps, but there is a yet larger issue involved: the inadequacy of *any* literature to the human impetuses beyond it. While I think literature interesting and important, I would argue (but have not yet) that it is a large fallacy of misplaced concreteness (or, if you prefer, idolatry) to mistake it for the full human motives and purposes. Or even to pretend that it adequately reflects them.

While the insufficiency, unto falsity, of literature is especially evident for formulaic fictions—romance, pornography, sci-fi, etc. (though even they may occasionally be violated or overreached so as to turn into something more)—the inadequacy is more general. Now, utopianizing taken in broader ways is not a formula, though some of its forms have been so used. As formula, the utopian is frequently boring and bleak. To wade through an additional few dozen classical utopias, or a handful of late nineteenth-century reformist utopias, or several dozen recent sci-fi fictions, or a pile of histories of utopias (all of which I conscientiously did as part of the prepatory context for this study, though sparing the reader much of it) may be to conclude that nowhere is no way. But is it all that different from reading, say, medieval poems (until one gets to Villon), or earlier romantic tales (until one gets to Laclos), or modern ambiguous fables (until one gets to "Bartleby") . . . or epics, or poems about nature, or recent novels (until one gets to the rare outstanding work)? Literary critical strategies, whether by genre, or subject, or period—or as here, by attempting to combine them—may be essentially wrong-headed. The categories as such, including utopian narratives (whether as type, issue, or intellectual history), may not only be falsifying but, equally bad, tedious.

Perhaps, then, some other dialectical strategy would better capture the utopianizing impetuses. That purpose (to repeat my opening emphasis), those ends, are rather more important than the strategy itself. Quite possibly, then, there might be better ways to grab onto the significance of, say, Zamyatin-Le Guin radical utopianizing, or femtopian aspiration, or pastoral vision, or erotic and thanatopian awareness, and still recognize that they are but local habitations of larger concerns. But the dialectics certainly do need some breadth, perhaps more than I can muster.

If in the concern with that enlargement my focus has been too ideological, especially with social questions, what better place to lean that way than with the utopian? Considerations of proposed alternative societies cannot decently ignore social issues. (Indeed, if I erred I suspect that it was less in my social emphasis than in not following it further out of the literature into other experiential social realities.) But a better objection might be that those concerns—such as with freedom and equality, community and resistance, eroticism and death—are certainly not confined to utopian narratives, nor even broader utopian materials, but are so basic as to be far more pervasive. Quite possibly utopianizing should be considered even further in nonutopian contexts. On my own premises, the utopian only suggests some dimensions of larger but quite tangible desires, denials, and needs. Perhaps better ways to deal with the utopian would include deutopianizing, demythicizing even further the quasifantasies that locate the immediate no where.

Detopianizing partly includes never treating the utopian as merely utopian, but as about the here and now. Yet it also goes beyond that. Early on I drew on the argument that most dystopias carried an at least implicit eutopia, and with the more radical (in the sense of getting to the root of the matter) it was more than just implicit. Antiutopia may be better understood as counterutopia. All too many eutopias turn out, of course, to be implicit dystopias. According to an early-considered argument, that was because actual society is too "complex" to be adequately contained in a projected literary vision of society. Of course. But does the "social novel"—or the social document or history or reportage—adequately present the complexity of social experience? Or, in spite of the remarkable literary efforts of Joyce and others, do we have truly adequate accounts of the complexity of actual psychological experience? Leaving aside considerable doubts as to whether complexity is itself always useful, interesting, or virtuous, most literature is a simplification of human actions in simplified images of society. Possibly the utopian is sometimes somewhat more so, but that is more likely to be a difference in degree than in kind. Therefore we might respond to the utopian as we respond to much else in, and out of, literature.

Detopianizing—that is, emphasizing the continuity of the utopian with other experiences—need not deny some peculiarities of utopianizing. It tends to be of other times and/or places. It tends to represent a somewhat alternative, or at least variant, society. It tends to use some recognizable conventions from "classical" utopias (More-Plato), or sci-fi (especially post-Wells), or modern dystopias (Huxley-Orwell), or new pastoral or old fable or whatever are the modish fictional forms. Or/and utopianizing uses conventions from nonliterary utopian activities (communes, collectives, kibbutzim, etc.), or conventions from utopianizing doctrines (millennial Christianity, socialism, capitalist reformism, radical schooling, revolutionary ecology, futurist technology, visionary city planning, feminism and antifeminism, erotic ideologies, religious cults, psychological theories, etc.). Or it combines several of them and/or parodies others. It tends to be expository, argumentative, tendentious, thus violating narrative and fictional conventions (including its own) for, shall we say, essay, report, dream, and sermon. Tends, tends, tends. While not everything goes, at least successfully, not much is excludable, at least in terms of utopianizing possibility.

There is, then, no clearly definable utopian literature. My selection of examples, partly conventional and partly a bit expansive, is considerably arbitrary, as are most selections. Detopianizing with a vengeance my utopianizing arguments? Rather more insisting on several other purposes. One emphasized here has been the countering, the reversing of other utopias, including even one's own, and the revision of social realities. But like most fundamental arguments, that is a bit circular. Define utopia as a counterordering; then, when faced with a fantasy that is not significantly countering, judge it not to be really utopian (as I have several times done). While probably unavoidable, the circularity suggests not only some self-skepticism but the need to regularly move the argument out and beyond itself. The issue may be less the condition of circularity than how big the circle, how much the discussion encompasses. So, too, with the arbitrariness of any selection. Let it at least be interesting, enlarging, provocative, countering. Even in critical method, proper utopianizing includes detopianizing.

Another example of this conclusion as introduction. I have often been treating utopianizing as the concern with "alternative societies." That is fairly commonplace, and, of course, not a little misleading. For the concern is not neutral, not the mere speculative engagement in variety, but the passionate desire for a quite different and considerably better society.

Different and better, I repeat again, because (as I have noted in several contexts) that provides a more plausible sense of utopianizing than the emphasis on the ideal and perfect, which can be smugly dismissed as unrealistic and impossible. Passionate desires, as we know all too well, are dangerous conditions. The passion for a different society draws on mixed motives. There are some good as well as many bad reasons that "utopian" is often a pejorative term. As I have been repeatedly quick to nail down with individual cases, utopianizing is full of fears, escapes, fantasies, resentments, destructions. No engagement with the utopian dare seriously ignore that recurrent underside. But to hammer the negative should not mean to consign the whole corpus to a terminally closed box. Critics may rightly be analogized to morticians but neither should be overeager to practice their talents. (Perhaps a few times I have impatiently done so.)

I have also applied my version of anarchism (as well as atheism and even a bit of neonihilism) to a number of utopian social and aesthetic cruxes. That is part of my passionate desire for the different and better. And not to do so would have been less than candid. Still, I have not proposed that any particular utopia, or even method of utopianizing, adequately meets my demands and aspirations. So I have been counterutopianizing all along. Detopianizing seems an essential part of the countering dialectics of utopianizing. May it contribute its mite to a different, possibly even a better, world, or at least to some counterings of this one.

Notes

Chapter 1

1. Michael Holquist, "How to Play Utopia," in *Game, Play, Literature,* ed. Jacques Ehrmann (Boston, 1968), pp. 106–23 (in sequence: pp. 107, 111, 119, 122–23). Gaming would more appropriately apply to science fiction, but even there one of the better practitioners holds that such an application defeats the innovation that intellectually justifies the mode. Stanislaw Lem, "Reflections on My Life," *Microworlds* (New York, 1984), p. 188

2. For example, see my discussion of T. E. Lawrence parodying war-game rules in the Battle of Tafileh, "The Intellectual as Soldier," in *T. E. Lawrence,* ed. Jeffrey Meyers (London, 1988).

3. Darko Suvin, "Defining the Literary Genre of Utopia: Some Historical Semantics, Some Genealogy, A Proposal, and a Plea," *Studies in the Literary Imagination* (1973): 121–45. I am quoting from his slightly revised version in his *Metamorphoses of Science Fiction,* "On the Poetics and History of a Literary Genre" (New Haven, 1979), quotations in sequence: pp. 38, 40, 42, 50, 53, 61.

4. Some examples are indicated at the end of this chapter.

5. See for illustrations, Ira Shor, "Learning How to Learn: Conceptual Thought in a Utopia Course," in *Critical Teaching and Everyday Life* (Boston, 1980), pp. 155–81.

6. In his final chapter, pp. 270–83, Suvin discusses Capek but denigrates *R. U. R.,* as against the sci-fi prose fiction *War against the Newts,* for form as well as politics.

7. Gary Saul Morson, *The Boundaries of Genre* (Austin, 1981), with quotes in order from pp. 73, 74, 75, 76, 115, 82, 92, 93.

8. Curiously, his definitions of "antiutopia" are much more open, so much so that Conrad's *Under Western Eyes* becomes a major example, p. 81, in spite of being without an alternative society, etc. Unexamined political bias, again, towards the radical.

9. As, among others, the Zamyatin and Le Guin discussed in chapter 2.

10. Frank E. Manuel, "Toward a Psychological History of Utopias," in *Utopias and Utopian Thought* (Boston, 1986), p. 95.

11. Frank E. Manuel and Fritzie P. Manuel, *Utopian Thought in the Modern World* (Cambridge, Mass., 1979), p. 814. For a sustained critique of the Manuels' suggestive but loose "constellations" of utopian thought, see J. C. Davis, "The History of Utopia: The Chronology of Nowhere," in *Utopias,* ed. Peter Alexander and Roger Gill (London, 1984), pp. 1–17. Davis'

own historical definition is the "institutional and organizational means of producing stable and ordered societies," p. 15. But since he carries this so far as to deny change—"The dynamic utopia is a myth," p. 13—not much since early utopias is allowed, which makes the definition not very useful and uninteresting.

12. David Bleich, *Utopia, The Psychology of a Cultural Fantasy* (Ann Arbor, 1984), p. 127.

13. I have developed some of this idea in "Twisting American Comedy," *Arizona Quarterly* 43 (Autumn 1987).

14. As has been mildly done by Peter Rupert, *Reader in a Strange Land: The Activity of Reading Literary Utopias* (Athens, Ga., 1986); see especially chapters 1, 6, and 7.

15. See Rupert, pp. 78–97; Robert C. Elliott, *The Shape of Utopia: Studies in a Literary Genre* (Chicago, 1970), pp. 25ff.

16. Voltaire, *Candide, or Optimism,* trans. John Butt (London, 1947), chapter 18.

17. Voltaire, chapter 19. I am modifying a bit the emphasis of Peter Gay, *The Englightenment,* v. 1 (New York, 1966), pp. 197–203.

18. Elliott, p. 139, emphasized the reversal.

19. D. H. Lawrence, *The Collected Letters,* v. 1, ed. Harry T. Moore, p. 307. For a fuller account, see Harry T. Moore, *The Priest of Love* (New York, 1974), p. 213.

20. D. H. Lawrence, *The Complete Short Stories,* v. 3 (London, 1977), pp. 722–46. I am modifying a bit the interpretation I first made in "D. H. Lawrence and the Art of Nihilism," *Kenyon Review* 20 (1958).

21. See my discussions of this major issue in Lawrence's fictions: "Desire and Denial, Dialectics of Passion in Lawrence," *D. H. Lawrence Review* 18 (Fall 1986); "Desire and Negation," in *The Spirit of D. H. Lawrence: Centenary Studies,* ed. Gamini Salgado and G. K. Das (London, 1988).

22. I have further placed this in various contexts in "Lawrence and the Nietzschean Matrix," in *D. H. Lawrence and Tradition,* ed. Jeffrey Meyers (London, 1985); and in "D. H. Lawrence," *Dictionary of Literary Biography,* ed. Thomas F. Staley (Detroit, 1985).

23. D. H. Lawrence, *Lady Chatterley's Lover* (New York, 1959). I am drawing on my heavily annotated "The Pertinence of Modern Pastoral: The Three Versions of *Lady Chatterley's Lover,*" *Studies in the Novel* 5 (1973): 298–313.

24. As in *Lady Chatterley,* p. 351, from where the other quoted phrases also come.

25. Paul Theroux, *Mosquito Coast* (Boston, 1982), hereafter cited in text *(MC).* As with some of the other subjects discussed below, I am not aware of any significant study.

26. Probably a dig, as with a number of points, at contemporary counterculture economics (see chapter 4).

27. John Fowles, *The Maggot* (New York, 1986), hereafter cited in text *(Maggot).*

28. Here is another problem in utopian definition. For example, see J. C. Davis, *Utopia and the Ideal Society: A Study of English Utopian Writing, 1516–1700* (Cambridge, England, 1981), who separates ideal-society rationales from the millennarian (and the arcadian, cockaygne, and moral-commonwealth) imperatives. The millennarian is seen as essentially different from the

others because attributed to the deity rather than man (p. 36). Fowles apparently holds the opposite, a point I will return to below.

29. For the generally accepted history, see Edward D. Andrews, *The People Called Shakers* (New York, 1963).

30. A contemporary feminist accolade of the long-enduring Shaker utopianism grants that though they showed exceptional equality of the sexes for the time, when it came to work, "gender roles among the Shakers were differentiated and traditional." Ruby Rohrlich, "The Shakers: Gender Equality in Hierarchy," in *Women in Search of Utopia,* ed. R. Rohrlich and Elaine Hoffman Baruch (New York, 1984), p. 58.

31. Fowles' concern with impassioned egalitarianism beyond playing the historian and novelist seems evident in James R. Baker, "An Interview with John Fowles," *Michigan Quarterly Review,* 25 (1986): 661–83. Not touched on are the difficulties in much of Fowles between egalitarianism and the exaltation of exceptional individuals.

32. See, for example, Judith N. Shklar, *After Utopia: The Decline of Political Faith* (Princeton, 1957, 1969). Her main theme seems to be the inevitability of the "decline of rational political optimisim" (p. ix), and she takes utopianism as in a broad way representing this (p. 219). The view was obviously more ideological than historical, as also with the more vehement antiutopianism of the very influential Karl Popper, "Utopia and Violence," *Conjectures and Refutations* (London, 1962), which restates a major issue of both volumes of his *The Open Society,* 4th ed. (London, 1950, 1962). As best I can order the intellectual history, such establishment doctrine changed the connotations of "utopia" from the positive value for change against established ideology, which had attached to it in Karl Mannheim's well-known 1920s definition, *Ideology and Utopia* (London, 1952), to utopianism as an outmoded, and often threatening, ideology. This sense influences a number of theories, including probably those of genre that I previously cited.

33. Ayn Rand, *Atlas Shrugged* (New York, 1957); the utopia section is pp. 701–815, though the justifying diatribe appears later, pp. 1019–69. For a rather simple-minded survey, see Mimi Reisel Gladstein, *The Ayn Rand Companion* (Westport, Conn., 1984), chapter 2, on the fiction.

34. The later "Introduction" (1968) to what is probably her best-known fiction, *The Fountainhead* (Indianapolis, 1943, 1968), p. x. This is not directly a utopia but centers on a utopianist-capitalist architect. Her earlier dystopian novel, *Anthem* (Caldwell, Idaho, 1946), is not only mercifully less redundant but draws on science fiction conventions (Zamyatin?) and includes the post-nuclear war reinvention of electricity (mentioned below) by a supposedly heroic entrepreneur.

35. Rand's emphasis on egoism is sometimes bracketed with Max Stirner's nineteenth-century reversed-Hegelian extreme individualism, including his "Union of Egoists." But Stirner was radically against "moral ghosts," which mark Rand's simple moralizing. For example, for Stirner "freedom of trade" was not to come from a market system (always antiindividual for most) but from "smuggling." *The Ego and His Own* (1844), ed. John Carrol (London, 1971), p. 230.

36. One of the more genial accounts of some of this is Jerome Tuccille, *It Usually Begins with Ayn Rand* (New York, 1972), though he does rather misuse my earlier comments on the movement. More ponderous academic-cult accounts appear in *The Philosophical Thought of Ayn Rand,* ed. Douglas Den Uly and Douglas Rasmussen (Urbana, Ill., 1984). Professor Rasmussen advised me (private conversation, July 1980) that the contemporary Libertarian Party was inconceivable

without Rand's influence. There are many other works in this tradition; for a collectivist dystopia transformed into a capitalist eutopia by historical cultural processes, see Henry Hazlitt, *The Great Idea* (New York, 1951).

37. Since I am not developing this example, see, for a balanced recent discussion, Howard P. Segal, "Vonnegut's *Player Piano:* An Ambiguous Technological Dystopia," in *No Place Else: Explorations in Utopian and Dystopian Fiction,* ed. Eric S. Rabkin, Martin H. Greenberg, and Joseph D. Olander (Carbondale, Ill., 1983), pp. 162–81. A useful fuller discussion is Stanley Schatt, *Kurt Vonnegut, Jr.* (Boston, 1976).

38. Walter M. Miller, Jr., *A Canticle for Leibowitz* (New York, 1960). There have been a number of discussions of this, for example the enthusiastic exposition of it (and its old-fashioned Catholicism) as "exemplary" (except for its lack of feminism) by David Dowling, *Fictions of Nuclear Disaster* (London, 1987), pp. 193–201.

39 *Canticle,* p. 69. The book shrewdly recognizes a variety of alternative societies, including the dominant pastoral: "simple clanfolk loosely organized into small communities . . . who lived by hunting, gathering, and primitive agriculture." In the sparsely populated North America of the first postbomb centuries, the main activities for most "were hunting, farming, fighting, and witchcraft—the last the most promising 'industry' for any youth with a choice of career," p. 61.

40. *Canticle,* p. 219.

41. *Canticle,* pp. 312 and 314. This is a countering response to a compassionate, atheistic doctor. With Miller's emphasis on conservative Catholic ritual and dogmatism (including taboos against abortion even of radiation monsters, one of whom is spiritually beatified at the end, and against suicide even for those dying of radiation), the meaning is not as heretical as this speculation suggests. But apparently a more respresentative traditional Catholic view is that of Thomas Molnar, *Utopia: The Perennial Heresy* (New York, 1967), which pronounces all utopianism to be "moral evil" against divine order.

42. For an uncritical exposition of Hobban's fiction, see Dowling, pp. 201ff. I grant that because of the movement towards community, this may be a disputable case.

43. See the previously cited studies of Suvin and of Davis.

44. I am drawing my examples from a variety of sources, of which the most useful may be Manuel, *Utopian Thought in the Western World,* but my emphasis rather differs.

45. Wells is further discussed (and studies cited) below.

46. H. G. Wells, *A Modern Utopia* (Lincoln, Neb., 1967), p. 60.

47. H. G. Wells, *Men Like Gods* (London, 1923). For the statement on education, p. 59. The rulers are called "samurai," a point often cited to confirm Wells' authoritarian tendency, but he seems to have been using it rather naively.

48. *Men Like Gods,* pp. 243 and 264.

49. Others, of course, have made similar points. "Utopias are . . . distinguished from fantasy because they presuppose no miracles of nature or improbable physiological developments." Elizabeth Hansot, *Perfection and Progress, Two Modes of Utopian Thought* (Cambridge, Mass., 1971), p. 3.

50. *Men Like Gods,* p. 212.

51. H. G. Wells, *Mind at the End of Its Tether* (New York, 1946), pp. 17–18.

52.   R. Buckminster Fuller, *Utopia or Oblivion: The Prospects for Humanity* (New York, 1967). Because of the time-frame—for example, using the right engineering, all mankind can be prosperous in twenty years, p. 346—the fantasy megalomania was misread as a program.

53.   R. Buckminster Fuller, *Operating Manual for Spaceship Earth* (Carbondale, Ill., 1969), p. 128.

54.   *Operating Manual*, pp. 36 and 132.

55.   Edward T. Hall, as quoted by Hugh Kenner, *Bucky: A Guided Tour of Buckminster Fuller* (New York, 1973), p. 257. But Kenner's quaint literary formalism does not encourage any larger perspective on technotopianism.

56.   John Gerber, *Utopian Fantasy* (London, 1957), p. 27. For a discussion of Stapledon, see Jack Kinnaird, *Olaf Stapledon* (West Linn, Ore., 1982). One might note, incidentally, the pervasive role of utopian fiction in modern British literature, from at least Wells (writing the genial social-realistic *Kipps* the same year he wrote *A Modern Utopia*) through Alan Sillitoe (writing studies of working-class life, but also *Travels in Nihilon* [1971], a satiric dystopia against competitiveness, etc.). It is, then, less a cast of mind than a tendentious alternative for social realists. Even a well-known novelist of moral manners, L. P. Hartley, ventures off into uncharacteristic satiric utopianism in *Facial Justice* (London, 1960), a version of Huxleyan motifs in a post-nuclear society which attempts to mock uniform egalitarian conditioning. The especially important role of utopianizing in modern British fiction is underrated and deserves more study.

57.   Alan Harrington, *The Immortalist* (Millbrae, Calif., 1977), pp. 275–84.

58.   F. M. Esfandiary, *Up-Wingers: A Futurist Manifesto* (New York, 1973), p. 32.

59.   T. S. Eliot, *Collected Poems* (New York, 1973), p. 32. Eliot, of course, was also a utopian in his *Idea of A Christian Society*.

60.   Timothy Leary, "Science," in *Millennium: Glimpses in the 21st Century,* ed. Albert Villoldo and Ken Dychtwald (Boston, 1981), pp. 277–98.

61.   Robert Anton Wilson, *The Illuminati Papers* (Berkeley, Calif., 1981), p. 55.

62.   *Illuminati,* p. 4. For Wilson's supposedly more fictional fantasies, see *The Cosmic Trigger* (New York, 1978), which, in the mode of the more sophisticated sci-fi, combines paranoia with put-on.

63.   John Passmore, *The Perfectability of Man* (New York, 1970), p. 326.

64.   With the exception of a few brief examples, I am not here further considering "futurists," sometimes mismerged with utopianists, and similar addicts. Herman Kahn, once the exploitatively best-known, was no more utopian than Nostradamus, and apparently no more accurate in seeing towards *The Year 2000* (New York, 1967), having missed inflation and energy problems in his lateral thinking as well as earlier miscalculating when nuclear war would come. (In the early 1960s, I listened to a Kahn lecture explaining the high probability of the bombs going off within the decade, which he took to be but a small problem.) Probably futurology, one of the less pretty forms of astrology, can no more be argued with than other addictions. Granted, we can discriminate among futurologists. Robert Vacca, for example, in *The Coming Dark Age* (Garden City, N.Y., 1973), interestingly provided systems analysis of coinciding large malfunctions; though probability denies by definition making those specific in kind or time, the issue does provide suggestive fantasy patterns for the anxieties engendered by our dependencies on large systems.

65. I was usefully led to the comparisons by Robert Fishman, *Urban Utopias in the Twentieth Century* (New York, 1977).

66. Ebenezer Howard, *Garden Cities of Tomorrow* (1902), ed. F. J. Osborne (Cambridge, Mass., 1965); Le Corbusier, *La villa radieuse* (Boulogne-Seine, France, 1935), and *Towards a New Architecture* (New York, 1960); Frank Lloyd Wright, *The Living City* (New York, 1958), which appeared in varying earlier versions, such as *The Disappearing City* (New York, 1932).

67. For the classic case of New York's Robert Moses, see Robert Caro, *Power Broker* (New York, 1974).

68. Paolo Soleri, *Arcology: The City in the Image of Man* (Cambridge, Mass., 1969). Soleri also holds to a large mystagoguery, partly derived from the mystical-evolutionary utopianism of Teilhard de Chardin, especially evident in *The Bridge between Matter and Spirit Is Matter Becoming Spirit* (Cambridge, Mass., 1979).

69. C. A. Doxiadis, *Building Entopia* (New York, 1975); see also *Between Dystopia and Utopia* (Hartford, 1966). I have, for the later discussions here, found a number of other studies suggestive. To mention just a couple: Dolores Haylor, *Seven American Utopias: The Architecture of Communitarian Socialism* (Cambridge, Mass., 1976), which mostly discusses the styles involved in seven diverse kinds of earlier intentional communities but also includes a section on 1960s communites, pp. 320ff. See also George R. Collins, *Visionary Drawings of Architecture and Planning, 20th Century through the 1960s* (Cambridge, Mass., 1979).

Chapter 2

1. H. G. Wells, *A Modern Utopia* (Lincoln, Neb., 1967). Wells' central role in the development of dystopianism is discussed by Mark R. Hillegas, *The Future as Nightmare: H. G. Wells and the Anti-Utopians* (New York, 1967).

2. In E. M. Forster, *The Eternal Moment and Other Stories* (New York, 1928).

3. For a summary, see Tom Moylan, *Demand the Impossible: Science Fiction and the Utopian Imagination* (New York, 1986), pp. 156–95.

4. For some of the resonances of the trope, see John Carroll, *The Break-Out from the Crystal Palace* (London, 1974).

5. Fyodor Dostoyevsky, *Notes from Underground and the Grand Inquisitor,* trans. and ed. Ralph E. Matlaw (New York, 1960), with the following quotes from p. 31. I did some interpretation in *Edges of Extremity* (Tulsa, Okla., 1980), pp. 13–16, and with "Bartleby," *The Ways of Nihilism: Herman Melville's Short Novels* (Los Angeles, 1970), pp. 91ff. Gary Saul Morson claims the novella to be "probably the most important single source of the modern dystopia." He then cleverly applies it to Zamyatin's, reducing the rebellion there to underground "caprice," with the mathematical metaphor's parody of the source. *The Boundaries of Genre* (Austin, 1981), pp. 130ff.

6. Yevgeny Zamyatin, *We,* trans. Mirra Ginsburg (New York, 1972), hereafter cited parenthetically in text. The first English translation, Gregory Zilboorg, *We* (New York, 1924, 1959), is the one cited in much of the criticism. Purely as a point of English style, I have adopted a phrase or two from Bernard G. Guerney's *My* in his *An Anthology of Russian Literature in the Soviet Period from Gorki to Pasternak* (New York, 1960). For biographical information, I have drawn from Alex M. Shane, *The Life and Works of Evgenij Zamjatin* (Berkeley, Calif., 1968).

7. For a discussion of Zamyatin's use of Wells (though not my point), see Christopher Collins,

Evgenij Zamjatin (The Hague, Netherlands, 1973), pp. 43–52. Some other details of Zamyatin's indebtedness to Dostoyevsky are provided by Richard A. Gregg, "Two Adams and Eve in the Crystal Palace: Dostoyevsky, the Bible, and *We,*" *Slavic Studies* 24 (1965): 68–87. See also the comparison in Gorman Beauchamp, "Zamiatin's *We,*" in *No Place Else,* ed. Eric S. Rabkin, Martin H. Greenberg, and Joseph D. Olander (Carbondale, Ill., 1983), pp. 62ff.

8. Following, of course, Michel Foucault, *To Discipline and Punish* (New York, 1978).

9. Collins provides what I take to be an oversystematic allegorizing of the colors, which he follows with a Jungian interpretation, pp. 52–70.

10. George Orwell, "Freedom and Happiness," *Tribune* (London), 471 (Jan. 4, 1946). Collins quotes a letter from Huxley saying he had not read *We,* p. 41. But the parallels are many.

11. E. J. Brown, *Brave New World, 1984, and We* (Ann Arbor, 1976), p. 24.

12. Morson, with an obviously gross misreading, believes that *"We* ends with a conclusion in which *everything* is concluded," p. 132 (italics his).

13. Also, both Zamyatin and Lawrence may have been influenced in their heightened libidinal views by the same Russian speculative thinker on the erotic and apocalyptic, V. V. Rozanov.

14. Quoted in Shane, p. 142.

15. Alexandra Aldridge is no doubt right in her conclusion about Zamyatin that "the sources of dystopia lie in scientistic thinking." But to claim that "the alternative to dystopia begins where a balanced inner life is allowed to flourish" is to impose a prudent moderation on an inappropriate subject. *The Scientific World View in Dystopia* (Ann Arbor, 1984), p. 44.

16. T. R. N. Edwards, *Three Russian Writers and the Irrational* (Cambridge, England, 1982), p. 67.

17. Aldous Huxley, "Foreword" (1946), *Brave New World* (1932; New York, 1969), p. viii.

18. Quoted in Shane, p. 145. More generally, see many of the essays in Zamyatin, *A Soviet Heretic, Essays,* trans. Mirra Ginsburg (Chicago, 1970).

19. "Zamyatin was an atheist, and he may have been influenced by the preoccupation with Satanism in pre-revolutionary Russia—and, of course, by Romantic Satanism." Edwards, p. 42. It is possible to put the issues reasonably within religious terms, as in the relatively compatible antinomian theology of Zamyatin's exile-contemporary, Nicolas Berdyaev, *Slavery and Freedom* (New York, 1948). Simply reduced to terms of cultural history, *We* is "a culmination of the essentially anti-Christian preoccupation with Prometheanism and sensualism" of the preceding period. James H. Billington, *The Icon and the Axe: An Interpretive History of Russian Culture* (New York, 1966), p. 510.

20. Frank E. and Fritzie P. Manuel, *Utopian Thought in the Western World* (Cambridge, Mass., 1979), p. 6.

21. Darko Suvin summarizes: "The basic values of *We* imply a stubborn revolutionary vision of a classless new moral world free from all social alienations, a vision common to Anarchism and libertarian Marxism." His "materialist utopia must subject itself to a constant scrutiny by the light of its own principles; its values are for Zamyatin centered in an ever developing human personality and expressed in an irreducible, life-giving, and subversive erotic passion." This constitutes, he wisely adds, a "dialectical utopianism." *Metamorphoses of Science Fiction* (New Haven, 1979), pp. 258–59.

22. "Contemporary Russian Literature," *A Soviet Heretic,* p. 51. The "neorealism" he defends in such essays—summarized by Edwards as "a fusion of Realism and Symbolism," p. 55—is an intensified, metaphoric, sometimes surreal, overreaching of the ordinary. The style of Nathanael West seems to me to provide some American parallels.

23. William Barrett, *The Illusion of Technique* (New York, 1979), p. 231.

24. Elizabeth Hansot held that the incorporation of change characterizes utopianism since the eighteenth century. *Perfection and Progress: Two Modes of Utopian Thought* (Cambridge, Mass., 1974), chapter 1. J.C. Davis finds change to be characteristic of sixteenth- and seventeenth-century utopians, who also "visualized not one form of society but many" and offered counterings to each other. *Utopia and the Ideal Society* (Cambridge, England, 1981), pp. 7–8. Other commentators do not emphasize change until the powerful effects of Darwin. But one suspects that some unconventional utopianizing minds, back at least to the Cynics, have always noted it. Such representative antiutopian charges as Barrett's are exceedingly ill-informed.

25. Put as a philosophical issue: "perfectibilism is dehumanizing," reasonably notes John Passmore, in its denial of a full range of human limitations and possibilities. But to jump from that to a total rejection of the utopian may commit a parallel dehumanization in refusing to recognize "that man is capable of becoming something much superior to what he now is." *The Perfectability of Man* (New York, 1970), p. 326. (By the same reasoning, of course, he could also become much worse.)

26. H. G. Wells, *A Modern Utopia,* pp. 3–4.

27. Quoted in Aldridge, p. 69.

28. Herbert Read, *The Green Child* (London, 1935). Read was also a libertarian utopianizer in many of his expository writings.

29. Paul and Percival Goodman, *Communitas,* rev. ed. (New York, 1960). For explication, see my *Paul Goodman* (Boston, 1980).

30. Ursula K. Le Guin, *The Dispossessed* (New York, 1975), with citations parenthetical in text *(Dis.).*

31. Ursula K. Le Guin, "Science Fiction and Mrs. Brown," in *Science Fiction at Large,* ed. Peter Nichols (New York: 1976), pp. 18–19.

32. As reported, for example, by Charlotte Spivak, *Ursula K. Le Guin* (Boston, 1984), p. 2.

33. As quoted by David Joravsky, reviewing Robert Oppenheimer, *Letters and Recollections* (1980), in *New York Review of Books,* 27 (July 17, 1980): 9. I recall a much earlier thoughtful discussion of this crucial scientist's attitude in Robert Jungk, *Brighter Than a Thousand Suns* (New York, 1958).

34. See W. Warren Wagar, *H. G. Wells and the World State* (New Haven, 1961).

35. Carol McGicirk grants that Le Guin avoids sci-fi clichés and inhumanisms but says it is at the price of "diminished emphasis on the unknowable" (?) and an optimistic antiscientific "humanist idealism" of traditional utopianism, which is "inherently anthropocentric." "Optimism and the Limits of Subversion in 'The Dispossessed' and 'The Left Hand of Darkness,'" in *Ursula K. Le Guin,* ed. Harold Bloom (New York, 1986), pp. 227, 251, 253.

36. Le Guin provides an earlier small sketch of Odo in "The Day before the Revolution," in *The Wind's Twelve Quarters* (New York, 1975). In the note to the story she identifies her sources for anarchism as Taoism, Shelley, Kropotkin, Goldman, and Goodman, p. 285.

37. Le Guin's utopianizing is briefly placed in the context of anarchist literature by Lyman Tower Sargent, with a good bibliography, in "A New Anarchism: Social and Political Issues in Some Recent Feminist Eutopians," in *Women and Utopia*, ed. Marleen Barr and Nicholas D. Smith (Lanhan, Md., 1983), pp. 3–16. The use of Kropotkin (mostly *Mutual Aid*) is spelled out by Philip E. Smither, "Unbuilding Walls: Human Nature and the Nature of Evolutionary and Political Thought in *The Dispossessed*," in *Ursula K. Le Guin*, ed. Joseph D. Olander and Martin Henry Greenberg (New York, 1979), pp. 77–96. Some additional discussion is given in the same volume by John P. Brennan and Michael C. Downs, "Anarchism and Utopian Tradition in *The Dispossessed*," pp. 116–52.

38. An overemphasis on the Taoist parallels is provided by Elizabeth Cummins Cogell, "Taoist Configurations in *The Dispossessed*," in *Ursula K. Le Guin: Voyager to Inner Lands and to Outer Space*, ed. Joe D. Bolt (Port Washington, N. Y.: 1979), pp. 153–79.

39. Le Guin's Taoism resembles that of such Western nonmystical exponents as Holmes Welch, *Taoism, the Parting of the Way*, rev. ed. (Boston, 1966), which may be one of her sources.

40. *Communitas*, pp. 153ff. The Morris is in *News from Nowhere* (discussed below), the Kropotkin primarily *Mutual Aid*. For a good recent discussion of the issues of urban proportion, see Kirkpatrick Sale, *Human Scale* (New York, 1980).

41. Victor Urbanowicz relates the hands-on learning for children to anarchist Herbert Read's *Education through Art*, and to Paul Goodman's libertarian psychology of self-regulation. "Personal and Political in *The Dispossessed*," in *Le Guin*, ed. Harold Bloom, p. 147.

42. Raymond Carr, reviewing David D. Gilmore, *Aggression and Community*, in *New York Review of Books* 34 (May 28, 1987): 42.

43. See my discussion of pastoral in chapter 4 below. Le Guin does quite self-consciously use pastoral in some of her other fictions, as in the peaceful feminist tribal order of *The Word for World Is Forest* (New York, 1972).

44. Urbanowicz sees this as having different sources than I suggest: "Le Guin's exaltation of poverty, a trait of the Christian anarchism of Tolstoy and the Catholic Worker movement, is central to the novel, as indicated by the title (which is also a sideswipe at Dostoyevsky)," Bloom, p. 153. Anthropologists Vera Mae and David Fredrickson, who studied in Le Guin's Kroeber tradition, provide general confirmation of my emphasis on the cultural theory background.

45. See, for example, Colin Ward, *Anarchy in Action* (New York, 1972).

46. In the late 1960s, in reply to a paper defending radical dissent that I presented at the Center for the Study of Democratic Institutions (Santa Barbara), a spokesman mockingly replied that I seemed to be arguing that "every institution have a Vice-President for Trouble-making." While I hope I was arguing for a bit more than that, it was not an altogether wrong wisecrack, with parallels to Le Guin's Syndicate of Initiative.

47. Urbanowicz reminded me of this again, but I cannot find the original text.

48. As noted, for example, by contemporary biological writer Lewis Thomas: "Maybe altruism is our most primitive attribute." Our DNA may well be coded "for usefulness and helpfulness." That application may "turn out to be the hardest test of fitness for survival, more important that aggression, more effective, in the long run, than grabbiness." *The Medusa and the Snail* (New York, 1979), p. 10.

49. It might also be recalled that Fourier, that crank nineteenth-century utopian genius, who has been, I suspect, of immense influence (from Hawthorne's Brook Farm and Dostoyevsky's subversive St. Petersburg to the Surrealists and the Situationists), suggested giving certain dirty work to young boys because of their disposition towards it. And he charmingly assigned the labor of prettily fluttering around, which also seems to be socially essential, to those with the "butterfly instinct," yet another of his 1,820 human types. See Charles Fourier, *The Utopian Vision,* ed. Jonathan Beecher and Richard Bienvenu (Boston, 1971); *Harmonion Man, Selected Writings of Charles Fourier,* ed. Mark Poster (Garden City, N.Y., 1971); and Nicholas Rianovsky, *The Teachings of Charles Fourier* (Berkeley, Cal., 1969).

50. A minor utopian fiction of a few years back by an academic had macho young American males eagerly doing the dangerous work, for its esprit and appropriate hip-perks, instead of contact sports and other virility psychodramas. James Brown, *The Troika Incident* (New York, 1968). But from a libertarian perspective, I would argue, some dirty jobs, including leadership, can only fairly be done by random selection.

51. "Is Gender Necessary?" *The Language of the Night,* ed. Susan Wood (New York, 1979), p. 163.

52. *Language of the Night,* p. 163.

53. Peter Rupert, *Reader in a Strange Land* (Athens, Ga., 1986), p. 149. He makes a similar relativist argument, contentless and neutralizing—"reader response theory" intellectual abeyance—about Zamyatin's *We,* p. 113.

54. Tom Moylan, pp. 101, 102, 103, 114. His contrasting total lack of criticism of his other main subjects—Joanna Russ, Marge Piercy, Samuel Delaney—reduces his dogmatism to fawning, leaving the anti-Le Guin his best chapter.

55. According to this faith, Le Guin fails because the structure of her "novel goes in a compensatory circle rather than a revolutionary spiral." Moylan, p. 116. The "circle" of the narrative pattern, if one yields to formalistic overreading of obvious devices, can also claim to be the stolid nonexistential "ethical," as with James W. Bittner's narrowly technical *Approaches to the Fiction of Ursula K. Le Guin* (Ann Arbor, 1984), pp. 119–24.

Chapter 3

1. See, for example, my *Reflections of a Male Housewife: On Being a Feminist Fellow-traveller* (Pittsburg, 1971); reprinted, *Exploring Contemporary Male/Female Roles,* ed. C. G. Carney and S. L. McMahon (La Jolla, Calif., 1977). I am indbted in this chapter for suggestions and objections from a number of feminists, including Vera M. Fredrickson, Eleanor Widmer, Penny Williams, Elsie Adams, Carey Wall, and Kathleen B. Jones.

2. Barbara Goodwin and Keith Taylor, *The Politics of Utopia* (New York, 1982), p. 211.

3. Anthony Burgess, *The Wanting Seed* (London, 1962).

4. Suggestive arguments, within a psychoanalytic framework, for defeminizing nurturance are made by Dorothy Dinnerstein, *The Mermaid and the Minotaur: Sexual Arguments and Human Malaise* (New York, 1976).

5. I wrongly took little account of feminist issues in my analysis of aggression theories in "Towards a Politics for *Homo Negans:* Libertarian Reflections on Human Aggression," *Personalist* 53 (1972).

6.   For some clever deployment of this, see Jane Gallop, *The Daughter's Seduction: Feminism and Psychoanalysis* (Ithaca, N.Y., 1982).

7.   Jewel Parker Rhodes, "Ursula Le Guin's *The Left Hand of Darkness:* Androgyny and the Feminist Utopia," *Women and Utopia,* ed. Marleen Barr and Nicholas Smith (Lanham, Md., 1983), p. 119.

8.   Joanna Russ, "Recent Feminist Utopias," in *Future Females: A Critical Anthology,* ed. Marleen S. Barr (Bowling Green, Ohio, 1981), p. 76.

9.   Daphne Patae, "Beyond Defensiveness: Feminist Research Strategies," in *Women and Utopia,* p. 164.

10.   Most of the interest in *Herland* seems to be as an ancestor, though a small case for such femtopianism is made by Sheila Delany, *Writing Women* (New York, 1983), pp. 164–73.

11.   Patae, p. 164.

12.   Russ, "Recent Feminist Utopias," p. 77. Perhaps the real, and more appropriate, context is the treatment of women in mainstream science fiction. A case, with Freudian overlay, for the misogyny of Arthur C. Clarke, Isaac Asimov, and Kurt Vonnegut, Jr., is made by Judith Spector, "Science Fiction and the Sex War: A Womb of One's Own," in *Gender Studies,* ed. Judith Spector (Bowling Green, Ohio, 1986), pp. 163–76.

13.   Robert Scholes, "A Footnote to Russ's 'Recent Feminist Utopias,'" in *Future Females,* p. 86. Scholes also interestingly reminds us of an oddly profeminist 1950s novel which eliminates gender in a suburban American near future, Philip Wylie's *The Disappearance* (New York, 1951).

14.   Scholes, p. 87.

15.   Carol Pearson, "Coming Home: Four Feminist Utopias and Patriarchal Experience," in *Future Females,* p. 65. The later *Herland* continues the smug sentimentalism. For a recent discussion of the Bulwer-Lytoon, see B. G. Knepper, *"The Coming Race:* Hell? Or Paradise Foretasted?" in *No Place Else,* ed. Eric S. Rabkin, Martin H. Greenberg, and Jos. D. Olander (Carbondale, Ill., 1980).

16.   Countering arguments by male utopianists are also of some vintage. The previously cited N. G. Chernyshevsky, for example, has a heroic dream woman announce that mere "worship" of women is a way of denying her equality and "human dignity." *What Is to Be Done?* as reprinted in Dostoyevsky's *Notes from Underground,* ed. Ralph E. Matlaw (New York, 1960), p. 160.

17.   See Dinnerstein's argument, previously cited, and Nancy Chodorow, *The Reproduction of Mothering: Psychoanalysis and the Sociology of Gender* (Berkeley, Calif., 1978).

18.   Russ, "Recent Feminist Utopias," p. 81.

19.   Joanna Russ, *The Zanzibar Cat* (Sauk City, Wisc., 1983), pp. 3–11.

20.   Since *The Female Man* (New York: 1975) does not substantially clarify the eutopian order, which is only part of the narrative, I have confined myself to the sketch rather than give the fragments explicatory attention they hardly merit. Tom Moylan gives lengthy uncritical exposition of them in *Demand the Impossible* (New York: 1986), pp. 55–90. Russ' inability to deploy consistent style, development, and ideas is also confirmed in her *The Two of Them* (New York, 1978).

21. *The Republic of Plato,* trans. F. M. Cornford (New York, 1945), p. 110.

22. Iris Murdoch, *The Fire and the Sun* (London, 1977).

23. Sally Miller Gearhart, *Wanderground: Stories of the Hill Women* (Boston, 1984), with citations parenthetical in text *(Wander).*

24. Perhaps the willful fragmentations and hyped poeticizing, as well as the homosexual exaltation, can be identified as part of a cultish subtradition. One apparent influence on this strain is Monique Wittig, *Les Guérilleres* (New York, 1971 [1969]).

25. My concern here is not with lesbian fiction as such, for which see, for both citations and thoughtful analysis, Catherine R. Stimpson, "Zero Degree Deviancy: The Lesbian Novel in English," in *Writing and Sexual Difference,* ed. Elizabeth Abel (Chicago, Ill., 1982), pp. 246–60. See also Tucker Farley, "Realities and Fictions: Lesbian Visions of Utopia," in *Women in Search of Utopia,* pp. 233–46.

26. Natalie M. Rosinsky, *Feminist Futures* (Ann Arbor, 1984), p. 82.

27. Judith Kegan Gardiner, "On Female Identity and Writing by Women," in *Writing and Sexual Difference,* p. 185.

28. Suzy McKee Charnas, *Motherlines* (New York, 1978), with citations parenthetical in text *(Mother).* Various references to it may be found in several of the critical anthologies previously cited. One of the most useful listings of such works is Lyman Tower Sargent, "A New Anarchism: Social and Political Ideas in Some Recent Feminist Eutopias," in *Women and Utopia,* pp. 3–33. Another discussion is contained in Lee Cullen Khanne, "Women's Worlds, New Directions in Utopian Fiction," *Alternate Futures,* 4 (1981): 47–60. A praising summary can also be found in David Dowling, *Fictions of Nuclear Disaster* (London, 1987), pp. 168–69.

29. An example of present maternal identification, however much in a patriarchal context, might be seen in the Israeli Law of the Return, in which Jewish identity is defined by the mother. (An Israeli official, who claimed to be charged with applying it, once explained to me at Tel Aviv University that "it was more certain" than identification by fatherhood.) If I understand a parallel genetic point, an essential element of genes is mitochondria, which is passed on exclusively in eggs, so we could "trace our ancestry, strictly down the female line." Richard Dawkins, *The Blind Watchmaker* (New York, 1986), p. 176. But isn't there something essentially reductive of the person in all this concern with motherlines, as with patriarchal fatherhood?

30. I forbear citation (but recall a film with two women and a pony seen in the officers' quarters on a U. S. aircraft carrier some years ago). The total elimination of fathers by parthenogenesis appeared early on in *Herland,* and continues in other fictions such as Mary Straton, *The Legend of Biel* (New York, 1975), where embryos are both conceived and tended by robotic machines.

31. Thomas Berger, *Regiment of Women* (New York, 1973), with citations parenthetical in text *(Regiment).* Joanna Russ has a denunciatory discussion of the novel in *"Amor Vincit Foeminam:* The Battle of the Sexes in Science Fiction," in *Gender Studies,* ed. Specter, pp. 244–45. Berger's theme is not primarily military (though that is his forte, as in his well-known *Rinehart* trilogy), but is taken from the representative Christian misogynist fulminations of John Knox, *The First Blast of the Trumpet against the Monstrous Regiment of Women* (1558).

32. Gerd Brantenberg, *Egalia's Daughters* (Seattle, 1985). Quotations from pp. 97, 172, and 229.

33. For a recent example, see Martin Amis' macho John Self, who discovers that "God is a woman. Look around! *Of course She is." Money* (London, 1986), p. 136. On male insistence on women

as witches, see, besides John Updike's jokey *Witches of Eastwick,* Norman Mailer's more earnest insistence, as discussed in my "The Perplexities of Protest: Some American Literature of the 1960s," *The Sphinx* (University of Regina, Canada) 3 (1980).

34. See Rene Dubos, *A God Within* (New York, 1972).

35. The arguments around Gaea worship have been variously developed since propounded by James E. Lovelock, *Gaea: A New Look at Life On Earth* (New York, 1979), until they have become stock ideology for such writers as William Irwin Thompson, *Pacific Shift* (San Francisco, 1986). (Thompson is further discussed in the next chapter, below.) Modern Gaeism, of course, goes back much earlier. Ernst Bloch, for example, discusses it as part of Johan Bachofen's mother-worship (*Maternal Law,* etc.) in the mid-nineteenth century: "Confrontation: Gaea-Themis and Its Survival in the Collective Schools of Natural Law," in *Natural Law and Human Dignity* (Cambridge, Mass., 1986), pp. 111–19. The worship has been somewhat seriously combined with "deep ecology" by Kirkpatrick Sale in *Dwellers in the Land: The Bioregional Vision* (San Francisco, 1985). See my critical review essay in *Social Anarchism* (Spring 1988). Sale has emphasized its currency with feminist groups in a later discussion. "Ecofeminism—A New Perspective," *The Nation* 245 (September 26, 1987): 302–5. The proper skeptical feminist retort below is from Angela Carter, *The Sadeian Woman, and the Ideology of Pornography* (New York, 1980), p. 5. There is something quite obscene as well as sad in the contemporary countering of patriarchy with neomatriarchy.

36. Sally Miller Gearhart not only fictionally practiced it (above) but found it characteristic of many feminist utopias which take an antitechnocratic view: "Future Visions: Today's Politics; Feminist Utopias in Review," in *Women in Search of Utopia,* ed. Ruby Rohrlich and Elaine Hoffman Baruch (New York, 1984), pp. 273–309.

37. Beya Weinbaum, "Twin Oaks," in *Women in Search of Utopia,* p. 158.

38. The apparent contradiction of freedom and primitivism has been plaintively noted, for example, by Krishan Kumar, "Primitivism in Feminist Utopias," *Alternate Societies* 4 (1981).

39. This is my cumulative impression from reading a scattering of anthropological studies: I have no single source to cite for it. Other current evidence on the relation of the "sacral" to "conservation" seems ambiguous, as indicated, for example, in a report on a worldwide conference around the subject: Liz Harris, "Brother Sun, Sister Moon," *New Yorker* (April 27, 1987): 90.

40. Marge Piercy, *Woman on the Edge of Time* (New York, 1976), with citations parenthetical in text *(Woman).*

41. Marge Piercy, *Dance the Eagle to Sleep* (New York, 1970), with citations parenthetical in text *(Dance).* I take a somewhat more sympathetic view of the novel than does Susan Kress, who judges it to be a "visionary dead end" which is "heavy-handed" in its political dogmatism. "In and Out of Time: The Form of Marge Piercy's Novels," in *Future Females,* p. 144.

42. Perhaps the most direct illustration of this is the documentary collection, which includes Piercy, *The Movement towards a New America,* ed. Mitchell Goodman (New York, 1970). Material on the communalism of the period will be cited later in another context.

43. I am drawing on memory here (though I had only limited association with the Students for a Democratic Society after such factions as Progressive Labor started taking over in late 1967). The charge of leftist rhetorical triteness is given qualified repetition from the reviewers by Jack Hicks, *In the Singer's Temple* (Chapel Hill, N.C., 1981), pp. 143–51.

44. I have elsewhere provided more detailed analyses of *Cuckoo's Nest*, as in "The Post-Modernist Art of Protest: Kesey and Mailer," *Centennial Review* 19 (1975).

45. It seems likely that Piercy was influenced in the split-narrative by the slightly earlier (and leftist-feminist) Doris Lessing, *Briefing for a Descent into Hell* (New York, 1973).

46. Sheila Delany, p. 180.

47. Lucy M. Freibert, "World Views in Utopian Novels by Women," in *Women and Utopia*, p. 83.

48. Kress, p. 117.

49. I have discussed some of the arguments of Marx, Arendt, and Marcuse, in "Culture and Alienated Work," in a symposium, "Marx and Critical Thought," *Paunch* 44–45 (1976).

50. For some discussion of feminist efforts to modify usage, including this one, see H. Lee Gershunn, "The Linguistic Transformation of Womanhood," *Women in Search of Utopia*, pp. 189–99.

51. I have elaborated arguments about ritualism as a dominant function of contemporary mass culture in "Sensibility under Technocracy: Reflections on the Culture of Processed Communications," in *Human Connection and the New Media*, ed. Barry N. Schwartz (Englewood Cliffs, N.J., 1973), and recently summarized the issue in "The Age of Showbiz," *American Book Review* (Jan.-Feb. 1987), and so will not repeat them here.

52. Rosinsky, *Feminist Futures*, p. 103. An elaborate and uncritical exposition is given by Moylan, pp. 121–55.

53. Margaret Atwood, *The Handmaid's Tale* (New York, 1987), with citations parenthetical in text *(Tale)*.

54. Her Canadian cultural nationalism appears in a number of writings, perhaps most controversially in *Survival: A Thematic Guide to Canadian Literature* (Toronto, 1972).

55. This perhaps leads one scholarly survey to describe her as a "crypto-feminist." Jerome H. Rosenberg, *Margaret Atwood* (Boston, 1984), p. 148.

56. Atwood's frequent centering on the ambiguous issues of female deception is apologetically summarized for the earlier fictions by Ann Parsons, "The Self-Inventing Self: Women Who Lie and Pose in the Fictions of Margaret Atwood," *Gender Studies*, pp. 97–109.

57. Speaking of Atwood's voluminous poetry, much of which preceded her fiction and determined her literary stature, one interpreter has defined her gender theme: "Man and woman do not exist separately. . . . They mutually construct and define each other's identities." Barbara Balkely, "The Pronunciation of Flesh: A Feminist Reading of Margaret Atwood's Poetry," in *Margaret Atwood*, ed. Sherrill E. Grad and Lorraine Weir (Vancouver, Canada, 1983), p. 33.

58. There are a number of arguments for redirecting character towards androgyny; for a simple case (with a bias towards feminization) see Ann Ferguson, "Androgyny as an Ideal for Human Development," in *The Philosophy of Sex*, ed. Alan Soble (Towtowa, N.J., 1980), pp. 232–55. The most recent feminist study at hand uncritically discusses a few feminoid motifs in some of the fictions (including some discussed here, and a number of others). Marleen S. Barr, *Alien to Femininity*, "Speculative Fiction and Feminist Theory" (Westport, Conn., 1987). It lacks utility because it shows little concern for larger patterns, values, and style. It also misdescribes its concern: "Speculative fiction by women is paving the way for nonsexist versions of reality" (p. 156). It would more accurately read "countersexist."

Chapter 4

1. I incline to a somewhat positive view of the neolithic, as with Claude Lévi-Strauss, *Triste Tropique* (New York, 1961), especially after considering the attacks on it, as in Jacques Derrida, *Of Grammatology* (Baltimore, Md., 1976). Background sources for the view of the pastoral here will be cited below.

2. For some discussion of Cynic utopianism, see my *The Literary Rebel* (Carbondale, Ill., 1965), chapter 1. For the millennial, see Marjorie Reeves, *The Influence of Prophecy in the Later Middle Ages: A Study of Joachimism* (London, 1969). The often cited broader account of Norman Cohn, *The Pursuit of the Millennium* (New York, 1957, and later editions) seems to me terribly biased in the sexual and political fears the subject often raises.

3. For some of this, including the later term "soft primitivism," see *A Documentary History of Primitivism*, ed. A. O. Lovejoy, et al. (Baltimore, Md., 1935). For the later period, see Harry Levin, *The Myth of the Golden Age in the Renaissance* (Bloomington, Ind., 1969), and Renato Poggioli, *The Oaten Flute* (Cambridge, Mass., 1975).

4. "The land of Arcadia is really the landscape of an idea." Peter V. Marinelli, *Pastoral* (London, 1971), p. 37.

5. Several of my points probably derive from William Empson, *Some Versions of Pastoral* (Norfolk, Conn., 1941).

6. For some of the social complications of the history of British ideas about pastoralism, see Raymond Williams, *The Country and the City* (New York, 1973).

7. Samuel Butler, *Erewhon, or Over the Range* (New York, 1955), which no doubt deserves fuller consideration here.

8. William Morris, *News from Nowhere, or, An Epoch of Rest: Being Some Chapters from a Utopian Romance* (New York, 1966), with citations in text *(News)*.

9. For doctrinaire reasons, Raymond Williams claims that the chapters on revolutionary actions "are strong and convincing," in spite of the heavy-handed writing, and a century of obvious historical evidence against what claims to be a historical interpretation. *Problems in Materialism and Culture* (London, 1980), p. 207.

10. Steven Lukes, "Marxism and Utopianism," in *Utopias*, ed. Peter Alexander and Roger Gill (London, 1984), p. 153.

11. E. P. Thompson's is probably the best known attempt to deny any contradiction between Morris' Marxisim and the rest of his utopianism. *William Morris* (New York, 1977). For this analysis Thompson relies mostly on works other than *News*, which he rather incoherently subsumes as a "Scientific Utopia," p. 693. While in his revision Thompson tries to avoid conflict between Marxism and utopianism, pp. 791ff., he wisely concludes: "We can now see that Morris may be assimilated to Marxism only in the course of a process of self-criticism and re-ordering within Marxism itself," p. 802. And in the sense of what Morris aspired to, he "can never be assimilated to Marxism," p. 807.

    The main texts on utopianism in historical Marxism should not be the few often-cited utopian passages in *The Communist Manifesto* and *The German Ideology* but Frederich Engels, *Socialism, Utopian and Scientific* (London, 1891), where the burbly argument often casts the utopian as a "mish-mash" while claiming that Marxism has the rigor of "science," p. 27. This is just religiosity. Yet a recent literary commentator writes: "What Engels did not realize in his otherwise useful critique was the more mediated effects that the utopian imagination can have on a set of readers at the level of ideological formation." Tom Moylan, *Demand the Impossible* (New York, 1986), p. 6. In other words, for such condescending priestliness, non-Marxist utopian literature is wrong but can be used as handy propaganda on the uninitiated.

12. Peter Faulkner suggests that Morris' eludes the technological crux by vaguely calling on a new "mechanical force" that "obviates the debasements of coal." *Against the Age: An Introduction to William Morris* (London, 1981), p. 141.

13. Gary Saul Morson is obviously in gross error in describing *News from Nowhere* as "uncompromising in its rejection of nineteenth century feminism." *The Boundaries of Genre* (Austin, 1981), p. 80.

14. George Woodcock rightly identified the work's politics as essentially Kropotkinesque anarchism in cast (in spite of Morris' disputes at the time with the London anarchists). *Anarchism: A History of Libertarian Ideas and Movements* (Cleveland, 1962), p. 24. Thompson, discussing the later scholarly research in the revisions of his biography, grants that the influence of Kropotkin and other anarchists was greater than has usually been acknowledged, by him or others, p. 792.

15. Faulkner gives this a rather positive twist, noting that "ordinary living is not transcended but raised to a higher quality," p. 142.

16. Even the most sympathetic commentators note the vagueness of the structure. Frederick Kurchoff, *William Morris* (Boston, 1979), p. 128. Raymond Williams granted Morris' artistic inadequacy and argued that his essays and lectures called forth his better writing. *Culture and Society* (London, 1958), p. 155. To my only partial acquaintance, he seems best on social aesthetics.

17. See, for example, Isabel F. Knight, "Alienation, Eros, and Work; The Good News from Nowhere," *Alternative Futures* 2 (Winter 1979): 3–28.

18. Edward Bellamy, *Looking Backward, 2000–1887* (New York, 1960), with citations in text *(Backward)*.

19. See Sylvia Bowman, *The Year 2000: A Critical Biography of Edward Bellamy* (New York, 1958), and *Edward Bellamy Abroad: An American Prophet's Influence* (New York, 1962).

20. Bellamy also totally ignores any "racial problem," past, future, or present, note William Nichols and Charles P. Henry, "Imagining a Future in America: A Racial Perspective," *Alternate Futures* 1 (Spring 1978): 41.

21. Ernest Callenbach, *Ecotopia* (Berkeley, 1975), with citations in text *(Ecotopia); Ecotopia Emerging* (Berkeley, 1981), with citations in text *(Emerging)*. Gerard K. O'Neill, *The High Frontier: Human Colonies in Space* (New York, 1977), with citations in text *(High); 2081: A Hopeful View of the Human Future* (New York, 1981), with citations in text *(2081)*.

22. From his citations *(High* 30, 228) as well as arguments, it seems that he especially wishes to counter the bleak overpopulation disaster predicted, to considerable attention at the time, by Robert Heilbroner, *An Inquiry into the Human Prospect* (New York, 1974). A similar concern can be found in other technocratic futurists, such as Willis H. Harman, *An Incomplete Guide to the Future* (Stanford, 1976). It can hardly be overemphasized how much a sense of countering argument is crucial to such works.

23. Hannah Arendt, *The Human Condition* (Garden City, N.Y., 1959), chapter 1.

24. On the first book, see Richard Frye, "The Economies of *Ecotopia*," *Alternative Futures* 3

(Winter 1980): 71–81, which gives sources for the "steady state" theory and its ecological base. While I think it confuses matters to describe such an economy as "primitive," I do call it "neoprimitive" to suggest the pastoral simplification to human scale. Frye points out the violations by Callenbach of such simplification in nuclear power, continuing into the sequel.

25. But Nichols and Henry's racial objections apply, as they dryly note, "Callenbach's willingness to acknowledge that he can imagine no utopian solution to [present American] racial conflict," p. 43. More importantly, Callenbach is partly doing handbooks for marginal living, luddite utopianism. See his *Living Poor with Style* (New York, 1972). In the more bellicose Edward Abbey (cited below) tradition of dissenting bohemianism, see George Heyduke, *Get Even: The Complete Book of Dirty Tricks* (Boulder, Colo., 1980), a manual on fighting the system. The subversive utopianizing of marginals certainly deserves further discussion.

26. I am drawing on a previously published discussion, "From Great War to Little Garden: Ford's Ford," *Antaeus* 56 (Spring 1986), but have dropped most of the discussion of the war and modified the argument.

27. Ford Madox Ford, *Parade's End* (New York, 1950).

28. Ford Madox Ford, *The Rash Act* (Manchester, England, 1982).

29. Besides Ford's memoir volumes, discussed below, see Frank MacShane, *The Life and Work of Ford Madox Ford* (New York, 1965).

30. For his wartime tracts, see *Between St. Dennis and St. George* (London, 1915) and *When Blood Is Their Argument* (London, 1915). They are placed in historical context by L. L. Farrar, Jr., "The Artist as Propagandist," in *The Presence of Ford Madox Ford,* ed. Sondra J. Stang (Philadelphia, 1981).

31. Ford Madox Ford, *No Enemy* (New York, 1929), with citations in text *(No); It Was the Nightingale* (New York, 1975), with citations in text *(Nightingale); Provence* (Philadelphia, 1935), with citations in text *(Provence); Great Trade Route* (New York, 1937), with citations in text *(Route).*

32. See my "Lawrence and the Nietzschean Matrix," in *D. H. Lawrence and Tradition,* ed. Jeffrey Meyers (London, 1985).

33. I have discussed some of this ideology in other contexts, as in "Melville and the Myths of Modernism," *A Companion to Melville Studies,* ed. John Bryant (Westport, Conn., 1986), and *The Literary Rebel* (Carbondale, Ill., 1965).

34. Nathanael West, *Miss Lonelyhearts, Complete Works of Nathanael West* (New York, 1957), p. 107. For context, see my *Nathanael West* (Boston, 1982), chapter 2.

35. I have qualified the interpretation suggested in my "The Prophet's Passional Ethos: Henry David Thoreau," *Paunch* (SUNY, Buffalo), 24 (October 1965).

36. See, for example, Kathleen Kincade, *A Walden Two Experiment* (New York, 1973), for the Twin Oaks intentional community in Virginia. There was even a Skinnerean commmune in England, according to Philip Abrams and Andrew McCulloch, *Communes, Sociology and Society* (Cambridge, England, 1976), which, not surprisingly, they found to be bureaucratic and rigidly controlled, p. 219. There would seem to be a disproportionate literature refuting Skinner. A measured humanist criticism is that of Joseph Wood Krutch, *The Measure of Man* (New York, 1953), pp. 56ff. George Kateb perseverates on issues surrounding Skinner in *Utopia and Its Enemies* (New York, 1963), pp. 141–217.

37. Helen and Scott Nearing, *Living the Good Life* (New York, 1970); *Continuing the Good Life* (New York, 1979).

38. Ralph Borsodi, *This Ugly Civilization* (New York, 1929); *Flight from the City* (New York, 1933, 1972). His influence, as I heard from several communalists, extended beyond his time.

39. Wendell Berry, *Recollected Essays, 1965–1980* (Berkeley, 1981); *The Unsettling of America: Culture and Agriculture* (New York, 1977); *Home Economics* (Berkeley, 1987).

40. Gary Snyder, *Earth Household* (New York, 1969); *The Real Work* (New York, 1980), quotes from pp. 138 and 88.

41. Snyder, *Real Work*, p. 145.

42. Snyder, *Real Work*, p. 149.

43. E. F. Schumacher, *Small Is Beautiful* (New York, 1973); *A Guide for the Perplexed* (New York, 1975); the posthumous *Good Work* (New York, 1979), chatty sermons on a positive utopian view of work, has an appended essay by Peter N. Gillingham, "The Making of Good Work," pp. 147ff., which is rather more apt than Schumacher. Examples of the continuation can be found in *The Schumacher Lectures*, ed. Satish Kumar (New York, 1981), with Ivan Illich, Hazel Henderson, Leopold Kohr, et al.

44. Leopold Kohr, *The Breakdown of Nations* (London, 1957); *The Overdeveloped Nations: The Diseconomies of Scale* (New York, 1977).

45. Kirkpatrick Sale, *Human Scale* (New York, 1980), p. 523.

46. Murray Bookchin, *The Ecology of Freedom: The Emergence and Dissolution of Hierarchy* (Palo Alto, 1982), with my points applying especially to the arguments on pp. 348ff.

47. Ivan Illich, *Toward a History of Needs* (New York, 1980), p. xiv.

48. Karl Hess, *Community Technology* (New York, 1979), with the following quotes from pp. 28, 7, 4, and 23. See also, with David Morris, *Neighborhood Power: The New Localism* (Boston, 1975). For his political shifts but supposed continuity of humane-scaled values, see his *Dear America* (New York, 1975).

49. Hazel Henderson, *Creating Alternative Futures* (New York, 1978).

50. Mark Satin, *New Age Politics* (New York, 1979), with quotes from pp. 109, 222, and 165. For an even more burbly pop version, see Marilyn Ferguson, *The Aquarian Conspiracy: Personal and Social Transformation in the 1980s* (Los Angeles, 1980).

51. See Martin Duberman, *Black Mountain* (New York, 1972); and Mary Emma Harris, *The Arts at Black Mountain College* (Cambridge, Mass., 1987). My treatment here of utopian education is only the barest of annotations. For further examples, see my "Subterranean Universities? Reflections on Utopian Institutions," *AAUP Bulletin* 57 (Winter 1971); and "Anarchism vs. Schoolism," *Social Anarchism* 1 (1980), among others.

52. A. S. Neill, *Summerhill: A Radical Approach to Childrearing* (New York, 1962); and Jonathan Croall, *Neill of Summerhill* (New York, 1983).

53. See Paul Avrich, *The Modern School Movement: Anarchism and Education in the United States* (Princeton, 1980); and my discussion of it in *Social Anarchism* 2 (1981).

54. Paulo Freire, *Pedagogy of the Oppressed* (New York, 1970); also, *Education for Critical Consciousness* (New York, 1973); *The Politics of Education: Culture, Power, and Liberation* (South Hadley, Mass., 1985); and my "Liberating the Illiterate?" *Social Anarchism* 12 (1986).

55. William Irwin Thompson, *At the Edge of History* (New York, 1971). See also his *Darkness and Scattered Light: Four Talks on the Future* (Garden City, N.Y., 1978).

56. William Irwin Thompson, *Passages about the Earth,* "An Exploration of the New Planetary Culture" (New York, 1974). For the Jeffersonian politics, see pp. 178ff.; for the explicit indebtedness to H. G. Wells, see pp. 56ff.

57. Or as he put it elsewhere, "now we need to miniaturize industrial civilization." Then he grossly jumps to arguments for "cosmic consciousness." *Evil and the World Order* (New York, 1976), pp. 10 and 17. He does not stick to his own principles, such as that "technology is not a tool, it is a culture," p. 21, but regularly uses it as a tool for an antithetical culture.

58. William Irwin Thompson, *The Time Falling Bodies Take to Light,* "Mythology, Sexuality, and the Origins of Culture" (New York, 1981), pp. 250 and 254 for the following quotes.

59. William Irwin Thompson, *Pacific Shift* (San Francisco, 1985), quotes from pp. 154, 23, 62, and 161.

60. See Gregory Bateson, *Steps to an Ecology of Mind* (New York, 1972). See also his *Mind and Nature* (New York, 1980).

61. William Irwin Thompson, *Islands out of Time* (Garden City, N.Y., 1985).

62. Theodore Roszak, *The Making of a Counter-Culture* (New York, 1969). For a more detailed sympathetic but skeptical response, see my review essay, *Village Voice* (October 30, 1969).

63. Theodore Roszak, *Where the Wasteland Ends,* "Politics and Transcendence in Postindustrial Society" (New York, 1973).

64. Theodore Roszak, *Unfinished Animal* (New York, 1975), quotes from pp. 106 and 264.

65. *Five Stages of Greek Religion* (London, 1912), chapter 5.

66. Theodore Roszak, *Person/Planet* (Garden City, N.Y., 1978), with the conclusion for the discussion of "scale," pp. 285ff. for the "monastic paradigm," and pp. 75ff. for Daniel Bell. For a fuller criticism of Bell's "functionalist" utopianism, see my "The Processed Culture: Wasting Sensibility in Post-Industrial Society," *Arts in Society* 12 (Winter 1974).

67. Robert Vacca, *The Coming Dark Age* (New York, 1973). Other postcollapse utopianizing is touched on in the next chapter, below.

68. Theodore Roszak, *Bugs* (New York, 1981); *Dreamwatcher* (New York, 1985).

69. Theodore Roszak, *The Cult of Information* (New York, 1986), with citations from pp. 201, 47ff., 135ff., 146, 148, 155, and 217. He draws upon what, in my limited reading on the subject, are two of the stronger discussions: Joseph Weizenbaum, *Computer Power and Human Reason* (San Francisco, 1976); and John Searle, *Minds, Brains and Science* (Cambridge, Mass., 1985).

70. For related critiques, see my "The Electric-Aesthetic and the Short-Circuit Ethic: The Populist Generator in the Mass Culture Machine," *Mass Culture Revisited,* ed. B. Rosenberg and David Manning White (New York, 1971), updated in my "The Age of Showbiz," *American Book Review* (Jan.-Feb. 1987).

71. Or as Roszak put it elsewhere, of Bay Area counterculturist technotopians, *"They insisted that they could have it both ways"* (italics his), and that "the technophiliac route forward would lead to a reversionary [libertarian neopastoral] future." *From Satori to Silicon Valley* (San Francisco, 1986), p. 32.

72. See, for example, *Autobiography of Brook Farm,* ed. Henry W. Sams (Englewood cliffs, N.J., 1958); *The Brook Farm Book,* ed. Joel Myerson (New York, 1957).

73. See Dorothy Day, *A Long Loneliness* (New York, 1952) and her earlier *House of Hospitality* (New York, 1939). See also William D. Miller, *A Harsh and Dreadful Love: Dorothy Day and the Catholic Worker Movement* (New York, 1973).

74. On Manson, see, among others, Ed Sanders, *The Family* (New York, 1971); Vincent Bugliosi, *Helter Skelter* (New York, 1974). On Jonestown, see James Reston, Jr., *Our Father Who Art in Hell: The Life and Death of Jim Jones* (New York, 1981).

75. Raymond Mungo, *Total Loss Farm: A Year in the Life* (New York, 1970); *Between Two Moons: A Technicolor Travelogue* (Boston, 1972). I am restating my discussion in "Hipped-Up Babes in the Woods," *Village Voice* (July 6, 1972).

76. As with Brook Farm, the less literary accounts of this long-lived commune are rather different: see Stephen Diamond, *What the Trees Said: Life on a New Age Farm* (New York, 1971); Richard Wezansky, et al., *Home Comfort: Life on Total Loss Farm* (New York, 1975); and Gilbert Zicklin, *Countercultural Communes* (Westport, Conn., 1983), pp. 84ff.

77. Judson Jerome, *Families of Eden: Communes and the New Anarchism* (New York, 1974). Not incidentally, anarchism is used in the opposite sense in his prior book, *Culture Out of Anarchy: The Reconstruction of American Higher Education* (New York, 1971), which proposes radical changes in academia. See my more elaborate discussin in "Professors and Communalism," *AAUP Bulletin* 60 (October 1974).

78. Ron E. Roberts, *The New Communes: Coming Together in America* (New York, 1971). Contrast the therapeutic emphasis with earlier surveys, sometimes of the same areas, such as Mark Holloway, *Heavens on Earth* (New York, 1966), and Robert Hine, *California's Utopian Colonies* (New Haven, 1966).

79. See the skeptical anecdotal survey of Kenneth Rexroth, *Communalism: From Its Origins to the Twentieth Century* (New York, 1974).

80. Keith Melville, *Communes in the Counter-Culture: Origins, Themes, and Styles of Life* (New York, 1972). Lewis Mumford suggested, long before, that much applied utopianism was only escapist, unlike the limited number that undertook social reconstruction, in *The Story of Utopias* (New York, 1922).

81. Rosabeth Moss Kanter, *Commitment and Community: Communes and Utopias in Sociological Perspective* (Cambridge, Mass., 1972).

82. Philip Abrams and Andrew McCulloch, *Communes, Sociology and Society* (Cambridge, England, 1976), quotes from pp. 189 and 194. The distortions of Marxist dogmatism are also evident in the dubious description of utopian communalism as "petty-bourgeois protest," p. 141.

83. Lawrence R. Veysey, *The Communal Experience: Anarchist and Mystical Communities in Twentieth Century America* (Chicago, 1978).

84. Zicklin, p. 62.

85. Bennett M. Berger, *The Survival of a Counterculture: Ideological Work and Everyday Life among Rural Communards* (Berkeley, 1981), with citations parenthetical in text. While more literate than some of the others cited, this book, too, is overwhelmed by debasing sociological ritualism, under the guise of discussing "methodology."

86. Frances FitzGerald, *Cities on a Hill: A Journey through Contemporary American Cultures* (New York, 1986), with citations in text *(CH)*. My only other sources here, drawn on generally, are running media reports (primarily *Los Angeles Times*).

87. In addition to the materials on Shakers in chapters 1 and 3 above, see Louis J. Kern, *An Ordered Love: Sex Roles and Sexuality in Victorian Utopias—The Shakers, the Mormons, and the Oneida Community* (Chapel Hill, N.C., 1981). For a standard discussion of the forms of earlier American communalism, see Arthur Bestor, *Backwoods Utopias: The Sectarian Origins and Owenite Phase of Communitarian Socialism in America, 1663–1827,* 2nd ed. (Philadelphia, 1970). For a brief discussion of later forms, see Maren Lockwood, "The Experimental Utopia in America," in *Utopias and Utopian Thought,* ed. Frank E. Manuel (Boston, 1966). For a discussion of some earlier interrelations of historical events and utopian efforts, see Arthur E. Morgan, *Nowhere was Somewhere: How History Made Utopias and Utopias Made History* (Chapel Hill, N.C., 1946).

Chapter 5

1. Robert Nozick, *Anarchy, State, and Utopia* (New York, 1974), pp. 295–334. The immediately following phrases, pp. 298 and 320. I am refashioning arguments made in my monograph, "Utopia and Liberty: Some Contemporary Issues within Their Intellectual Traditions," *Literature of Liberty* 4 (Winter 1981): 5–62. This ranges over many of the other examples used here.

2. Nozick, pp. 312 and 309.

3. Charles J. Erasmus, *In Search of the Common Good: Utopian Experiments Past and Future* (New York, 1977), p. 286. He also undercuts one of Nozick's few specific examples, the Israeli *kibbutz,* as being peculiar and problematic in utopian terms, pp. 167–199.

4. Nozick, pp. 310ff. for the argument from "complexity." There is little connection between a simple variety of alternate communes and complexity. But probably Nozick intends to adapt such positions as F. A. Hayek's "The Theory of Complex Phenomena," in *Studies in Philosophy, Politics and Economics* (Chicago, 1967), which holds that modern economies are complex beyond rational possibilities of central planning. That is quite different from making complexity a social-moral principle of organization. Hayek, of course, has been an influential antiutopian (see *The Road to Serfdom* [London, 1944], especially chapter 2, "The Great Utopia"). There seems to me a general confusion in this tradition as to whether socialist utopianism is bad because it cannot work (contrary to nature, to social complexity, to rational powers, etc.), or bad because it can work all too well (uniform, totalitarian, antirich, etc.). Yet, naturally, the opponent of rationalistic social "constructivism" even consciously proposes his own conservative "Utopia," such as a new constitutional form in "Economic Freedom and Representative Government," in *New Studies in Philosophy, Politics, Economics, and the History of Ideas* (Chicago, 1978), pp. 105–18. More generally, such views also rest on a fantastic utopianism of purified "free markets."

5. Nozick does criticize Ayn Rand in "On the Randian Argument," in *Reading Nozick,* ed. Jeffrey Paul (Totowa, N.J., 1981), pp. 206–31. But his notes draw on the long speech of Galt in *Atlas Shrugged,* and he calls her novels "exciting, powerful, illuminating, and thought provoking"; he claims to hold similar values, just not the specific arguments.

6. See Robert Owen, *A New View of Society, and Other Writings,* ed. G. D. H. Cole (London, 1927) and John F. C. Harrison, *Quest for the New Moral World: Robert Owen and the Owenites in Britain and America* (New York, 1969).

7. Wayne Hudson, *The Marxist Philosophy of Ernst Bloch* (New York, 1982), p. 50.

8. Hudson, p. 51.

9. Dennis J. Schmidt, Introduction, Ernst Bloch, *Natural Law and Human Dignity* (Cambridge, Mass., 1986), p. x.

10. Ernst Bloch, *A Philosophy of the Future*, trans. John Cumming (New York, 1970), pp. 84–144.

11. Bloch, *Future,* pp. 88–89.

12. Bloch, *Future,* p. 93.

13. Bloch, *Future,* p. 95.

14. Bloch, *Future,* p. 144. "Concrete utopia is a projective ontological concept, not a metaphysical reality which is already actual." Hudson, p. 101. For a longer summary of Bloch, with a quite different and obscurist emphasis, see Fredric Jameson, *Marxism and Form* (Princeton, N.J., 1971), pp. 116–59.

15. Vulgar Marxism, of course, is notorious for arbitrary readings of texts. On the subject here, see A. L. Morton, *The English Utopia* (London, 1952), which is better on the "Cockaygne" tradition, where the Marxist can patronize the socially lower orders, than on Huxley, Orwell, etc., where he just focuses the usual dogmatic clichés.

16. Fredric Jameson, *The Political Unconscious: Narrative as a Socially Symbolic Act* (Ithaca, 1981), p. 291. The following quotes are from pp. 293 and 299. For his relation to Bloch, see the earlier book cited, as well as the many references in this one.

17. On Jameson's role as coterie-careerist ideologue, see Fredrick C. Crews, *Skeptical Engagements* (New York, 1986), pp. 137ff. For an example of Jameson's practical criticism, see the charts and ill-informed and arbitrary impositions on Conrad, *Political Unconscious*, pp. 206ff.; for a drastically different ideological analysis, see my "Conrad's Pyrrhonistic Conservativism: Ideological Melodrama Around 'Simple Ideas,'" *Novel* 7 (1974).

18. I am drawing on parts of earlier discussions of Marcuse: "Society as a Work of Art," *Nation* 211 (July 6, 1970); "Marcuse's Allegory," *Anarchy* (London) (Sept. 1970); "Marcuse's Cultural Mystification," *Village Voice* (Sept. 28, 1972); and "Some Radical Criticism, Mostly Late-Marcusean," *The End of Culture* (San Diego, 1975).

19. Herbert Marcuse, *Counterrevolution and Revolt* (Boston, 1972), p. 130. Following quote, p. 134. *An Essay on Liberation* (Boston, 1969).

20. While there is little feminism in the earlier Marcuse, it becomes strong in the 1970s. See, for example, his "Marxism and Feminism," *Women's Studies* 2 (1974). Since, he holds, women have been virtually excluded from patriarchal-capitalist roles, their group character is less malformed, and they more freely connect with the aesthetic-erotic dimension. More tangibly, Marcuse had a quite romantic response to women.

21. Herbert Marcuse, *One-Dimensional Man* (Boston, 1964), throughout.

22. Herbert Marcuse, *Eros and Civilization: A Philosophical Inquiry into Freud* (New York, 1962), p. ix.

23. Herbert Marcuse, *Negations: Essays in Critical Theory* (Boston, 1968), p. xx.

24. The defiant point of "more subversive potential" in classic modernism is made at the end of the Preface to *The Aesthetic Dimension: Toward a Critique of Marxist Aesthetics* (Boston, 1978), p. xiii.

25. *Eros and Civilization,* p. 142.

26. "The End of Utopia," *Five Lectures: Psychoanalysis, Politics, and Utopia* (Boston, 1970), p. 63. Following quotes are pp. 66 and 68.

27. As Douglas Kellner, in the most useful book I know of on Marcuse, summarizes it: "Marxism is not utopian enough, for the technical-material possibilities at hand make possible even more radical and emancipatory social transformation than Marx envisaged." *Herbert Marcuse and the Crisis of Marxism* (Berkeley, 1984), p. 324. To the objections that technological forms would then be dominant, Marcuse responded with the vague call for a newly humanized technology, and science.

28. *One-Dimensional Man,* pp. 241ff.

29. Ivan Illich, *Toward a History of Needs* (New York, 1978) and his later work as well, such as *Shadow Work* (London, 1981), which utopianizes for modesty, small scale, immediate authenticity, etc. (and for confined roles for women).

30. Eliseo Vivas, *Contra Marcuse* (New York, 1971), on the last page of his diatribe. I have elsewhere (earlier articles cited) discussed some of the other criticism of Marcuse, such as that of Alasdair MacIntyre, *Herbert Marcuse* (New York, 1970).

31. *Five Lectures,* pp. 83ff.

32. Contra Melvin Lasky, *Utopia and Revolution* (Chicago, 1976).

33. In Herbert Marcuse, Barrington Moore, and Robert Paul Wolff, *A Critique of Pure Tolerance* (Boston, 1965).

34. Marcuse specifically cites Fourier as a source of the aesthetic work-play community in *Essay on Liberation,* p. 22.

35. *Aesthetic Dimension* citations are in text *(AD).*

36. Kellner, p. 358.

37. *Counterrevolution and Revolt,* pp. 79–128.

38. Part of the difficulty, as Marcuse made clear to me (in a number of personal conversations, 1966–72), was his centering on an earlier Continental tradition and lack of relation to later developments. At a Free University where we both lectured, he complained that there was Rock instead of Bach for the celebratory music. Similarly, his views of violence, censorship, elitism, etc., came out of a matrix quite removed from the American scene (as when he sniffily lectured me on my not responding with more anger and paranoia to the hate mail I was getting).

39. Alasdair MacIntyre, *Herbert Marcuse: An Exposition and a Polemic* (New York, 1970), p. 50.

40. Helen Hazen, *Endless Rapture: Rape, Romance, and the Female Imagination* (New York, 1983), p. 18. It should be acknowledged that my generalizations are based on reading only a very small sample of contemporary romances (and a few other studies in addition to those cited here).

41. Janice A. Radway, *Reading the Romance; Women, Patriarchy, and Popular Literature* (Chapel Hill, N.C., 1984). Quotations from pp. 147, 55, 218, and 22.

42. With some reluctance, I am following current usage which has merged "obscenity" into the now pervasive term "pornography." Contrast D. H. Lawrence's emphatic distinctions between sexual explicitness and sexual exploitation in his various late essays on the issues. *Sex, Literature, and Censorship,* ed. Harry T. Moore (New York, 1959). For a recent analysis, see Donald Gutierrez, "D. H. Lawrence's 'Pornography and Obscenity'—Sex, Society, and the Self," in

The Dark and Light Gods (Troy, N.Y., 1987), pp. 156–77. The earliest citation in the *OED Supplement* for "pornotopia" is Steven Marcus (*The Other Victorians,* 1966), though the term is apparently a bit earlier.

43. My sketchy survey draws upon *The Complete Justine, Philosophy in the Bedroom, and Other Writings* (New York, 1965); *120 Days of Sodom* (Paris, 1957); and Ronald Hayman's biography, *De Sade* (London, 1978).

44. Roland Barthes, *Sade/Fourier/Loyola* (New York, 1976). Quotations from pp. 171, 129, and 167.

45. A similar point was made by D. H. Lawrence about Edgar Allen Poe's love-obscenity: *Studies in Classic American Literature* (New York, 1951), pp. 74–76.

46. Jane Gallop, *Intersections: A Reading of Sade with Bataille, Blanchot, and Klassowski* (Lincoln, Neb., 1981), pp. 33 and 16.

47. Angela Carter, *The Sadeian Woman, and the Ideology of Pornography* (New York, 1980). Quotations are from pp. 17, 36, 138, and 150.

48. Barthes, pp. 80–81, and p. 113. Granted the qualification that, with the skittish pretenses now fashionable, Barthes is not talking about the subject but about the "semiotic" in and of it.

49. Susan Sontag, "The Pornographic Imagination," appended to Georges Bataille, *Story of the Eye* (London: 1982), pp. 83–118 (orig. *Styles of Radical Will* [1967]). Following quote, p. 113.

50. Bataille, *Story of the Eye,* with the quotation from p. 42.

51. Pauline Reage, *Story of O* (New York, 1965); *Return to the Chateau: Story of O (Volume 2)* (New York, 1971). Page citation for the first lost.

52. *Return to the Chateau,* quotations from pp. 9, 23, and 64. For the view of it as "moral allegory," see Peter Michelson, *The Aesthetics of Pornography* (New York, 1971), pp. 53–60. Why this belongs to the special order of "complex pornography" is unclear to me.

53. See, for example, the discussion (and literature cited) in Alan Soble, "Male and Female Sexuality in Capitalism," *Pornography: Marxism, Feminism, and the Future of Sexuality* (New Haven, 1986), pp. 55–102. The view seems to be so commonplace that further citation would be gratuitous. My bias is that those arguments which root gender differences in biology are not only unpersuasive in details but dubious in the premise of what we know about human eroticism. Yet it must be granted that contrary arguments attempting to link porn-visualization with patriarchy, in the objectification of the inferior other, seem arbitrary. See Susanne Kappeler, *The Pornography of Representation* (Cambridge, 1986).

54. Sontag, p. 113; other quotations, pp. 102 and 88.

55. Theodore Sturgeon, *Godbody* (New York, 1987). Ff. quotations from pp. 33, 32, 67, 181.

56. Sturgeon, p. 191.

57. Soble, p. 175.

58. It is considered a radically utopian view to hold that "self-regulation . . . has never been tried on a large enough scale over a long enough time span to have yet had its experiential test." Arthur Efron, *The Sexual Body: An Interdisciplinary Perspective* (New York, 1985), p. 280. But the self-regulatory view has a "naturist" premise outside social-cultural ordering. I take as a partial drastic qualification of it such evidence as the following: "One of the striking things about the concentration camp experience—and there is enormous evidence on this point—is

that under conditions of privation and horror the need for sex disappears. It simply is not there, neither in feeling nor in fantasy." Terence Des Pres, *The Survivors: An Anatomy of Life in the Death Camps* (New York, 1976), p. 189. Neither the Sadean nor the Reichean takes adequate account of how determining the social-cultural context is of sexuality.

59. For a consideration of some of these examples, see my *The Literary Rebel* (Carbondale, Ill., 1965).

60. Denis Diderot, *Supplement to Bougainville's Voyage* in *Rameau's Nephew and Other Writings*, ed. Jacques Barzun (New York, 1956), pp. 187–237.

61. Wilhelm Reich, *The Sexual Revolution: Toward a Self-Regulating Character Structure* (New York, 1974). For his later, less "naturist," views, see *Selected Writings: An Introduction to Orgonomy* (New York, 1961). See also M. Sharaf, *Fury on Earth: A Biography of Wilhelm Reich* (New York, 1983).

62. Norman O. Brown, *Life against Death* (New York, 1959); *Love's Body* (New York, 1965). A balanced account of some of the erotic utopianisms is Richard King, *The Party of Eros* (Chapel Hill, N.C., 1972).

63. While resembling patriarchal sexuality in form, Noyes' "regulated promiscuity" had considerably different effects, argues Robert David Thomas in *The Man Who Would Be Perfect, John Humphrey Noyes and the Utopian Impulse* (Philadelphia, 1977), p. 175. Somewhere Aldous Huxley has a defense of Noyes and male incomplete coitus as a desirable future sexuality (reference lost).

64. Robert Rimmer, *The Harrad Experiment* (New York, 1966); *The Rebellion of Yale Marratt* (New York, 1967); and *Proposition Thirty-One* (New York, 1968).

65. Murray S. Davis, *Smut: Erotic Reality/Obscene Ideology* (Chicago, 1983), p. 243; for Sadean Gnosticism, pp. 178ff.

66. Mary Shelley, *The Last Man* (London, 1985). The reference below to Olaf Stapledon, *Last and First Men: A Story of the Near and Far Future* (London, 1930) is, of course, to the conclusion.

67. Stanislaw Lem, "Science Fiction: A Hopeless Case—With Exceptions," in *Microworlds*, ed. Franz Rottensteiner (New York, 1984), pp. 74–75.

68. See Richard Dawkins, *The Blind Watchmaker* (New York, 1986). I used another biological notion (so far as I can understand it) in the sense of Jacques Monod, *Chance and Necessity* (New York, 1970).

69. William Golding, *The Inheritors* (New York, 1955). Epigraph from Wells is p. 9. The use of Wells is discussed by Bernard F. Dick, *William Golding*, rev. ed. (Boston, 1987), pp. 30–31. More generally, see James R. Baker, *William Golding: A Critical Study* (New York, 1965). Parallel points, of course, have been made in sci-fi. The example noted parenthetically is given by a spokesman from another world, who rejects earthlings because they eliminated the more gentle, vegetarian, artistic Neanderthal. Stanislaw Lem, "The Eighth Voyage," in *The Star Diaries* (original 1971; New York, 1976), p. 35. But on another cosmic trip, Lem's sardonic commentator suggests a positive side to the limitations of *homo sapiens:* "It's comforting to know, when you think about it, that only man can be a bastard," p. 85.

70. Jonathan Schell, *The Fate of the Earth* (New York, 1982).

71. "American Apocalypse: Notes on the Bomb and the Failure of Imagination," in *The Forties*, ed. Warren French (De Land, Fla., 1969), pp. 141–54. I now recognize this discussion as inadequate but will not substantially revise it here.

72.   Robert Jay Lifton, *Death in Life* (New York, 1967). My objection that such accounts underplay the real issues, especially those of the technocratic state, also applies to the later attempts to compound nuclear awareness, as in the literary anthology *In a Dark Time,* ed. Robert Jay Lifton and Nicholas Humphrey (Cambridge, Mass., 1984). See my review, "Dark Literary Lunch," *Social Anarchism* 5 (1985).

73.   "Incarceration and Torture," in *The Dark and Light Gods,* pp. 178–216.

74.   Tim O'Brien, *The Nuclear Age* (New York, 1985), with the following quotes from pp. 200 and 312. For didactic purposes, time is frequently in the very near future in such fictions. In Whittey Steriber and James Kunelka, *War Day* (New York, 1985), the incomplete nuclear armageddon is in 1988, the relentlessly commonplace postwar fictional documentary in 1993.

75.   David Dowling, *Fictions of Nuclear Disaster* (London, 1987), the chapter "Post-Nuclear Society," pp. 83–113.

76.   *The Survivors,* p. 188. Qualification: survivors were likely often not the best people, I suspect.

77.   Leo Tolstoy, "The Death of Ivan Ilyich," in *Classics of Modern Fiction,* ed. Irving Howe (New York, 1972), p. 168.

78.   D. H. Lawrence, *Reflections on the Death of a Porcupine* (London, 1934), p. 17; Paul Tillich, "Critique and Justification of Utopia," in *Utopias and Utopian Thought,* ed. Frank Manuel (Boston, 1966), p. 309; Nicholas Berdayev, *Slavery and Freedom* (New York, 1948), repeatedly.

Bibliography

Abbey, Edward. *The Monkey Wrench Gang*. New York, 1975.

Abrams, Philip, and Andrew McCulloch. *Communes, Sociology and Society*. Cambridge, 1976.

Aldridge, Alexandra. *The Scientific World View in Dystopia*. Ann Arbor, 1984.

Amis, Martin. *Money*. London, 1986.

Andrews, Edward D. *The People Called Shakers*. New York, 1963.

Arendt, Hannah. *The Human Condition*. Garden City. N.Y., 1959.

Aristophanes. *The Clouds,* Ed. J. K. Dover. New York, 1968.

Atwood, Margaret. *The Handmaid's Tale*. New York, 1987.

———. *Lady Oracle*. New York, 1987.

———. *Life after Man*. New York, 1983.

———. *Survival: A Thematic Guide to Canadian Literature*. Toronto, Can., 1972.

Avrich, Paul. *The Modern School Movement*. Princeton, N.J., 1980.

Baker, James Rupert. *William Golding*. New York, 1965.

Baklely, Barbara. "The Pronunciation of Flesh; A Feminist Reading of Margaret Atwood's Poetry." In *Margaret Atwood*. Ed. Sherrill E. Grad and Lorraine Weir. Vancouver, Can., 1983.

Barr, Marleen S. *Alien to Femininity: Speculative Fiction and Feminist Theory*. Westport, Conn., 1987.

Barrett, William. *The Illusion of Technique*. New York, 1979.

Barthes, Roland. *Sade/Fourier/Loyola*. New York, 1976.

Bataille, George. *Story of the Eye*. London, 1982.

Bateson, Gregory. *Steps to an Ecology of Mind*. New York, 1972.

Beauchamp, Gorman. "Zamiatin's *We*." In *No Place Else*. Ed. Eric S. Rabkin, Martin H. Greenberg, and Joseph D. Olander. Carbondale, Ill., 1983.

Bellamy, Edward. *Looking Backward, 2000–1887*. New York, 1960.

Berdyaev, Nicholas. *Slavery and Freedom*. New York, 1948.

Berger, Bennett M. *The Survival of a Counterculture*. Berkeley, 1981.

Berger, Thomas. *Regiment of Women*. New York, 1973.

Berneri, Marie Louise. *Journey through Utopia*. London, 1950.

Berry, Wendell. *Home Economics*. Berkeley, 1987.

———. *Recollected Essays*. Berkeley, 1981.

———. *The Unsettling of America: Culture and Agriculture*. New York, 1977.

Bestor, Arthur. *Backwoods Utopias*. 2nd ed. Philadelphia, 1970.

Billington, James H. *The Icon and the Axe*. New York, 1966.

Bittner, James W. *Approaches to the Fiction of Ursula K. Le Guin*. Ann Arbor, 1984.

Blake, William. *The Marriage of Heaven and Hell. The Poetry and Prose*. Ed. David V. Erdman. Garden City, N.Y., 1965.

Bleich, David. *Utopia, The Psychology of a Cultural Fantasy*. Ann Arbor, 1984.

Blish, James. *Earthman, Come Home*. London, 1974.

Bloch, Ernst. *Natural Law and Human Dignity*. Cambridge, Mass., 1986.

————. *A Philosophy of the Future*. Trans. John Cumming. New York, 1970.

Bookchin, Murray. *The Ecology of Freedom*. Palo Alto, Cal., 1982.

Borsodi, Ralph. *Flight from the City*. New York, 1972.

Bowman, Sylvia. *Edward Bellamy Abroad: An American Prophet's Influence*. New York, 1962.

————. *The Year 2000: A Critical Biography of Edward Bellamy*. New York, 1985.

Brantenberg, Gerd. *Egalias's Daughters*. Seattle, 1985.

Brennan, John P. and Michael C. Downs. "Anarchism and Utopian Tradition in *The Dispossessed*." In *Ursula K. Le Guin*. Ed. Joseph D. Olander and Martin H. Greenberg. New York, 1979.

Brown, E. J. *Brave New World, 1984, and We*. Ann Arbor, 1976.

Brown, James. *The Troika Incident*. New York, 1968.

Brown, Norman O. *Life against Death*. New York, 1959.

————. *Love's Body*. New York, 1965.

Buber, Martin. *Paths in Utopia*. Boston, 1958.

Bulwer-Lytton, Edward. *The Coming Race*. London, 1960.

Burgess, Anthony. *The Wanting Seed*. London, 1962.

Butler, Samuel. *Erewhon, or Over the Range*. New York, 1955.

Callenbach, Ernest. *Ecotopia*. Berkeley, 1975.

————. *Ecotopia Emerging*. Berkeley, 1981.

————. *Living Poor with Style*. New York, 1972.

Capek, Karl. *R. U. R.* New York, 1948.

Carroll, John. *The Break-out from the Crystal Palace*. London, 1974.

Carter, Angela. *The Sadeian Woman, and the Ideology of Pornography*. New York, 1980.

Charnas, Suzy McKee. *Motherlines*. New York, 1978.

Chodorow, Nancy. *The Reproduction of Mothering: Psychoanalysis and the Sociology of Gender*. Berkeley, 1978.

Coetzee, J. M. *Waiting for the Barbarians*. London, 1982.

Cogell, Elizabeth Cummins. "Taoist Configurations in *The Dispossessed*." In *Ursula K. Le Guin: Voyager to Inner Lands and to Outer Space*. Ed. Joe D. Bolt. Port Washington, N.Y., 1979.

Collins, Christopher. *Evgenij Zamjatin*. The Hague, Netherlands, 1973.

Collins, George R. *Visionary Drawings of Architecture and Planning, 20th Century through the 1960s*. Cambridge, Mass., 1979.

Crews, Frederick. *Skeptical Engagements*. New York, 1986.

Davis, J. C. "The History of Utopia: The Chronology of Nowhere." In *Utopias*. Ed. Peter Alexander and Roger Gill. London, 1984

————. *Utopia and the Ideal Society*. Cambridge, England, 1981.

Davis, Murray S. *Smut: Erotic Reality/Obscene Ideology*. Chicago, 1983.

Dawkins, Richard. *The Blind Watchmaker*. New York, 1986.

Day, Dorothy. *A Long Loneliness*. New York, 1952.

Delaney, Sheila. *Writing Women*. New York, 1983.

Delany, Samuel. *Triton*. New York, 1976.

Des Pres, Terence. *The Survivors*. New York, 1976.

Dick, Bernard F. *William Golding*. Rev. ed. Boston, 1987.

Dick, Philip K. *Valis*. New York, 1984.

Diderot, Denis. *Supplement to Bougainville's Voyage. Rameau's Nephew, and Other Writings*. Ed. Jacques Barzun. New York, 1956.

Dinnerstein, Dorothy. *The Mermaid and the Minotaur: Sexual Arguments and Human Malaise*. New York, 1976.

Dostoyevsky, Fyodor. *Notes from Underground and the Grand Inquisitor*. Trans. Ralph E. Matlaw. New York, 1960.

Dowling, David. *Fictions of Nuclear Disaster*. London, 1987.

Doxiadis, C. A. *Building Entopia*. New York, 1975.

Duberman, Martin. *Black Mountain*. New York, 1972.

Dubos, Rene. *A God Within*. New York, 1972.

Edwards, T. R. N. *Three Russian Writers and the Irrational*. Cambridge, England, 1982.

Efron, Arthur. *The Sexual Body*. New York, 1985.

Elliott, Robert C. *The Shape of Utopia*. Chicago, 1970.

Empson, William. *Some Versions of Pastoral*. Norfolk, Conn., 1941.

Engels, Frederich. *Socialism, Utopian and Scientific*. London, 1891.

Erasmus, Charles J. *In Search of the Common Good*. New York, 1977.

Esfandiary, F. M. *Upwingers*. New York, 1973.

Evans, Sara. *Personal Politics: The Root of the Women's Liberation Movement in the Civil Rights Movement and the New Left*. New York, 1979.

Farley, Tucker, "Realities and Visions: Lesbian Visions of Utopia." In *Women in Search of Utopia*. Ed. Ruby Rohrlich and Elaine Hoffman Baruch. New York, 1984.

Faulkner, Peter. *Against the Age: An Introduction to William Morris*. London, 1981.

Ferguson, Ann. "Androgyny as an Ideal for Human Development." In *The Philosophy of Sex*. Ed. Alan Soble. Totowa, N.J., 1980.

Fishman, Robert. *Urban Utopias in the Twentieth Century*. New York, 1977.

FitzGerald, Frances. *Cities on a Hill*. New York, 1986.

Ford, Ford Madox. *The Great Trade Route*. New York, 1937.

––––––. *It Was the Nightingale*. New York, 1975.

––––––. *No Enemy*. New York, 1929.

––––––. *Provence*. Philadelphia, 1935.

––––––. *The Rash Act*. Manchester, England, 1982.

Forster, E. M. "The Machine Stops." In *The Eternal Moment and Other Stories*. New York, 1928.

Foucault, Michel. *To Discipline and Punish*. New York, 1978.

Fourier, Charles. *Harmonian Man: Selected Writings*. E. Mark Poster. Garden City, N.Y., 1971.

––––––. *The Utopian Vision*. Ed. Jonathan Beecher and Richard Bienvenu. Boston, 1971.

Fowles, John. *The Maggot*. New York, 1986.

Freire, Paulo. *Pedagogy of the Oppressed*. New York, 1970.

––––––. *The Politics of Education, Culture, Power, and Liberation*. South Hadley, Mass., 1985.

Freibert, Lucy M. "World Views in Utopian Novels by Women." In *Women and Utopia*. Ed. Marleen Barr and Nicholas Smith. Lanham, Md., 1983.

Frye, Richard. "The Economics of Ecotopia." *Alternative Futures* 3 (Winter 1980).

Fuller, R. Buckminster. *Operating Manual for Spaceship Earth*. Carbondale, Ill., 1969.

––––––. *Utopia or Oblivion: The Prospects for Humanity*. New York, 1967.

Gallop, Jane. *The Daughter's Seduction: Feminism and Psychoanalysis*. Ithaca, N.Y., 1982.

––––––. *Intersections*. Lincoln, Neb., 1981.

Gardiner, Judith Kegan. "On Female Identity and Writing by Women." In *Writing and Sexual Difference*. Ed. Elizabeth Abel. Chicago, 1982.

Gay, Peter. *The Enlightenment*. Vol. I. New York, 1966.

Gearhart, Sally Miller. "Future visions: Today's Politics; Feminist Utopias in Review." In *Women in Search of Utopia*. Ed. Ruby Rohrlich and Elaine Hoffman Baruch. New York, 1984.

––––––. *Wanderground*. Boston, 1984.

Gerber, John. *Utopian Fantasy*. London, 1957.

Gershun, H. Lee. "The Linguistic Transformation of Womanhood," In *Women in Search of Utopia*. Ed. Ruby Rohrlich and Elaine Hoffman Baruch. New York, 1984.

Gilman, Charlotte P. *Herland*. New York, 1915.

Gladstein, Mimi Reisel. *The Ayn Rand Companion*. Westport, Conn., 1984.

Golding, William. *The Inheritors*. New York, 1955.

Goodman, Paul and Percival. *Communitas*. Rev. ed. New York, 1960.

Goodwin, Barbara, and Keith Taylor. *The Politics of Utopia*. New York, 1982.

Gorer, Geoffrey. *The Life and Ideas of the Marquis de Sade*. New York, 1963.

Greg, Richard A. "Two Adams and Eve in the Crystal Palace: Dostoyevsky, The Bible, and *We*." *Slavic Studies* 24 (1965).

Griffin, Susan. *Pornography and Silence*. New York, 1981.

Gutierrez, Donald. *The Dark and Light Gods*. Troy, N.Y., 1987.

Hansot, Elizabeth. *Perfection and Progress: Two Modes of Utopian Thought*. Cambridge, Mass., 1971.

Harman, Willis H. *An Incomplete Guide to the Future*. Stanford, 1976.

Harrington, Alan. *The Immortalist*. Millbrae, Cal., 1977.

Harris, Liz. "Brother Sun, Sister Moon." *New Yorker* (April 27, 1987).

Harrison, John F. C. *Quest for the New Moral World: Robert Owen and the Owenites in Britain and America*. New York, 1969.

Hartley, L. P. *Facial Justice*. New York, 1960.

Hayek, F. A. *New Studies in Philosophy, Politics, and the History of Ideas*. Chicago, 1978.

––––––. "The Theory of Complex Phenomena." In *Studies in Philosophy, Politics and Economics*. Chicago, 1967.

Haylor, Dolores. *Seven American Utopias: The Architecture of Communitarian Socialism*. Cambridge, Mass., 1976.

Hazen, Helen. *Endless Rapture: Rape, Romance, and the Female Imagination*. New York, 1983.

Hazlitt, Harry. *The Great Idea*. New York, 1951.

Henderson, Hazel. *Creating Alternative Futures*. New York, 1978.

Hess, Karl. *Community Technology*. New York, 1979.

––––––. *Dear America*. New York, 1975.

Hess, Karl, and David Morris. *Neighborhood Power*. Boston, 1975.

Heyduke, George. *Get Even: The Complete Book of Dirty Tricks*. Boulder, Colo., 1980.

Hicks, Jack. *In the Singer's Temple*. Chapel Hill, N.C., 1981.

Hillegas, Mark R. *The Future as Nightmare: H. G. Wells and the Anti-Utopians*. New York, 1967.

Holloway, Mark. *Heavens on Earth*. New York, 1966.

Holquist, Michael. "How to Play Utopia." In *Game, Play, Literature*. Ed. Jacques Ehrdmann. Boston, Mass., 1968.

Howard, Ebenezer. *Garden Cities of Tomorrow*. Ed. F. J. Osborne. Cambridge, Mass., 1965.

Hudson, Wayne. *The Marxist Philosophy of Ernst Bloch*. New York, 1982.

Huxley, Aldous. *Brave New World*. New York, 1969.

––––––. *Island*. New York, 1963.

Illich, Ivan. *Shadow Work*. London, 1981.

––––––. *Toward a History of Needs*. New York, 1980.

Jameson, Fredric. *The Political Unconscious*. Ithaca, N.Y., 1981.

––––––. *Marxism and Form*. Princeton, 1971.

Jerome, Judson. *Families of Eden*. New York, 1974.

Jungk, Robert. *Brighter than a Thousand Suns*. New York, 1958.

Kahn, Herman. *The Year 2000*. New York, 1967.

Kappeler, Susanne. *The Pornography of Representation*. Cambridge, England, 1986.

Kanter, Rosabeth Moss. *Commitment and Community, Communes and Utopias in Sociological Perspective*. Cambridge, Mass., 1972.

Kateb, George. *Utopia and Its Enemies*. New York, 1963.

Kellner, Douglas. *Herbert Marcuse and the Crisis of Marxism*. Berkeley, 1984.

Kenner, Hugh. *Bucky*. New York, 1973.

Khanne, Lee Cullen. "Women's Worlds: New Directions in Utopian Fiction." *Alternate Futures* 4(1981).

Kincade, Kathleen. *A Walden Two Experiment*. New York, 1973.

King, Richard. *The Party of Eros*. Chapel Hill, N.C., 1972.

Kinnaird. Jack. *Olaf Stapledon*. West Linn, Ore., 1982.

Knepper, B. G. *"The Coming Race:* Hell? Or Paradise Foretasted?" In *No Place Else*. Ed. Eric S. Rabkin, Martin H. Greenberg, and Joseph D. Olander. Carbondale, Ill., 1980.

Knight, Isabel F. "Alienation, Eros, and Work: The Good News from Nowhere." *Alternative Futures* 2(Winter 1979).

Kress, Susan. "In and Out of Time: The Form of Marge Piercy's Novels." In *Future Females*. Ed. Marleen S. Barr. Bowling Green, Ohio, 1981.

Krieger, Ronald A. "The Economics of Utopia." In *Utopias: The American Experience*. Ed. G. B. Moment and Otto F. Kraushaar. Metuchen, N.J., 1980.

Kropotkin, Peter. *Mutual Aid*. New York, 1970.

Krutch, Joseph Wood. *The Measure of Man: On Freedom, Human Values, Survival and the Modern Temper*. New York, 1953.

Kurchoff, Frederick. *William Morris*. Boston, Mass., 1979.

Kumar, Krishan. "Primitivism in Feminist Utopias." *Alternate Societies* 4 (1981).

Lasky, Melvin. *Utopia and Revolution*. Chicago, 1976.

Lawrence, D. H. "The Man Who Loved Islands." In *The Complete Short Stories*. Vol. 3, London, 1977.

———. *The Plumed Serpent*. New York, 1951.

———. *Lady Chatterley's Lover*. New York, 1959.

———. *Sex, Literature and Censorship*. Ed. Harry T. Moore. New York, 1959.

Leary, Timothy, et al. *Millennium: Glimpses in the 21st Century*. Ed. Albert Villoldo and Ken Dychtwald. Boston, 1981.

Le Corbusier. *Towards a New Architecture*. New York, 1960.

Le Guin, Ursula K. *The Dispossessed*. New York, 1975.

———. *The Language of the Night*. New York, 1979.

———. *The Left Hand of Darkness*. New York, 1969.

———. *The Wind's Twelve Quarters*. New York, 1975.

———. *The Word for World Is Forest*. New York, 1972.

Lem, Stanislaw. *Microworlds*. Ed. Franz Rottensteiner. New York, 1984.

———. *Star Diaries*. New York, 1976.

Lessing, Doris. *Briefing for a Descent into Hell*. New York, 1973.

Levin, Harry. *The Myth of the Golden Age in the Renaissance*. Bloomington, Ind., 1969.

Lévi-Strauss, Claude. *Triste Tropique*. New York, 1961.

Lifton, Robert Jay. *Death in Life*. New York, 1967.

Lockwood, Maren. "The Experimental Utopia in America." In *Utopias and Utopian Thought*. Ed. Frank E. Manuel. Boston, 1966.

Lovejoy, A. O., et al. *A Documentary History of Primitivism*. Baltimore, Md., 1935.

Lovelock, James E. *Gaia: A New Look at Life on Earth*. New York, 1979.

Lukes, Steven. "Marxism and Utopianism." In *Utopias*. Ed. Peter Alexander and Roger Gill. London, 1984.

McGicirk, Carol. "Optimism and the Limits of Subversion in 'The Dispossessed' and 'The Left Hand of Darkness.'" In *Ursula K. Le Guin*. Ed. Harold Bloom. New York, 1986.

MacIntyre, Alasdair. *Herbert Marcuse*. New York, 1970.

MacShane, Frank. *The Life and Work of Ford Madox Ford*. New York, 1965.

Manuel, Frank E. and Fritzie P. *Utopian Thought in the Western World*. Cambridge, Mass., 1979.

Marcuse, Herbert. *The Aesthetic Dimension*. Boston, 1978.

———. *Counter-revolution and Revolt*. Boston, 1972.

———. *Eros and Civilization*. New York, 1962.

———. *An Essay on Liberation*. Boston, 1969.

———. *Five Lectures*. Boston, 1970.

———. *Negations*. Boston, 1968.

———. *One-Dimensional Man*. Boston, 1964.

Marinelli, Peter V. *Pastoral*. London, 1971.

Martin, James J. *Men against the State: The Expositors of Individualist Anarchism in America, 1827–1908*. Colorado Springs, 1970.

Michelson, Peter. *The Aesthetics of Pornography*. New York, 1971.

Miller, Walter M., Jr. *A Canticle for Leibowitz*. New York, 1960.

Miller, William D. *A Harsh and Dreadful Love: Dorothy Day and the Catholic Worker Movement*. New York, 1973.

Molnar, Thomas. *Utopia: The Perennial Heresy*. New York, 1967.

Montaigne, Michel de. "Of Cannibals." In *Selected Essays*. Trans. D. A. Frame. New York, 1963.

Moore, Harry T. *The Priest of Love*. New York, 1974.

More, Thomas. *Utopia*. London, 1960.

Morris, William. *News from Nowhere, or, An Epoch at Rest*. New York, 1966.

Morson, Gary Saul. *The Boundaries of Genre*. Austin, 1981.

Morton, A. L. *The English Utopia*. London, 1952.

Moylan, Tom. *Demand the Impossible*. New York, 1986.

Mumford, Lewis. *The Story of Utopias*. New York, 1922.

Mungo, Raymond. *Between Two Moons*. Boston, 1972.

Murdoch, Iris. *The Fire and the Sun*. London, 1977.

Myerson, Joel, ed. *The Brook Farm Book: A Collection of First-Hand Accounts of the Community*. New York, 1987.

Nearing, Helen and Scott. *Continuing the Good Life*. New York, 1979.

———. *Living the Good Life*. New York, 1970.

Neill, A. S. *Summerhill*. New York, 1962.

Nelson, William, et al. *Twentieth Century Interpretations of Utopia*. Ed. William Nelson. Englewood Cliffs, N.J., 1968.

Nichols, Robert. *Exile*. Vol. 4 of *Daily Lives in Nghsi-Attai*. New York, 1979.

Nichols, William, and Charles P. Henry. "Imagining a Future in America: A Racial Perspective." *Alternate Futures* 1 (Spring 1978).

Nietzsche, Friedrich. *On the Genealogy of Morals*. Trans. R. J. Hollingwood and Walter Kaufmann. New York, 1968.

Nozick, Robert. *Anarchy, State, and Utopia*. New York, 1974.

———. "On the Randian Argument." *Reading Nozick*. Ed. Jeffrey Paul. Totowa, N.J., 1981.

O'Brien, Tim. *The Nuclear Age*. New York, 1985.

Ogilvey, James. *Many Dimensional Man*. New York, 1977.

O'Neill, Gerard K. *The High Frontier*. New York, 1977.

———. *2081: A Hopeful View of the Human Future*. New York, 1981.

Orwell, George. "Freedom and Happiness." *Tribune* (London) 471 (Jan. 4, 1946).

———. *Nineteen Eighty-Four*. New York, 1949.

Owen, Robert. *A New View of Society, and Other Writings*. Ed. G. D. H. Cole. London, 1927.

Parsons, Ann. "The Self-Inventing Self: Women Who Lie and Pose in the Fictions of Margaret

Atwood." In *Gender Studies*. Ed. Judith Spector. Bowling Green, Ohio, 1986.

Passmore, John. *The Perfectability of Man*. New York, 1970.

Patae, Daphne. "Beyond Defensiveness: Feminist Research Strategies." In *Women and Utopia*. Ed. Marleen Barr and Nicholas Smith. Lanham, Md., 1983.

Pearson, Carol. "Coming Home: Four Feminist Utopias and Patriarchal Experience." In *Future Females: A Critical Anthology*. Ed. Marleen S. Barr. Bowling Green, Ohio, 1981.

Piercy, Marge. *Dance the Eagle to Sleep*. New York, 1970.

————. *Woman on the Edge of Time*. New York, 1976.

Piercy, Marge, et al. *The Movement Towards a New America*. Ed. Mitchell Goodman. New York, 1970.

Plato. *The Republic*. Trans. F. M. Cornford. New York, 1945.

Poggioli, Renato. *The Oaten Flute*. Cambridge, Mass., 1975.

Polak, Frank L. *The Image of the Future*. Trans. E. Boulding. Dobbs Ferry, N.Y., 1961.

Popper, Karl. "Utopia and Violence." In *Conjectures and Refutations*. London, 1962.

Radway, Janice A. *Reading the Romance: Women, Patriarchy, and Popular Literature*. Chapel Hill, N.C., 1984.

Rand, Ayn. *Atlas Shrugged*. New York, 1957.

————. *Anthem*. Caldwell, Idaho, 1946.

Rasmussen, Douglas, et al. *The Philosophical Thought of Ayn Rand*. Ed. Douglas Den Uly and Douglas Rasmussen. Urbana, Ill., 1984.

Read, Herbert. *The Green Child*. London, 1935.

Reage, Pauline. *Return to the Chateau*. New York, 1971.

————. *Story of O*. New York, 1965.

Reeves, Marjorie. *The Influence of Prophecy in the Later Middle Ages: A Study of Joachism*. London, 1969.

Reich, Wilhelm. *Selected Writings*. New York, 1961.

————. *The Sexual Revolution*. New York, 1974.

Rexroth, Kenneth. *Communalism: From Its Origins to the Twentieth Century*. New York, 1974.

Rhodes, Jewel Parker. "Ursula Le Guin's *The Left Hand of Darkness*: Androgyny and the Feminist Utopia." In *Women and Utopia*. Ed. Marleen Barr and Nicholas Smith. Lanham, Md., 1983.

Rianovsky, Nicholas. *The Teachings of Charles Fourier*. Berkeley, 1969.

Rimmer, Robert. *The Harrad Experiment*. New York, 1966.

Roberts, Ron E. *The New Communes*. New York, 1971.

Rohrlich, Ruby. "The Shakers: Gender Equality in Hierarchy." In *Women in Search of Utopia*. Ed. Ruby Rohrlich and Elaine Hoffman Baruch. New York, 1984.

Rosenberg, Jerome H. *Margaret Atwood*. Boston, 1984.

Rosinsky, Natalie M. *Feminist Futures*. Ann Arbor, 1984.

Roszak, Theodore. *The Cult of Information*. New York, 1986.

————. *From Satori to Silicon Valley*. San Francisco, 1986.

————. *The Making of a Counter-Culture*. New York, 1969.

————. *Person/Planet*. New York, 1978.

————. *Unfinished Animal*. New York, 1975.

————. *Where the Wasteland Ends*. New York, 1973.

Rupert, Peter. *Reader in a Strange Land*. Athens, Ga., 1986.

Russ, Joanna. *"Amor Vincit Foeminam:* The Battle of the Sexes in Science Fiction." In *Gender Studies*. Ed. Judith Spector. Bowling Green, Ohio, 1986.

————. *The Female Man*. New York, 1975.

————. "Recent Feminist Utopias." In *Future Females: A Critical Anthology*. Ed. Marleen S. Barr. Bowling Green, Ohio, 1981.

————— . *The Two of Them*. New York, 1978.

————— . "When It Changed." *The Zanzibar Cat*. Sauke City, Wisc., 1983.

Sade, Marquis de. *The Complete Justine, Philosophy in the Bedroom, and Other Writings*. New York, 1965.

————— . *120 Days of Sodom*. Paris, 1957.

Sale, Kirkpatrick. *Dwellers in the Land: The Bioregional Vision*. San Francisco, 1985.

————— . "Ecofeminism—A New Perspective." *The Nation* 245 (September 26, 1987).

————— . *Human Scale*. New York, 1980.

Sargent, Lyman Tower. "A New Anarchism: Social and Political Ideas in Some Recent Feminist Utopias." In *Women and Utopia*. Ed. Marleen Barr and Nicholas Smith. Lanham, Md., 1983.

Satin, Mark. *New Age Politics*. New York, 1979.

Schatt, Stanley. *Kurt Vonnegut, Jr.* Boston, 1976.

Schell, Jonathan. *The Fate of the Earth*. New York, 1982.

Scholes, Robert. "A Footnote to Russ's 'Recent Feminist Utopias.'" In *Future Females: A Critical Anthology*. Ed. Marleen S. Barr. Bowling Green, Ohio, 1981.

————— . *Structural Fabulation*. London, 1975.

Schumacher, E. F. *Good Work*. New York, 1979.

————— . *A Guide for the Perplexed*. New York, 1975.

————— . *Small Is Beautiful*. New York, 1973.

Segal, Howard P. "Vonnegut's *Player Piano:* An Ambiguous Technological Dystopia." In *No Place Else*. Ed. Eric S. Rabkin, Martin H. Greenberg, and Joseph D. Olander. Carbondale, Ill., 1983.

Sennet, Richard. *The Uses of Disorder*. New York, 1970.

Shane, Alex M. *The Life and Works of Evgenij Zamjatin*. Berkeley, 1968.

Sharaf, Myron. *Fury on Earth: A Biography of Wilhelm Reich*. New York, 1983.

Shelley, Mary. *The Last Man*. London, 1985.

Shklar, Judith N. *After Utopia: The Decline of Political Faith*. Princeton, N.J., 1969.

Shor, Ira. *Critical Teaching and Everyday Life*. Boston, 1980.

Sibley, Mulford. *Technology and Utopia*. Minneapolis, 1971.

Sillitoe, Alan. *Travels in Nihilon*. London, 1971.

Skinner, B. F. *Walden Two*. New York, 1948.

Slater, Philip. *Earthwalk*. Garden City, N.Y., 1974.

Smither, Philip E. "Unbuilding Walls: Human Nature and the Nature of Evolutionary and Political Thought in *The Dispossessed*." In *Ursula K. Le Guin*. Ed. Joseph D. Olander and Martin Henry Greenberg. New York, 1979.

Snyder, Gary. *Earth Household*. New York, 1969.

————— . *The Real Work*. New York, 1980.

Soble, Alan. *Pornography*. New Haven, 1986.

Soleri, Paolo. *Arcology: The City in the Image of Man*. Cambridge, Mass., 1969.

Sontag, Susan. "The Pornographic Imagination." In *Styles of Radical Will*. New York, 1967.

Spector, Judith. "Science Fiction and the Sex War: A Womb of One's Own." In *Gender Studies*. Ed. Judith Spector. Bowling Green, Ohio, 1986.

Spivak, Charlotte. *Ursula K. Le Guin*. Boston, 1984.

Stapledon, Olaf. *Last and First Men: A Story of the Near and Far Future*. London, 1930.

Steriber, Whittey, and James Kunelka. *War Day*. New York, 1985.

Stimpson, Catharine R. "Zero Degree Deviancy: The Lesbian Novel in English." In *Writing and Sexual Difference*. Ed. Elizabeth Abel. Chicago, 1982.

Stirner, Max. *The Ego and His Own*. London, 1971.

Straton, Mary. *The Legend of Biel*. New York, 1975.

Sturgeon, Theodore. *Godbody*. New York, 1987.

Suvin, Darko. *Metamorphoses of Science Fiction*. New Haven, 1979.

Swift, Jonathan. *Gulliver's Travels, and Other Writings*. New York, 1955.

Theroux, Paul. *Mosquito Coast*. Boston, 1982.

Thomas, Lewis. *The Medusa and the Snail*. New York, 1979.

Thomas, Robert David. *The Man Who Would Be Perfect*. Philadelphia, 1977.

Thompson, E. P. *William Morris*. New York, 1977.

Thompson, William Irwin. *At the Edge of History*. New York, 1971.

_____ . *Evil and the World Order*. New York, 1976.

_____ . *Islands Out of Time*. Garden City, N.Y., 1985.

_____ . *Pacific Shift*. San Francisco, 1985.

_____ . *Passages about the Earth*. New York, 1974.

_____ . *The Time Falling Bodies Take to Light*. New York, 1981.

Thoreau, Henry David. *Walden*. New York, 1981.

Tolstoy, Leo. "The Death of Ivan Ilyich." In *Classics of Modern Fiction*. Ed. Irving Howe. New York, 1972.

Tuccille, Jerome. *It Usually Begins with Ayn Rand*. New York, 1972.

Urbanowicz, Victor. "Personal and Political in *The Dispossessed*." In *Ursula K. Le Guin*. Ed. Harold Bloom. New York, 1986.

Vacca, Robert. *The Coming Dark Age*. Garden City, N.Y., 1973.

Vaneigem, Raoul. *The Revolution of Everyday Life*. London, 1983.

Veysey, Lawrence R. *The Communal Experience: Anarchist and Mystical Communities in Twentieth-Century America*. Chicago, 1978.

Voltaire. *Candide, or Optimism*. Trans. John Butt. London, 1971.

Vonnegut, Kurt, Jr. *Player Piano*. New York, 1954.

Wagar, W. Warren. *H. G. Wells and the World State*. New Haven, 1961.

Walsh, Chad. *From Utopia to Nightmare*. New York, 1962.

Ward, Colin. *Anarchy in Action*. New York, 1972.

Weinbaum, Beya. "Twin Oaks." In *Women in Search of Utopia*. Ed. Ruby Rohrich and Elaine Hoffman Baruch. New York, 1984.

Welch, Holmes. *Taoism: The Parting of the Way*. Rev. ed. Boston, 1966.

Wells, H. G. *Men Like Gods*. London, 1923.

_____ . *A Modern Utopia*. Lincoln, Neb., 1967

_____ . *Mind at the End of Its Tether*. New York, 1946.

West, Nathanael. *Miss Lonelyhearts. Complete Works of Nathanael West*. New York, 1957.

Wezansky, Richard, et al. *Home Comfort: Life on Total Loss Farm*. New York, 1975.

Williams, G. H. *The Radical Reformation*. Boston, 1952.

Williams, Raymond. *The Country and the City*. New York, 1973.

_____ . *Culture and Society*. London, 1958.

_____ . *Problems in Materialism and Culture*. London, 1980.

Wilson, Robert Anton. *The Cosmic Trigger*. New York, 1978.

_____ . *The Illuminati Papers*. Berkeley, 1981.

Wittig, Monique. *Les Guerillères*. New York, 1971.

Woodcock, George. *Anarchism: A History of Libertarian Ideas and Movements*. Cleveland, 1962.

Wright, Frank Lloyd. *The Living City*. New York, 1958.

Wylie, Philip. *The Disappearance*. New York, 1951.

Zamyatin, Yevgeny. *A Soviet Heretic: Essays*. Trans. Mirra Ginsberg. Chicago, 1970.

_____ . *My: An Anthology of Russian Literature in the Soviet Period from Gorki to Pasternak*. Trans.-ed. Bernard G. Guerney, New York, 1969.

_____ . *We*. Trans. Mirra Ginsburg. New York, 1972.

_____ . *We*. Trans. Gregory Zilboorg. New York, 1959.

Zicklin, Gilbert. *Countercultural Communes*. Westport, Conn., 1983.

Index

OHIO UNIVERSITY LIBRARY

Please return this book as soon as you
have finished with it. In order to avoid a
fine it must be returned by the latest date
stamped below.

JAN 1 0 1996

NOV 0 9 1995

AUG 0 8 1988